On steel by John Sartain Phil^a

Your affectionate Mother
Jane Swisshelm

THE AUTOBIOGRAPHY OF JANE FAIRFIELD;

EMBRACING

A FEW SELECT POEMS

BY

SUMNER LINCOLN FAIRFIELD.

BOSTON:
PUBLISHED BY BAZIN AND ELLSWORTH.
1860.

STEREOTYPED AT THE
BOSTON STEREOTYPE FOUNDRY.

TO

MY NOBLE AND ENDEARED COUNTRYMEN,

WHO HAVE SO LONG AND SO GENEROUSLY SUSTAINED ME,—
FOR WHOSE SYMPATHY, CHEERFUL ENCOURAGE-
MENT, AND UNFAILING KINDNESS,
I AM EVER GRATEFUL,—

THIS WORK IS RESPECTFULLY

DEDICATED,

BY

JANE FAIRFIELD.

NEW YORK, April 5, 1857.

TO MRS. SUMNER LINCOLN FAIRFIELD.

Dear Madam: Marked as your life has been by events and circumstances of no common order, an intimate acquaintance with the varied phases of society, — the little and deceitful, the high born, the generous and the good, — basking, at times, in the sunshine of prosperity; at others sinking, from untoward circumstances, into the depths of despondency; again rising from its descent by an innate and irresistible energy, breasting the storm, and riding securely through the whirlwind, your forthcoming volume cannot but be properly appreciated by good taste, fellowship, and generous and kindred feeling.

That this souvenir to your country may, as I am sure it will, long outlive the ephemeral productions which dance their hour upon the stage, then pass to the land of neglect and oblivion — that it may form in the future a recompense for the past, — is the sincere desire of yours,

Very truly,

JNO. BARBER.

PREFACE.

JUSTICE to myself, and compliance with a long established and very proper custom, require that I should introduce my book to the public by a PREFACE.

I style my work an "Autobiography," as it is written by its subject; though the plan was complete, its execution is but partial, for reasons that will suggest themselves to the reader.

The record of the life of an individual, and that too of a woman! how pitiful the subject! how insignificant the space of a lifetime, in comparison with that eternity to which we are all hastening! and how slight the probability that the events of threescore years, or even of fourscore, in the passage of a soul across the stage of time, can interest or instruct the mass of readers! With all the multitudinous events of childhood, maturity, and decline, — of love, marriage, and maternity, — of joy and sorrow, disease and death, — how few will dare to unveil to the eye of the world the complete record of a life? Indeed, the lives of many, perhaps of most, of my sex, in the middling and upper ranks of society, consist of little but childish pleasures, transitory sorrows, flirtations, with their accompaniments of fashionable frivolity, envy, jealousy, and petty scheming, ending in disappointed single-blessedness, or a business-like, thoughtless marriage, with the monotonous routine of ordinary wedded life, and the closing of an eventless career in the family tomb. Even in the rare instances where the union of hands is also one of souls, the joys of true love and the scenes of a happy home are not the proper objects for the public gaze.

The course of my life, at all events, is not open to the reproach of being tame, spiritless, or void of incident. My life! in these two little words, what a gulf of misery have I to look back upon! the pain of the retrospect is almost as acute as that at the time of the actual suffering.

Crushed in spirits and failing in health, — with a sick, mind-clouded, and perishing family dependent on me for support, — with a sad and weary heart, I had reconciled myself to the idea of laying bare my very soul to the world's inspection, as a last resource against the ruin which stared me in the face. The struggles of mind and the torturing anxiety through which I came to this desperate decision, will be appreciated by every noble and sensitive reader. I addressed myself zealously to the task of recording my varied experiences, and had written, in my anguish, an account, alas! too complete; it reflected severely, but justly, upon the principal authors of my life's bitterness, who have now passed beyond the boundaries of time to the eternal unknown; but more mature reflection and the advice of friends induced me to blot out many a dark page of suffering and indignity, that the world might have no occasion to pass harsh judgment upon those whom even I, their victim, am forbidden to judge. For this partial disclosure, this fragmentary record, I may perhaps be censured; but considerations of family ties, and an unwillingness to wound the feelings of innocent living kindred, forbid the moral wrong I should commit by rehearsing the whole story of my wrongs.

> "I could unclasp a secret book,
> And to your quick-conceiving discontent,
> Could read you matter deep and dangerous, —"

but I refrain, not desirous of reopening wounds which, though never healed, at least have lost some of their sensitiveness. Suffering has been so long the normal condition of my life, that griefs which would wear out one accustomed to the happiness of this world rest kindly and even cheerfully upon me— the patient, scarred sufferer of more than twenty years. Indeed, were I to write all the interesting events of my life, I should fill volumes, whose sad and strange truths would appear fabulous; I should positively be accused of speaking untruths, were I to unfold my life in all its cruel disappointments and wrongs; and should render myself liable to the charge of attempting to excite, unworthily, the pity of my readers. Such, therefore, of my history as is here omitted, is better concealed in the most secret chambers of my heart, known only to the All-seeing Eye, which alone can read our thoughts, and pity and console.

The great happiness of my life has been to provide for the wants of my unfortunate children, to whose still more unfortunate father I devoted the flower of my days and all the energies of my mind. Though anguish and injustice, poverty and affliction, have been my constant companions, I have hitherto been enabled to wear a smiling face, and to extract pleasure even from gall and bitterness, under the guiding star of Hope and the sustaining encouragement of my children's love. My eventful history, though it has modified, has never extinguished the naturally buoyant and cheerful element in my character; and it is my prayer that I may drain to the very dregs, if need be, my bitter cup with a smiling countenance, as long as any of my loved ones look up to it for solace and support.

Of course, a work written amid such anxieties and interruptions as was this, cannot be expected to present a uniformly smooth current of narrative; like my life, it is irregular, startling, at times rambling and digressive, but never, I trust, dull or inanimate; like my thoughts and acts, rendered mercurial by necessity, my pen cannot move within the narrow lines of conventionalism, and may often have transgressed the limits of classical English style. Elegance of language and polished periods I have not aimed at; but clearness and conciseness I have endeavored always to preserve. The circumstances under which this work has been written, I am sure, will protect me from the keen shafts of learned criticism; and will induce my readers to pardon much for the inexperience and natural emotion of the writer.

Such as it is — with all its faults — I present this my life-picture, sombre though its colors be, to my generous countrymen. If it afford them even transitory amusement — and especially if it enable any of my countrywomen to avoid the rock upon which my happiness was wrecked — an ill-judged and thoughtless marriage, — I shall feel amply repaid for all the pain of its preparation.

In obedience to a wish expressed by many kind friends, I add to my work some of the most popular pieces of my husband's composition, that strangers, while they read the record of my sufferings, may recognize and do justice to the genius which I claim for him.

Adieu, kind reader.

"Weave we the woof — the web is spun —
The web is wove — the work is done."

JANE FAIRFIELD.

BOSTON, November, 1860.

CONTENTS.

CHAPTER I.

CHAPTER II.

CHAPTER III.

CHAPTER IV.

CHAPTER V.

CHAPTER VI.

CHAPTER VII.

CHAPTER VIII.

CHAPTER IX.

CHAPTER X.

CHAPTER XI.

CHAPTER XII.

CHAPTER XIII.

CHAPTER XIV.

CHAPTER XV.

CHAPTER XVI.

CHAPTER XVII.

CHAPTER XVIII.

CHAPTER XIX.

CHAPTER XX.

POEMS.

THE AUTOBIOGRAPHY

OF

JANE FAIRFIELD.

CHAPTER I.

I WAS born in Rahway, New Jersey, of poor but industrious parents, noble by all the ennobling qualities of the heart, personal worth, and individual merit. Under Heaven, their home, their life, their lot, were all of their own making. They made for themselves a place in the new world. They began life together at a period when living, in its best sense, was rough and practical. My mother's name was Grummond, of French extraction: she was a native of South Orange, New Jersey, and the daughter of a farmer. My maiden name was Frazee.

My father was of Scotch origin; he possessed equally the philosophy, capacity, and genius of that noble and unswerving people. He believed that the superstructure of life for enjoyment must be a foundation for solid work. Thus, with my beloved mother, they set themselves together steadily to seek out and fulfill the universal *law of life*, which is labor, life's natural and indispensable necessity. The better to assist them, love came; not that wild passion or fancy miscalled love, but the fervent, the deep and hallowed worship of the heart, that finds its happiness, *only*, in kindness, unselfishness, and sympathy.

My father was a true patriot; and though he never cherished a thirst for war or military glory, he always possessed a warm and unwavering spirit of patriotism, which he inherited from his ancestors on both sides, who were all whigs during the American revolution, and who fought bravely and suffered much to wrest their beloved country from the iron grasp of intolerance and oppression.

As time wore on, my parents found themselves quietly happy, surrounded by loving little ones, among whom I was the second daughter.

My first impressions were of the diverse tastes and dispositions of the family. My sister being the eldest, I observed the most her nature, which was pensive and sad.

I was an impulsive and energetic child. It was this difference in our characters that made us competitors in affection for each other; though this could hardly be otherwise, with the example set us by our beautiful and affectionate mother, whose sweet smiles acted as a charm upon our childish hearts, and made home the very nucleus of cheerfulness and happiness. Bitter or sweet as was her lot, no murmurs ever escaped her: no restless longings after what Heaven had denied her, of the superfluities of wealth, ever troubled her. Her life was a chronicle, the "title page" of which could be read upon her charming and benign countenance; her manner gentle, cheerful, and at ease; her unfailing interest in every thing around her, and in all people. Religion sat upon her soul, and her profession of it was neither hollow nor false. Single-hearted and pure-minded she walked through life, suffering as all must, but never defenseless, recognizing solely and above all her dependence upon God.

In those days of frugality and self-reliance, people were sensible, and ignored extravagance; they were not lavish on their dwellings, dress, and entertainments, but used their means in the cultivation of their rural homes and the education of their children.

The household of my mother was conducted on quite a different plan from those of the present time. Quick and attentive in her simple home, making all matters straight, she was one of those whom the wise man delighted to praise.

"She layeth her hands to the spindle, and her hands hold the distaff; she stretcheth out her hand to the poor; yea, she reacheth forth her hands to the needy."

Idleness was never known in my mother's dwelling. The taxation on all imported articles was so great after the war, that none except the most wealthy could furnish them. Industry, therefore, and prudence, were the words most in use in our little home. All articles of clothing for the male portion of the family, as well as bed and table linen, from the flax and wool to the material ready for use, were prepared by the incessant and individual energy of my mother. This noble economy lessened the personal wants of many families in those days, and left the people free from the ridiculous and contemptible tyranny into which fashion and extravagance would otherwise have plunged them.

The village of Rahway, at the time of my birth, was small. It contained a few wooden houses, distant neighbors, a physician, and a church. In this church I was baptized when a child. My mother had adopted its creed: it was orthodox; of course, her children, while young and under her control, bowed at its altar. The catechism was learned at an early age, and recited to the good old pastor; but it had little effect upon my childish understanding.

CHAPTER II.

"I remember, I remember the house where I was born,
The little window where the sun came peeping in at morn."

ATTACHED to the small two-story frame house was a finely cultivated garden, of fruit and flowers of every hue. Here my sister and myself, when we had finished our lessons and duties, repaired together; and if there had been any thing to mar our happiness, here we would come to sympathize and encourage each other. She inherited a nature so pure and so innocent that she seemed incapable of a fault.

Our garden was our paradise. My father had an aged gardener, a very old, faithful, and honest negro, who had lived in our family for years; his name was Gray; he derived his name from his age and his very gray hair. This old man was fond of children; he had arrived at second childhood, and their prattle and simplicity suited him.

It was his habit to get a number of us near him and tell our fortunes by palmistry. I well remember the delight he would manifest at our credulity. When it came to my turn, he would always repeat the same thing; for he had told it many times. "Your path lies across the stormy waters, little missus; great traveler — danger, and work, and trouble for you, little missus. O, I can't tell you all I see — so much trouble; but faint not on the journey it is appointed for you to go." This man was nearly ninety years old, and had passed his life in the village, respected alike for his industry and honesty.

We had now attained the ages of nine and seven. During those few years since our birth, there had been changes in our family; human existence brings little else. My father had experienced losses — the same that every man meets who begins life with nothing but labor and luck to sustain him. As our family increased, perplexities, toils, and anxieties increased with it. These things change sometimes the most patient and lovely natures, and bring antagonisms of which we little dream. I pass over here many recollections of incidents so commonly known by all in the dawning of life. Childhood is a torturing and most bitter portion of our existence, from which all suffer nearly alike. Reproof, inflicted mortifications, unanswered questions, heartaches and tears, are its guerdon. A few incidents, only, of my earlier life I shall note here, but pass on to years which brought their melancholy hues of experience and vicissitude.

Though young, my mind had already caught a tone of romance.

There had been living for some years near us a lady of great personal beauty and talent, whose beautiful, cultivated mind, gave something of romance and poetry to her appearance — a Mrs. N——n, from Rhode Island. There was a mystery attached to her history, which caused her to leave her native home and seek refuge among strangers. She had been living for several years in the neighborhood, unsought, and unseeking society. Silent and lonely, she was never seen except at church, where she had furnished herself with a pew, and sat quite alone. Her walks for exercise were through an avenue which led from her dwelling and back again. I had, though a child, strange and vague thoughts of this lady, and longed for nothing so much as to attract her attention. One day, late in the afternoon, in company with my sister, we took it into our heads to stroll near the avenue, so as to be seen by her. She at once spoke to us, with a very sweet and gentle tone, with a subdued and tranquil air and manner, but her voice had something in it of sadness which affected me almost to tears. She said, "My dear children, will you come in with me? I live alone with Annette, my adopted child; perhaps you will join us in a cup of tea." I replied by thanking her, and said, "We shall be happy to do so, but must return hastily, as our mother may feel anxious concerning us."

Her apartments, though plain and simple, were hallowed with the memories of other and happier years — books, music, paintings, and statues, the relics of the past.

Born in a country town, among a people who had neither knowledge nor taste for the beautiful, this accidental and delightful visit was the opening of a new life, new influences; and to this charming woman and this visit, in connection with my social intercourse with her in after years, I am indebted for the early sympathy I felt for literature, poetry, and genius. Her reverence for the good and her perception of the gen erous were exalted and strong from nature's sympathy with her high-toned and ideal mind; she was eminently calculated to win one of my excitable imagination. She loaded us with books, authors of whom I had never heard, of history, biography, and poetry: for these enchanting and soul-absorbing works I neglected my school lessons; for these I was often punished, which caused me sadness and embarrassment.

Among the works this lady wished me to read were Madame Cottin's beautiful work, "Elizabeth, or the Exile of Siberia," "Paul and Virginia," "Rasselas, or the Happy Valley," and "Young's Night Thoughts." "These," she said, "will animate and stimulate your mind to self-dependence — to heroic and noble deeds."

One cold and stormy night, after the toils and frettings of the day were over, I prevailed on my parents to allow me to read to them one of the books I had borrowed of the stranger. Though I had that morn ing wept bitterly over the sorrows of poor Elizabeth, to read it again would be a sweet task. Evening came; the fire burned brightly, the old fashioned fire in the open chimney place, giving an air of cheerfulness and comfort to all around. Our little family drew near the hearth, around the little work table; my father sat smoking his pipe, my mother with her knitting-work, — her favorite evening employment, — eagerly waiting the commencement of the story. I read on. When I came to the departure of Elizabeth with the old missionary, the farewell with her parents for her lonely pilgrimage through the cold snows of Siberia to obtain their release and pardon, we wept the sweet tears of sympathy. My father, especially, was deeply moved. O, how I wished that future years might bring the trial of my affections in some such sacrifice! Poor child as I was, I little dreamed these wishes, made in helplessness, would, in after life, become sadly fulfilled.

In our village there lived the envious and the ill-natured; they exist every where — people who are happy at the sorrows and misfortunes of others; it gives them something to talk about. My charming friend Mrs. N——n was a subject for speculation: who she was, and where she came from, and why she came there, greatly interested the gossips and the scandal-mongers. Stories were circulated, and the gossips were busy; for *there*, as every where, were not wanting tongues to babble of the dead and wrong the living. Human nature revenges itself by suspicion.

I think Byron says, or quotes, "Many people have the reputation of being wicked with whom we should be too happy to pass our lives;" and so I felt toward this lovely woman.

I was a fitful child, full of changes, passions, and sympathies. Reading now became almost my only occupation. I had been suffering with severe attacks of chills and fever, which lasted for two long years. This terrible illness had so broken my constitution as to render me unfit for study; consequently I was taken from school. Half my time, during the long summer months, was spent in my little favorite grotto in the garden, reading to my sister and my friend Mary Marsh. She was the daughter of a sea captain. Our parents were near neighbors; we were inseparable for years; she was the only girl I ever loved: we read together many volumes; from these I contracted early in life an existence of my own. These works inspired me with love, courage, energy, and fidelity; many were highly picturesque, and highly false. It was well, however, I could do so, for the true and the real came, alas! too soon.

The illness from which I had been suffering rendered my appearance shadowy, and greatly impaired my nervous system. These severe chills brought on that strange and mysterious affection of somnambulism, from which I suffered, and which often endangered my life. In those nocturnal seasons, although I was very feeble, I was stronger, and manifested my natural disposition more than when awake; I laughed, and sang, and danced, and was always merry, to the great discomfort of my parents. It was not so pleasant a thing to be kept awake night after night by such antics as I was accustomed to perform; I was placed for safety in a small room from which there was no egress except through my parents' apartments, and generally performed my exploits in their presence; my father's patience often became worn out; he could not be persuaded but that I knew what I did.

I had a horror of darkness, from having heard ghost stories repeated to me by a negress, a slave, who belonged to the family of my young friend Mary, so that on no account could I be persuaded to enter a room at night, alone, even though I had a light. My eyes, my mother said, appeared of uncommon size, as though encased in glass, and never winked. To me there was always a mystery about one thing: unconscious entirely as I was of what I did, if my mother, on my going to bed, would remember to warn me against rising in my sleep, I never failed to have a quiet night; but if she forgot to do so, I invariably arose. I recollect on one occasion of being awakened and forcibly dragged from off my sister's head, she screaming with fright, I shouting and dancing. On another and last occasion of these night perambulations, I sprang from my bed, ran through the room to the top of a flight of winding stairs, crying fire at the top of my lungs. Before my mother could reach me I fell headlong to the bottom. I was taken up apparently lifeless. This had the decided effect of curing me of this strange malady. I never more walked in my sleep.

My father never made companions of his children; his impressions were, that they must be kept at a distance; there were six of us; three noisy, mischievous boys, who were the youngest, did little else than pester and persecute their sisters, as boys usually do. My sister was shy and sensitive, and therefore not amusing; a word of reproof or unkindness would chill her heart. When alone with her in our garden, among the fruit, the birds, and the green foliage, my heart beaming with joyousness, she would look into my face and wonder what could make me so happy; then a sudden grief would come over me at seeing her tears fall on the bright and shining leaves. I could not understand the difference in our natures. I received the same reproof and underwent the same corrections with herself. It is true, I would suffer for a moment, then brush the tears away and turn a minuet, and off I would run, as happy as ever. How well I remember her sweet face, with her large black eyes, though always pensive, always sad. My first real sorrow was of my sister.

The restraint we felt in our father's presence made us glad in his absence; his business often called him from home, which always added to our delight, for then we could have a good time; we were free to romp, laugh, sing, and tell stories, in all of which I was the happy ringleader. My parents were both musical; my mother's voice had the sweetest melody in it, the very echo of the pensive airs she taught us; my father's songs were more spirited and impassioned; I admired his choice in all that pertained to cleverness; his Scotch nature made him passionately fond of Burns. A thousand times have I sung sweet "Bonnie Doon," feeling all the helplessness and sadness its sentiments inspire.

My uncle, my father's brother, possessed great genius for music and art; he discovered my early taste for the beautiful, and when he had a leisure hour, would devote it cheerfully to my instruction. He had the finest tenor voice I ever heard; joined to this was an impassioned, noble, and soul-stirring nature, which, when he sang, affected the heart to tears. My fondness was for the sentimental. Gay as was my nature, I could not bear the comic in music; I loved the sad and plaintive. Tom Moore's songs enchanted me; among these my favorite one was "The Meeting of the Waters."

I have a thousand times blessed the opportunities I had in my youth to cultivate this divine — this soul-absorbing gift. It has whiled away many a wretched, many a desolate and sad hour. Dr. Watts inspired me with a love for sacred music — "not through his tame versions of King David, for in these he has abused the sacred Psalmist, by neutralizing, with his conventional metres and silly rhymings, the sublimity and poetic beauty of those divine compositions." It was his lyric poems that touched my heart for poetry; there is in some of these pieces a sweet and touching truthfulness that I loved, and often, when strolling along by the streams and solitary places, I have sat down upon the green grass, or some rough stone, and sang them to the scenery around me.

"The history of childhood images forth our after life;" even such has been mine; it has only repeated what it learned from the first, — sorrow and disappointment. Alas! the familiar objects which surround poverty did not wait for me, but greeted me early with all its honors.

I was called the sunny-eyed brunette; the soft tinge of my complexion was the color of the rose-leaf; my dark-brown hair floated unbound in long, soft tresses, the eyes of those who loved me dwelt upon me with mingled pride and tenderness, for there was mind in the lofty brow, and heart in the warm, flushed cheek; but what are beauty, mind, and heart to a poor girl but sad gifts, that in after life involve her in an infinitude of trials? That future lay before me like a vast desert.

A change had come upon my father's fortunes, and we were about to leave the home of our birth and childhood for new scenes and new associations. My father had for some time been preparing himself to reveal the unexpected news of his failure to my mother, who had already observed a change in him; he grew petulant, abstracted, and nervous.

September has always been a fatal month to me. I was born in it. Early one September morning, while my parents were seated at breakfast, I sat looking over my lessons, when on a sudden I heard my mother sigh. I looked up, and saw the big tears falling from her eyes. I never saw her weep, though ignorant of the cause, that I did not also weep with her. I would have flown to her and kissed them away, as often I had done before; but my father, whose manner was stern toward us, and who always checked these sympathies by terming them weaknesses, prevented. O, how, at that moment, every tear I had seen her shed, every sorrow of the past, seemed to rise up as a recollection of her sufferings, each of which, in my childish affection, seemed an omen of what was before her.

A fearful discontent had for some time been gnawing at my father's heart; he informed my mother that morning that all was lost; he had failed in business; that our home and lands together, all, had the day before been attached — that, in short, we must prepare as soon as possible to remove from the place, —

as soon, at all events, as he could decide where to choose.

We had, all of us, become heart and soul in love with our little home, — with its garden, grounds, and flowers. We had never seen any thing of life, or been farther from home than its environs.

It was the dearest privilege of my mother to soothe the sorrowing, to renovate exhausted nature, by awakening it with hope and elevating it with the spiritual. Her faith in God was too strong ever to give way to emotions of despair. She sought her chamber, peculiarly appropriated to her own use. There, in my grief and heart ache, I found her seated by the window, sunk into a state of sad and listless reverie.

CHAPTER III.

EARLY the next day, as soon as I had breakfasted, I hastened to the house of my friend Mary, with a cloud upon my brow and heart, to inform her of our family misfortunes. I asked my mother's permission to pass the day with her. We immediately prepared to pass it in our accustomed rambles. We set off. We had not gone far on our way, when our attention was suddenly arrested by a cat in the act of charming a bird. She sat crouching with a most strange and eager look, with ears erect, her eyes fixed upon those of the poor little trembling thing, quivering and coming nearer and nearer. In a moment more, but for our accidental interference, the little songster must have perished. So, like this little bird, my pathway, during helpless childhood, had been beset by dangers from which I had been saved by the kind interference of a watchful and overruling Providence.

Proceeding in our walk, we passed through the orchards and fields, where often our occupation had been to pluck the fruit and gather the luxuriant strawberry, then onward beyond, a short distance, till we had gained the running brook. There, many a bright and clear morning, Mary, my sister, and myself had bathed in its stream with gladness and merriment in our young hearts. When we came here, we sat down upon the green earth, entwined our arms around each other, and wept the *sincere and poignant tears of childhood.* Returning, we made our way home through a beautiful wood cleared of underbrush. Here Mary and myself had often come attired in simple white, reclining on the green grass, reading some enchanting story. We were the happiest of the happy. How I realized the descriptions of romance, as we sat in the foreground, with our crooks by our side, fancying ourselves the shepherdesses we had read of! The sheep, however, could never be seen. They were somewhere in the background. We thought ourselves images of loveliness.

We returned to our homes after having spent a sad but tranquil day amid the dear familiar scenes of childhood.

On entering the tea room, I found the family seated at table. My mother's eyelids were swollen and red; they had evidently been talking over matters. "And yet," continued my father, after a pause, "it matters not in what shape our trials come to us. I am convinced that in this life there is no such thing as happiness. So, my dear wife, let us be as philosophical as we can for the sake of our children." I kissed them both good night. Weary and fatigued, I went to my room, feeling, for the first time in my life, that vague presentiment of evil which is its certain forerunner. The time drew rapidly near when we were to remove. My father had returned from New Brunswick, about twelve miles distant, where he had hired a house, and a building suitable to resume his business. I remember well the cloud of sadness that settled on my mother's face on his return, when she said, "Must we leave all to make our home among strangers? Must we leave the home which smiled on us on our wedding day, and the dear friends and neighbors with whom we have so long exchanged kindnesses? — the church, too, where, with our children, we have worshiped; the graves of loved ones, never more to enjoy their sweet consolation and influences?"

My mother was not what is termed a "strong-minded woman," who, when shut out from the natural sphere of her affections, could resort for enjoyment to her consciousness of power; her happiness was in the affections. It was a bitter trial to leave forever the home of her youth. To my young heart it was sadder than death to leave the paths that had been haunted by my childish dreams — to quit the green fields and the pleasant garden and grounds in which from infancy my heart delighted. It is true, in our home there had been sorrows. What cottage or palace is without them? Long vigils, sickness, prayers, and tears had been there. My beloved mother, whose best affections were with the child most unhappy, most afflicted, — now perceived that the dejection of my sister had become a settled melancholy; that the life-springs of life and thought of her dearest first-born had been crushed. Alas! "the body and the soul are not friends, but enemies." The one curbs and confines; the other wears and shatters. Yet for all these associations, we loved our abode, for here we had shared its joys and sorrows together.

I passed my time, for the few days we had left us, in visiting the old familiar faces and places. I lingered for hours in the old churchyard, amidst the graves of departed loved ones, and in the church where my ancestors had prayed and worshiped. My visit to their graves awakened all my childish memories — the closing scenes in the lives of my grandparents, my cousins, and many of my schoolmates. They had gone beyond the scenes of that calm and quiet morning; the breathing of a holy stillness rested upon their graves, where the green grass and the wild flowers, as they slept in repose, bloomed so sweetly above them.

CHAPTER IV.

ARRIVED in our new home, it was the happiness of each to assist in arranging the affairs for a comfortable, if not a luxurious one. It was not long before all matters were adjusted, and we were again, each, pursuing our avocations.

New Brunswick contained at that time about seven thousand inhabitants, chiefly of a Dutch population, though mixed with others.

After we had become settled, I rather liked the change. I had then just entered my teens.

My father, who was a manufacturer, began business with a new zeal, determined not to retrace or think of the past. Novelty sometimes pushes us on. Obstacles increase the ardor of some natures. For myself, young as I was, I saw plainly that my parents were too poor for me to think of remaining as a burden to them, and I determined soon to begin the work of life for myself. My education was very imperfect. The best advantages in those days were bad enough. The teachers themselves knew but little, especially in those small places.

In this interval of time, I occupied myself industriously by getting all the information I could from books. History, travel, and poetry, and biographies of great men and women were my delight. I loved antiquity, and always sought the oldest authors. The lives of poets enchanted me. The works of Petrarch, and Virgil, and Torquato Tasso, and Alfieri, and Lady Mary Wortley Montagu's Letters, I read with inexpressible happiness. With the English poets, also, I had become quite familiar, so that my character was formed more from reading than any other opportunity I had had of improvement.

I was, by nature, ambitious, and began thus early to feel an inexhaustible desire for the society of the great and intellectual. I loved my family, but I longed for intercourse and congeniality. The only persons I had ever met at that time who had interested me, were my uncle, who was then living in New York, and Mrs. N——n, who had evidently discovered in my young heart a strong desire for knowledge. My uncle, John Frazee, Esq., was fast gaining both wealth and fame as a sculptor. I had been long enough in New Brunswick to discover that it had no interest for me. Restless and impatient, feeling a certainty that my path in life lay *far* apart from the dull monotony of the unambitious people that surrounded me, I proposed to my parents that they should permit me to reside with my uncle. Once there, I should be introduced into the society of his friends. I should find myself in an element better suited to my wishes and future success.

There is nothing a firm and resolute mind can not accomplish. The moment for my departure was at hand. I embraced my dear sister and brothers, while we wept the bitter tears of parting for the first time in our lives. I then kissed my dear mother in silence, for words could not express the deep suffering I felt at parting with her.

My father, according to my wishes, made ample preparations for my departure, and accompanied me to New York. Our journey thither was by the old turnpike road, by stage coach, to Jersey City. At that time there were no steam conveyances. My uncle and his family received me with as much kindness as though I had been their daughter. This was, indeed, a change for me, in which my heart took intense delight. My uncle was engaged in an extensive marble business, independent of his art. I took infinite delight in going into his studio to watch the slow progress of the busts on which he was at work.

I now began to cultivate a taste for art, as I had for literature. I was introduced to several celebrities in painting; among them were Mr. Inman and Colonel Trumbull, both highly distinguished as artists. Colonel Trumbull was advanced in life, and did but little at that time. Among his finest productions is the Battle of Yorktown, and the surrender of Lord Cornwallis to General Washington at Saratoga. These paintings ornament the rotunda of the Capitol at Washington.

The art of sculpture at that time was in its infancy in this country. My uncle was the *first* native American artist in that line. Crawford, the sculptor, was a pupil of my uncle's.

During the perils and misfortunes of my early life, he did so much to relieve me, that I feel it obligatory on me, since I have it in my power, to show some mark of my gratitude. I therefore extract here a few passages from a Journal kept by him.

"At the instance of my friend, Mr. G. C. Verplanck, Congress, in 1831, appropriated five hundred dollars for a bust of Chief Justice Jay. In 1833, Messrs. Prime, Ward, and King gave me an order to execute the bust of Mr. Nathaniel Prime. This opened my way to Boston; it having been seen while in progress by Mr. Thomas W. Ward, of that city, while on a visit here. Immediately on his return to Boston, he proposed to his friends to have the busts of Daniel Webster and Dr. Bowditch executed by me for the Athenæum. I was sent for immediately, to proceed thither and take the models. Away I went, and soon found myself in the society of *great and distinguished men.* This was in October, 1833. When I arrived at Boston, and found Mr. Ward, he straightway took me to the house of Dr. Bowditch, where I was soon introduced to this great astronomer and mathematician. I found the doctor in fine health and spirits. He had not before, it seems, been apprised that I was a native artist; but, from the orthography and sound of my name, he had believed that I was a sculptor of some considerable celebrity, from either France or Italy; and when we came to converse upon the object of my mission, and I was revealed to him as a native and self-taught artist, who had never trod a foreign soil, he began to show symptoms of uneasiness; and the many interrogatories he put to me, concerning what works I had done, and with what success, clearly betrayed the anxiety of his mind. I saw plainly that he was fearful of being caught in the hands of a charlatan, whose unworthy chisel never sought integrity, and whose marble would be an enduring libel upon his finely formed head and features. Misgivings like these were not calculated to cheer the mind of an artist — a stranger, too, after being called a distance of two hundred and fifty miles from his home, upon an engagement like mine. Still, I could not say that the doctor's inquiries were by any means improper; he made them, I am sure, with feelings of delicacy and reserve. But it wounded my pride to be obliged to speak for myself, or of my own works and their merits; and, indeed, I said little in reply to his questions, except to state the leading facts as to the number of busts I had made, leaving their merits to be discussed by my employer, Mr. Ward, who assured the doctor, that those of my works he had seen and examined gave him the fullest confidence in my ability and competency as a sculptor. This seemed to reconcile the old gentleman, and brighten up his countenance with a more cheering and confiding aspect. In less than a week from this time, I had modelled the doctor's head in clay, to the entire satisfaction of himself and friends.

"The Hon. Daniel Webster was now called upon to sit for his bust, which was completed with equal success and approbation. In commencing with Mr. Webster, I found him extremely solicitous in regard to his likeness. He said he hoped I might succeed in obtaining a good likeness, which had never been accomplished yet, in his own opinion, either by painters or sculptors;

all that had hitherto been taken of him, he said, except the one by Stuart, were complete caricatures, and the model of him in wax, by Hughes, was of the same stamp. He added, 'I am the more anxious that you should succeed, because this is the last time I ever intend to sit for my portrait to any one.' I replied that I had no fears of being able to do ample justice to the work; and on we went very cheerfully together, until the third sitting, when he made use of a few expressions that did not please me. The truth is, his face is a peculiar one, and remarkably different when the muscles are in repose, from what it is when under the influence of inward emotion. To give myself full time, therefore, to study the best expressions which played around his mouth and changeable muscles of his face, I did not, in the first sittings, hasten to bring out these parts, but kept them back while I worked up the cranium and less flexible parts of the head. This course gave nothing very promising as to the portrait of the face, even to the third sitting. Mr. Webster entered my room this morning with his usual salutations, and walked up to where the model stood, while I was preparing some clay at the other end of the room. 'Well,' said he, in a low tone, as if talking to himself, 'I can see no likeness there. I am afraid it is going to follow in the track of all the rest.' He then took his seat for the work, as usual. I distinctly heard every word, and felt somewhat *touched* that he should have expressed his opinion so prematurely, and, as I thought, invidiously.

"I walked up to my work, and as I began to model,

thus addressed him: 'Now, sir, there is one thing about this work, which, to insure success, requires our mutual good faith and exercise; that is, we must endeavor *to keep cool.* If, sir, we but *keep cool*, there will be no sort of difficulty in this business, and success is sure.'

"While uttering these words, I could discover by the flashing of his great dark eyes and the play of his lips, that he understood me, that we might pass receipts; and the moment I paused, he broke out very good humoredly in reply, thus: 'O, I'll keep cool, I'll keep cool, if that will do it; I'll be as cool as a cucumber, sir.' And the joke passed off with a hearty laugh between us. I had no further trouble. The last sitting he gave was, at my request, by candlelight. He had been seated a while, when I observed to him how much I regretted my misfortune in never having seen him in public debate; that could I have once seen him delivering a speech in the Senate Chamber upon some important topic, it would have enabled me to delineate with greater force the higher mental qualities. To this he quickly replied, 'If that, Mr. Frazee, will be of any service to you, I can go through the business for you here right off; I can show you how we do business *down yonder*.'* I said it would oblige me very much; when he at once arose and began, first, by stating the preliminaries by the clerk, on the opening of the Senate, and then the services of the chaplain, personating himself as he usually stands during prayer.

* Meaning at the Capitol.

"'Now,' said he, 'it is my turn to speak.' He then put himself in a most grave and dignified attitude, looking as if he really saw the president of the Senate before him; then, compressing his keen lips a moment, he began, 'Mr. President,' and went on in a very animated and impressive speech for a quarter of an hour, I working with my might the while in the clay, to catch, flying as it were, the vivid and noble traits as they flashed upon his strong features. It was well done; and the inspiration of that hour lives, and may it long live, in the marble of Daniel Webster.

"These were finished in last July. Previous to their completion, however, in the month of May, I received a letter from Colonel Perkins, of Boston, requesting me to repair to Richmond, and model the bust of Chief Justice Marshall. 'We intend it,' said he, 'for our Boston Athenæum.' I started immediately for Old Virginia, and reached Richmond on the 21st of May. I found Judge Marshall at his residence, where I met with a frank and friendly reception from him. The next day he commenced sitting for his bust. On the 26th it was finished, packed up, and put on board a packet for New York, and I packed in the stage for home. I had some business to transact in Washington for another person, which obliged me to remain there for a week; and as much of that time was likely to be frittered away, I concluded to employ my leisure hours in taking the bust of President Jackson. I am certain of my complete success with the likeness. Shortly after my return home, I was called upon by Miss Ann Jay, who commissioned me to execute in marble a copy of the bust of her father, the late Chief Justice. It is now nearly finished. Having completed the busts of Webster and Bowditch, I started with them for Boston on the 26th of July; and in a few days they were delivered safely at the Athenæum. As an evidence of the approbation they received, I had not been in Boston a week before I was engaged to model and execute in marble four more busts, for the Athenæum, of distinguished individuals, namely, Judge Story, of the United States Court, Judge Prescott, Colonel Thomas H. Perkins, and Mr. John Lowell. Of all these gentlemen I have undoubted likenesses, acknowledged to be so by their friends, their families, and themselves. Thus, reckoning the head of C. D. Colden, Esq., I have, within the space of one year, modeled nine busts, — seven of which are for the Boston Athenæum, — and have executed four of them in marble."

Thus much have I narrated of the life, of the industry and the success of my kind uncle, at whose house and with whose family I found much happiness and consolation during the few fleeting years of my girlhood.

The home of my uncle was always gay during the time of his prosperity. Conversational parties, suppers, musical *soirees*, — of which he was fond, — mirth, and jests, were his delight. His pleasantry, wit, and gayety were contagious. His nature was generous and free. He received his friends with the greatest *empressement*, and was always in excellent humor; added to this he never failed, when occasion required, to feel deeply and with sympathy the sorrows of others, and was ever ready to assist when in his power.

I occupied my time in study, and in rendering to my good aunt the assistance she needed in sewing and needlework, in which I was quite perfect. My uncle often improved on the patterns I had with his beautiful taste. If I were embroidering a rose, he would discover some defect in the want of a bud or a leaf. We were fond of the drama. Large parties of us often attended the Park, the Old Drury, as it was called. It was there I first saw the young, the beautiful Malibran,—that immortal songstress,—make her *first* appearance. I had never witnessed an opera before. She could not have been more than sixteen years old. The streets were lined with carriages, and a gay and fashionable crowd filled the house. I saw her years afterward, when she had been racked by mental agony and sorrow, which, with her genius, added, no doubt, greatly to her success. Her large, gleaming eyes, so passionate and so wild, the soft tones of her lute-like voice, have haunted me long after I have heard them. My impression is, that none who ever saw her forget her to their dying day.

It was now the opening of the spring of 1826. Four years of my youth had passed since I had parted with my parents and family. I had written and received letters over which I had wept the scalding tears of sorrow. Early youth has a degree of *acute* anguish that after years can not know. A sweet instinct told me that I was beloved, that anxious and loving hearts were open to receive me.

I had been long enough in New York already, and had seen enough of society, even thus early, to change my impressions of what I had fancied so truthful and so fascinating.

I hastily made preparations to leave. I provided myself with sufficient wardrobe to remain with my mother during the summer. I left my uncle and family with regret, to return the following winter.

CHAPTER V.

ARRIVED at New Brunswick, with a beating heart and with feelings no words can describe, I found myself once more beside my mother's hearth. Tears plentifully were shed at our first meeting. She had changed. Her sweet, lovely face bore the expression of heartache; deep and bitter anguish sat upon it. She had avoided in her letters speaking of my sister; she did not wish to give me pain. But the truth must come, and I was not unprepared to meet it. My sister had lost her reason. "You would scarcely know her again," said my mother, "she is so altered. Sometimes she raves, then she will sit and not speak for hours." She was placed in a room that had been arranged for her, and seldom came out of it.

My parents now found me a grown woman, altered in mind and manner, perhaps improved. My father questioned me as to my happiness and my liking for city life. He too seemed changed, but more contented than when I left him. He was again hopeful from business prosperity.

My brothers had grown, and gone from home. In this dull, monotonous town there was nothing to vary the scene except church-going. Opposite our residence stood the old Episcopal church in which the Reverend

Bishop Croise had long officiated. In this church my cousin, William Brookfield, Esq., held a pew; he kindly invited me to occupy a place in it whenever I felt disposed. While in New York I had visited alternately churches of all denominations, after the Catholic Cathedral. If I had any preference for any, it was for these two, on account, chiefly, of the music. Like King David of old, the truest worship seemed to me that of "singing unto the Lord" — to praise him with the psaltery and harp. What worship is there so inspiring, so elevating, as music? It is intellectual, and therefore the heart and mind are in it. My mother had enforced upon me, from a child, much Bible reading. I was, therefore, thoroughly acquainted with its wonderful and inspired contents. Born with an independent nature, I was inclined, early, to think and seek out for myself — not to rely upon what others thought, said, or had done.

The principles of Christianity my mother taught me were all good. To creeds, however, I could not subscribe. When I came to an age to think and reflect for myself, how changed I became! One Sabbath morning, while listening to a sermon by the bishop, the life of Christ came to my mind in all its purity and simplicity; all passed before me like a beautiful vision. The poverty of his birth, the manger in which he was laid — how different, thought I, from the birthplace of his successors in the priesthood! — his after life, when he taught his pure and holy precepts to the poor people! The temple in which he worshiped was not a costly edifice, but the holy temple of nature; the mountains and hills echoed forth his divine teachings to the houseless *poor*. Alas! thought I, the successors of poor fishermen have forgotten their origin. They march, covered with gold and with purple, proud of the spoils of the poor. Instead of the little boats in which those gained their living on the Lake of Genesareth, these inhabit *superb palaces*. To the most simple repasts have succeeded the most sumptuous feasts; and where the apostles went on foot, priests are now seen driving in ornamented carriages.

I could never *profess* to be any thing. It is the same in friendship as religion; although I knew my heart sincere, the moment I began to assert it I would doubt my sincerity. If I attended church or joined in church service, the moment I heard my voice repeating after the clergyman I doubted my sincerity, simply because I was making a show of what ought to be done in my closet, in secret, before God. There was always an enthusiastic love which I felt for the Inexhaustible Goodness,—for the Supreme Being,—before whom, *in my heart*, I ever prostrated myself. When my thoughts take the highest flight of which they are capable, in gratitude they raise themselves in a sort of invocation with these words: Thy name, O God, is wisdom. "Thy name is love." Have pity upon thy poor, dependent child. This is not precisely prayer, but rather homage.

During the early spring of that year I did all I could to console my family, especially my poor, afflicted sister. She seemed to have thought me dead. She grieved and grew worse after I had left home. I could fill a volume with the intense sufferings I underwent during my short stay, from spring to the ensuing autumn; there is enough before me without lingering long on the sorrows of the past.

The July of that summer was an intensely hot month. I had taken a severe cold from walking out with my acquaintances during evenings, which, in a short time, laid me on a bed of illness; a severe attack of bilious fever set in, which terminated in the dangerous type of typhoid. My father's family physician was called in, who informed my parents that my illness was a dangerous one.

My dear mother's vigils and prayers for me were unremitting, as nightly she sat by my bed watching the short breathing occasioned by the burning fever that had prostrated me. In a few days I had become entirely insensible, and lay as one dying. So low was I, that my death had been circulated through the town. My physician, Dr. Jacob Dunham, to whose devoted attention and care (under Providence) I owe my life, when the crisis arrived, which, during the day, would decide my fate, came in the morning, and remained the entire day. He sat by my bedside with his watch in his hand, faithfully administering the medicine. My father and mother had retired to another room; there, in hopelessness and grief, to await the will of Heaven toward their child.

The doctor sat holding my hand, with his finger on my pulse, listening most intently to my breathing, when suddenly I opened my eyes; consciousness was returning; a perspiration was perceptible. I spoke for the first time for several days. I asked for my mother. My kind and endeared physician hastily arose and joined my parents, with the happy assurance that, with care and prudence, I should get well.

My strength, with convalescence, gradually returned, so that in a few days the doctor thought I might venture to walk with my mother a half a square. I took her arm, for I was too feeble to sustain myself. Nature never looked so lovely as it did at that moment; the earth, the sky, — all things seemed so joyous; the air that fanned my cheek seemed purer than I had ever felt it. The singing of the wind, like a natural lute, plaining through the leaves of some fine old trees we passed, — all combined to carry me out of myself. I felt grateful and subdued, as all do, coming out of a dangerous illness; a thousand vague and sweet emotions came over me, and I was happier and better for this affliction.

A few days in August had flown by, when I received an affectionate letter from my uncle, inviting my return. I again bade adieu to home and parents, but with less acute feelings than when I first left them.

CHAPTER VI.

"The maiden leaves her childhood and her home,
All that the past has known of happy hours, —
Perhaps her happiest ones: well may there be
A faint van color on those orange flowers."

MY aunt and uncle received me with caresses and open arms, for I had by some means won their sincere affections. Many inquiries had been made about me, and cards and notes had been left. Some months before I left my uncle's to visit my parents, I had been introduced to a Colonel S., a gentleman of talent and position as a lawyer. During our short acquaintance he had often spoken to me of a young friend of his, then traveling in Europe. This friend was the poet Fairfield. He had also presented me with the copies of a literary paper, which contained his letters of travel in England and France, which I had read with much interest. The periodical containing these letters was edited by the poet James G. Brooks, Esq. Mr. Fairfield had arrived in New York, from Paris, during the month of July. The following August I was introduced to him at the house of a young friend I then had residing at Jersey City. It was on the occasion of a small party given by the beautiful Miss Bucknor, who, at my request, had extended an invitation to the poet, through Colonel S.

A few moments only had passed after the introductions were given, when the poet seated himself by me, at an open window, greatly to the chagrin of many of the young ladies present, who, like myself, had a *penchant* for poets. Our conversation was upon his travels. His eloquence and powers of description were so graphic as to enchant me; his appearance I thought remarkable; his complexion was dark, with strongly-marked features. It was one of those faces one might term great, without being fascinating. There was something wanting of softness in his countenance, as well as manner. I was captivated by his intelligence and genius. At eleven o'clock our party dispersed. We took the last ferry-boat for that night which crossed to the city. It was too late to find a carriage; so we walked to my uncle's. As the gentleman left me, Mr. F. asked my permission to visit me the following morning, to which request I politely consented.

The next morning the poet made his appearance, with a huge portfolio under his arm. Seating himself, he immediately presented me with a sonnet he had written the previous night after leaving me, addressed "to a lady's eyes." I thanked him, blushing, but did not read it in his presence. He appeared confused, as all do who are about to make a proposal on a *grave* subject, on doubtful grounds of acceptance. With a woman's instinct I saw it all.

He sat a half hour without saying much, and left. I received a letter the next morning early, by post. I opened and read it. It was a proposal. I had not the slightest idea at that moment of accepting his or any other offer of marriage. I was young, and had thus early begun to prize my liberty too well to part with it so soon.

I answered his letter, and told him so. So far from chilling, it only renewed his ardor. The day following he came again. We had a long conversation, in which I told him frankly my position and situation — that I was the daughter of poor but respectable parentage; so that if he had entertained any thoughts of a pecuniary advantage, he was at once undeceived. He then related to me his own prospects, which were chiefly dependent on his future literary career.

I immediately informed my uncle of this strange offer of marriage. He seemed surprised, and did not, of course, on account of its suddenness, encourage me; bade me ponder well before embarking on a voyage which, as he said, at best was rough enough.

I then wrote to my father, stating the matter precisely. His answer came as a *veto* to any such sudden arrangement; beside, he said, "the gentleman is too poor to support a wife, and can never do it by poetry."

Human nature is so strange and unaccountable! I had felt no fervent attachment for Mr. Fairfield; the acquaintance had been too short, and most likely, if I had not met with opposition, I should have ceased thinking of him.

My father wished me to marry a business man. Like all fathers, he felt anxious for the future of his child. I cared not for wealth. Money was a thing I never thought of. I lived in ethereal creations of love, hope, and happiness; these appeared to me actual existences. I felt that the future owed me happiness, and thought I was in a fair way to find it. I was an imaginative, romantic girl. Sweet dreams of life had I then. Health had returned; once more my heart was light and gay.

It was during September, the anniversary of my birth. The poet's visits were constant, beside the love epistles that I daily received.

My mind was fully made up. In my infatuation, I said no more to my uncle or parents, but wrote a long letter to my cousin, at New Brunswick, William Brookfield, Esq., to which he at once replied, assuring me that his house was at my disposal; that he would himself be most happy to supply all things for my wedding; that all preparations should be made in any way that I might be pleased to suggest. All, so far as the wedding was concerned, was tastefully arranged, thanks to my cousin.

The twentieth day of September was the day set for the ceremony. One hundred guests had been invited, few of whom I had ever seen.

It was now the fifteenth of the month. I had five days left in which to prepare. All the fortune I had in the world was embraced in a few hundred dollars. This amount I had deposited in the hands of Mrs. Fairfield, the poet's mother, to furnish a small house he had taken in Elizabethtown, New Jersey.

He had hastily chosen this place to establish an academy for young men. I had intrusted to his mother the purchase and arrangement of the furniture, so as to be able to enter our new home immediately after our marriage.

The morning of the 20th dawned with that golden sunshine so usual in September; happy voices greeted me on all sides; but those who should have been the happiest — my loving parents — were lonely and anxious. This thought cast a shadow over my heart, which, with all my efforts at gayety, I could not well conceal. My spirits were forced. I requested to be left alone in my room. There, in the solitude of my heart, I sat down and wept bitterly.

Late in the afternoon I heard a carriage stop before the door. I stepped hastily to the window of my room, and saw Mr. F. and his mother alight. I turned quickly away, and sat down. In that moment a sickness of the soul came over me; my heart foretold me its doom. In a moment more they were at my side.

The evening drew rapidly on. The noise and stir of the crowd below, the gathering of the people, reminded me of the approaching hour. With the assistance of my cousin's wife I made my toilet. I had no bridemaids. I wished for none. My dress was simply white tulle, over white satin, looped with flowers, without a single ornament; a small bouquet of orange blossoms fastened in front of the low bodice, a wreath of the same in my hair, white kid gloves, and satin slippers completed my toilet. When all was finished, I turned from the mirror as I had from the window, with a deep feeling of desolation.

At the hour of eight we were summoned to the

drawing room; the bishop was waiting; all was ready. I took the arm of the groom. In company with a few dear friends, I walked slowly down the stairs with a beating heart. No one who had ever known me in my gay and happy moods could have believed me the same being.

I will not stop here to describe what all have seen — a marriage. Suffice it to say, the ring had been placed on my finger, the ceremony over, many congratulations given, and many kind wishes for my future happiness. The good old bishop took my hand with emotion; he kissed my brow, and said, with a tenderness I shall never forget, "God bless and keep you, my dear child; look to him as your Guide and Counselor; you will have need of such support." These words sank deep into my heart.

Supper was now announced. I was seated between the groom and the bishop; the guests followed and took their seats; all seemed gayety and mirth, which were greatly increased after the wine had passed plentifully around; many sparkling cups were drank to the health of the poet and myself. The supper was a sumptuous one, and all gave good evidence of their liking for the pleasures of the table. After this scene was over, the good bishop took his leave of the company, at which time the gayeties of the night began in music, dancing, and conversation. It was to the guests a gay festival.

Early the next morning our carriage was got ready for our departure for Elizabethtown, the place that I supposed would be my future home. We breakfasted with my cousin's family. Before taking my leave I had a duty to perform — to visit my parents and bid them adieu. In company with my cousin I set off for that most painful purpose, a distance of a quarter of a mile. I passed into the house trembling, though with a buoyant step, forcing a smile. I met my mother at the door. She kissed me with that same kindness of heart, that sweet, affectionate disposition, which nothing could change. My father's manner and look were so cold and stern that I did not approach nearer him, but sat by my mother, feigning cheerfulness, when my inmost heart was ready to burst. My sister sat eating her breakfast, gazing at me with that vacant smile so painful to behold in one whose mind is extinguished.

I could bear it no longer; tears and sobs burst forth. My mother wept with me, but there was no time for melancholy meditation. I arose to bid them adieu, when my father, who had not spoken before, said, "So, Jane, you have settled the business for yourself; but mark my words: the day will come when, instead of despising your poor father's house, you will be glad to return to it, and will do so with broken hopes and heart." This, though a cruel prophecy, was spoken in such a tone and manner, and with such an appeal to my feelings, my own sad heart secretly assenting to what he had said, that I turned mournfully away, deeply impressed with what I myself feared might be the result. I shall never forget the yearning, yet trusting and hopeful expression, of my mother's sweet face, when she impressed a kiss on my cheek, and said, with that earnestness none but a mother can feel, "God bless you, my dear child; trust in Heaven." *Volumes* could not express all that was intended in that blessing.

Returning, I found my party ready and waiting to leave. My kind cousin had witnessed all my sadness, and as if he wished to say something to create a smile at parting, (he had a jovial and happy nature,) said, "Coz, life is like a fairy tale, and it don't become a fairy to look sad; so cheer up and laugh before you go." So drolly he said this that we all burst into a laugh together, and so drove off.

The morning was beautiful. We chatted and amused ourselves with the scenery of country life. We passed through Rahway. I pointed out to my husband the house where I was born, and told him much of my early life. The distance to Elizabethtown was only twenty miles; we arrived early in the afternoon. I found the house a very comfortable one, two stories high, of brick, adjacent to the Episcopal church, on the main street; all things within were neatly adjusted; to say the least, it was comfortable. I now decided in my own mind to make matters pleasant, and to be as happy as possible. My husband's mother hastened to prepare tea. I seated myself by an open window in the front parlor. I was admiring some sweet brier that stood within reach of the window, impaled by a low fence, to secure its safety. I had not sat long, before a loud and repeated knocking came at the door—so loud that it startled me. Just at that instant I recollected the injunction that Mrs. Fairfield had given me before leaving the room, "not to go to the door if any one came," adding, "it would not seem well for a bride to be seen opening the door." There was no servant. The knocking by this time became alarming. Neither my husband nor his mother made their appearance, and I sat petrified with terror. In a moment more, I saw two rough banditti-looking men come rapidly to the window, and before I had power to move from it, each, in succession, planted his feet on the little paling, and in an instant swept past me, through the window, landing in the center of the room. In their loud and rough voices, they demanded of me where Mr. Fairfield was. Almost fainting with fright, I could not speak. At that moment my husband and his mother made their appearance. In this bedlam let loose, I heard, amid the uproar, many violent expressions. By this time I saw how it was. The officers declared they would not leave the house without the money or security. At that moment I began to feel certain that Mr. Fairfield had not even the sum demanded, for that single debt, in the world. O, how my romance of poetry, poets, and "love in a cottage," at that moment faded out! To have a truce, and before I could know the cause of this sudden outbreak, my husband permitted these outrageous desperadoes to take an inventory of all in the house. If I had possessed a million I would have laid it quietly at the feet of these terrorists, to have been saved the shame and mortification I knew it would bring on us. This, thought I, is a new phase of "honey moon." I still think there never was an incident in *any* life precisely like it.

We were now in the midst of a dilemma. My husband begged my forgiveness; he explained to me, as soon as his feelings would allow him, the cause of this scene. It was for a debt contracted after he had arrived in New York, from Europe, which, no doubt, would have been paid, had he been allowed sufficient time to have established the school he had in contemplation. What I most blamed him for was, that, expecting this trouble, or fearing it, — as evidently he did, — he should so thoughtlessly have taken all I had for the furnishing of a house, when the money would have made us comfortable for some time.

The next thing to be considered was the debt, and the money with which it was to be paid. There was none, any where, at least within our reach. One trouble never comes alone; the landlord, having heard of this affair, became alarmed for himself. The money could not be obtained, so that at the end of a fortnight, the time allowed by the officers, the furniture was sold under the sheriff's hammer. Feeling assured that this would be the result, we had made preparations to give up all; to go, we knew not where.

The news flew swiftly, as bad news does. My parents and my uncle had heard of my misfortunes, but offered me no assistance, and I was too proud to ask it; beside, I had no right to expect any favors after taking the independent course I had. I decided to bear silently all my trials, come what might.

Homeless and penniless we arrived in New York; we repaired to miserable lodgings, where, Mr. Fairfield said, we would remain until he could hear of something that might better our condition. So at the present we lived upon

> "Nothing a week, and that uncertain — very."

The hue and cry now was, that I had married imprudently, and that I deserved all I got. Be it so; it was myself who suffered. I never asked any favors of these croakers about imprudence. I believe that, taking life as a whole, it consists not in the abundance we have, but in the capacity of enjoying a little. There are nobler things, and dearer, than ease or wealth, or freedom from care. "How much of cowardly selfishness," says a writer, "weakness and falsehood are, in both sexes, under the names of *prudence*, *honorable feeling*, or *obedience to parents*." *There is many an act petted under the name of virtue*, which is a *blacker* crime before God, and of far more fatal results to society at large, than the *worst* of the so-called improvident marriages.

Never lived there a being who felt more deeply her situation than I at that moment.

I caught an omen of what must be my ultimate wretchedness from what I had already suffered. Even so soon, my spirits began to sink, and hope only appeared a more gentle word for fear.

Mr. Fairfield was greeted cordially by his literary acquaintances, among whom were General Morris, editor of the "New York Mirror," James G. Brooks, Esq., Dr. Bartlett, of the "Albion," and Major Noah. For these gentlemen he sometimes wrote articles and poetry. The remuneration, however, was very slight.

We occupied small and dreary-looking apartments in one of the retired streets, where all was quiet as if it had not been in the center of that busy metropolis. Here, one evening, as we sat talking over matters, what were best to be done, we were startled at a visit from my aunt and uncle, who had heard we were in the city, and sought out our lodgings. We passed a pleasant evening, had an animated conversation on those topics of art and literature, which delighted both parties.

My uncle evidently was highly pleased with his visit, and charmed with the intelligence of my husband — so much pleased, that he ceased to be astonished at my preference. We were cordially invited to visit them, and my uncle nobly offered to do any thing in his power to serve us.

If it were true that poets were actually what their genius, conversation, and writings seem to represent them, what irresistibly fascinating beings they might be! In spite of all I could do to encourage Mr. F., he felt despondent, for he saw no cause for hope, from his pecuniary situation. The weeks passed like ghosts flitting by, till at length, and on a sudden, he determined to make a change, and decided to go to Boston.

I was for the first time impressed with the instability of genius — that a creative and poetical mind was a fatal gift.

In one of the most original and thoughtful works of our day, it is said, —

"It is a fatal gift; for, when possessed in its highest quality and strength, what has it ever done for its votaries? What were all those great poets of whom we talk so much; what were they in their lifetime? The most miserable of their species — depressed, doubtful, obscure — or involved in petty quarrels and petty persecutions; often unappreciated — utterly uninfluential; beggars; flatterers of men unworthy of their recognition. What a train of disgustful incidents, what a record of degrading circumstances, is the life of a great poet!"

A few weeks had passed. My husband began to think earnestly, and to hasten preparations to make his appearance, during that winter, on the Boston stage.

I knew him to be unfitted, entirely, for the profession. With his young and enthusiastic views, he only saw the bright spots of the picture. He had a passion for histrionic fame, but he little dreamed of the days and nights of painful toil, mortifications, and insults that awaited him, perhaps before he might attain even a moderate estimation. His nature was haughty, unbending, and reserved; he could not brook personal or newspaper attacks. I have seen him writhe under mental pain even upon a criticism of a poem. How, then, with his quick sensibility, could he sustain the jeers and scoffs of public caprice? Any little reputation he might gain in the profession, in an instant, with his uncontrolled temper, might be destroyed by even the slightest and most unintentional offense. These things I mildly suggested to him.

The people now began to feel a sympathy for the poet. Frederic S. Hill, Esq., the actor, became his warm advocate and friend. The principal motive, it must be confessed, that induced him to try the stage, was his really melancholy pecuniary situation. He found literature a miserable dependence, and he was utterly without business faculties, or a profession of any kind.

A list of characters was given to him, from which he chose "Norval," in the play of "Douglas," in which to make his appearance. Nathaniel Green, Esq., kindly presented him with his dress for the character.

The night came. I was sick at heart, and would not have gone to witness the performance on any account. I found a friend, who was kind enough to return from the theater at the end of each act, to inform me of the events of the night.

A large and elegant assemblage greeted the poet's appearance. The liberal and indulgent kindness of the people had enabled him to proceed well through this first effort, which would have been encouraging but for one of those blunders so common and so mortifying to novices. In the closing scene, after Norval is dead, the curtain falls. Norval had died in the wrong place, and the heavy drop-curtain was falling across his body. Thump, thump, rap, rap, went the house. "Run, run," cried one. "He'll be killed," cried another. The curtain had now nearly reached him, before he discovered what all this noise was about. Then, with the agility of a deer, he was not long getting from under. For minutes after the shouting was vociferous. During the few moments they were enjoying the death scene, my husband had rapidly changed his dress, and while they were calling him out, he was making a speedy exit to his lodgings from these unfortunate scenes.

The gentleman whom I had commissioned to bear the news of the night to me had preceded him a few minutes. It is my nature to enjoy any thing so ridiculous, even though it be at my own expense; and while my friend was relating to me, what I have narrated here, I was enjoying this rich scene hugely.

In a moment more my husband opened the parlor door. Such had been the tragic scenes that had been enacted during the few months of my married life, that he had never heard me laugh, or seen me joyous. He stood a moment, looking at me in amazement, then, pointing to the door, requested me to leave for my room. He had no relish for farce occasioned by his own mistakes, either on or off the stage. He could not laugh over these things; could he have done so, how different would have been his fate in life!

"So," said he, "you can rejoice over the ruin of your husband." He suffered so much under this mortification, — he seemed to take it so much to heart, — that I grew grave, and assured him that I was sorry to have been amused, since he felt so unhappy. I tried to console him by saying that such mstakes were common to the stage, and begged him to think nothing of it. He wept the tears of mortification, and declared he would leave Boston, never to step a foot upon the stage again.

CHAPTER VII.

It was a cold and inclement winter. We took the route to New York by land, in the stage coach. We came to Providence. Here my husband's purse gave out, and he was obliged to leave me behind, and proceed alone. I was to remain until he could remit the sum requisite to take me thither. He had a friend in Providence, to whom he was to send the money to defray my expenses. A few weeks passed lonely enough, when I received, through this gentleman, a letter from Mr. F., containing the funds to continue my journey. I was placed under the care of one of his acquaintances, and onward I journeyed to join my husband.

During the interval of our separation, Mr. F. had advertised for a situation as preceptor, to go south. He soon received an answer from Mr. Bryan, postmaster of Alexandria, Virginia. This gentleman stated that there was an opening of this kind in Charlestown, of that state, and invited us to leave New York, and to accept his hospitality, until further knowledge could be obtained regarding the place and the school.

It was now the beautiful summer. We had been joined in the *holy bonds* of wedlock nearly a year when we set out on this new expedition. Arrived at Alexandria, we were kindly received by Mr. Bryan and his wife. I was pleased with her gentle Virginian air and manner, and for the short time we remained, I found in her a congenial and sympathizing friend. This lady was a sister to Governor Barbour, of Virginia.

We had not been long at the house of Mr. Bryan before the two poets quarreled. Mr. B., I believe, prided himself as a poet, and member of that immortal fraternity; they parted, however, apparently friends.

We arrived in Charlestown, and were invited to remain at the house of a Mr. Gallagher, editor of a small village paper. The place was small and obscure, and the village poor. The spot Mr. F. had chosen to locate his school was five miles distant from the village, among the farmers, whose children had little opportunity of cultivation. Here he found a vacant log cabin, which he had fitted up for the purpose, about a half mile distant from the farm house where we boarded. So fatigued and disgusted had I become with the succession of trials I had had, that I longed for nothing so much as peace and quiet — for

"Peace, O virtue, peace is all thine own."

I verily believe I could have felt happy to have been at *peace* on an island lonely as that of Robinson Crusoe.

The following is a letter from my husband to my uncle, in New York, written soon after our arrival in Charlestown: —

CHARLESTOWN, July 23, 1827.

MY DEAR SIR: Nearly a fortnight has elapsed since we left Alexandria. It was then my intention to proceed immediately to

Frederick; but a very violent attack of erysipelas confined me at the house of my friend Mr. Barry, of Georgetown, for several days of extreme suffering. The attack, however, was ordered in wisdom, not the less consummate because inscrutable, for it saved me from a bilious fever, which, in this climate, is almost always either presently or ultimately fatal. Copious bleeding relieved me, but left me in a state of debility from which I have not yet recovered. On our arrival at Frederick, it soon became apparent to me that the trustees would consult much less the credentials submitted to them than the caprices of favoritism and the interests of party. Therefore, after a delay of two days in that place, we came hither, and have been very busy collecting scholars, making friends, and purchasing furniture for the house we shall rent at Bellefontaine. Mr. Bryan, of Alexandria, is a man of much merit in some respects, but by no means such a high-hearted fellow as Mr. Gallagher, who was the first to discover this situation, and has been the agent in all that has been done in relation to it. From all, however, with whom we have been associated since our arrival at the south, we were uniformly met with a generous welcome. The utmost kindness has been extended toward us, and the greatest interest manifested in our success. The path, which has thus been opened, we shall now steadily pursue; and I fervently hope that all things will advance according to the ardor of our industry, and the hopes we can not but consider well founded on rational plans. My school is situated in a beautiful country, and the plain people who will patronize it, if not much cultivated, are purely honest.

The country is singularly luxuriant, the inhabitants warm-hearted and hospitable, and the means of living abundant and economical. Congratulate me, therefore, that the darkness of my fortune is dissolving away, and that brighter prospects are unfolding before us.

Your letter gratified and amused me. I regret that this searching weather has made me thoroughly prosaic, and that I can not return your song in kind. When the Muses favor me with their smiles again, however, I will endeavor to send you a few loose rhymes, which may repay the toil of perusal. All I can do now is to thank you for your affectionate prognostications of good, while I rationally hope that they may not be falsified by any untoward events.

We are going into the country this afternoon. I shall commence business on Monday next. Let us hear frequently from you, (direct as before;) present our respects to Mrs. Frazee, our remembrance to Anson; and believe me,

Very affectionately yours,

John Frazee, Esq. S. L. FAIRFIELD.

A few children were obtained, who knew nothing even of the rudiments.

This was a trying situation for a poet and a scholar, to come down to an assemblage of stupid children; his pride was wounded, and were it not that the place was far distant from his literary friends, he would have felt much mortification. His most flattering prospect did not exceed six hundred dollars a year; then we found no domestic purpose in the arrangement of boarding. I had become, heart and soul, sick with this bond of union among boarding-house lodgers.

I proposed housekeeping. Mr. F. seemed delighted at the idea of having a home of his own. He went at once to Charlestown, and purchased, on credit, articles to the amount of nearly a hundred dollars, with Mr. Gallagher's name as security. With this pittance we were about to commence housekeeping. We had been some weeks in the place. Our board bill had amounted already to more than we could command, and we were called upon to pay it. People took advantage of my husband's ignorance to do business; human nature *he could not* comprehend. Instead of arranging with the farmer to pay his bill at the end of six months, giving himself *time*, he said nothing about it. This want of judgment brought on another disaster, and the articles we had purchased for housekeeping were taken for board.

Thus it ever was with the poet. If unsuccessful in the execution of *any* plan he attempted, he would become disgusted, give up all, and leave. But dwelling on these trials was of no use. *My heart was strong; my path was onward.*

> "And if my voice break forth, 'tis not that now
> I shrink from what is suffered: let him speak
> Who hath beheld decline upon my brow,
> Or seen my mind's convulsion leave it weak:
> *But in this page a record will I seek.*"

I began to feel that human life had in reserve for me its darkest cup — that fate had predestined for me a path to weariness and sorrow.

Arrived safely in Philadelphia, I begged Mr. F. to allow me to rest there, at least for a time; he was as anxious as myself for repose. He set himself at work to prepare for the press a volume of his poems, — "The Cities of the Plain," — with a few fugitive pieces. He soon got the work under way, through the kind printer and publisher, Mr. Maxwell, then residing in that city. It was not long after his poems appeared, when several editors and well-known literary gentlemen found their way into our society; among them was the talented poet, Robert Morris, Esq., the able editor of the "Pennsylvania Inquirer." About that time, there came a young poet here from New England, Willis Gaylord Clarke, Esq. This young man submitted many of his earliest effusions to the inspection of my husband, before committing them to the public.

It can not be denied that Mr. Fairfield's genius was of a high and imaginative order, which was often a benefit to others — even his worst enemies admitted this truth. His knowledge of the literature and the history of all nations, and of all ages, was perfect. It was only the intellectual that enjoyed his society. Young and rising talent especially gained his sympathy and encouragement.

His nature was generous toward his compeers. He loved all that was good of talent among all people, though always severe toward rhymesters and poetasters.

Our stay in Philadelphia lasted some months. The poems were out, and sold well, and brought us the comforts of life. Our acquaintances and friends increased. We had not long been in the city, when, one day, Mr. F. accidentally met with William Badger, Esq., one of his college classmates. This was a pleasant reunion. An hour spent occasionally by this gentleman at our house was very agreeable. The two friends entertained each other with many recollections and incidents of college life. The tricks, fun, and frolic played upon each other were really immensely amusing. Humor and wit were my delight; and these were the first pleasant days I had passed since my marriage.

CHAPTER VIII.

DECEMBER had come. Nothing had occurred to mar, so far, our tranquillity. I was now a mother. A flood of happiness poured down upon my heart. I forgot the terrors and tumults of life, as I gazed into the face of my first-born boy.

"A woman's character is developed by the affections; when once they come into action, how rapidly are the latent qualities called forth, and in how brief a time what a wonderful change is wrought!"

One morning, after I had become convalescent, I sat with my infant, looking from the window of my chamber, when I saw, on a lamp-post opposite, a large placard, and on it the name of my husband, in huge letters. I could not make out the smaller type. I informed Mr. F.'s mother, and requested her to hasten and bring it to me, lest he should see it. It was a shameless, cowardly, and wicked attempt to ruin the poet. A more dark and demoniacal act was never perpetrated, than the circulation of this placard throughout the country.

A few weeks before this placard appeared, my husband had met with a volume of poems, written by Daniel Bryan, Esq., the gentleman I have mentioned heretofore, at whose house we visited in Alexandria.

These poems he reviewed—the review was a sarcasm. It were better it had never been written. My husband was in the habit of using his pen in epigrams and satire for retaliation. To say the least, it was unwise and impolitic to make enemies, especially in his unfortunate situation. I had not dreamed these placards had been so extensively circulated in the city. I thought the one I saw had been placed there for the especial benefit of my husband.

On his return home that day, he came into my room, holding one of them before me, and in a state of frantic despair, asked me to read it. I had hoped he might not see it, and so escape the torture I knew he would feel.

Mr. Gallagher, of Charlestown, and Mr. Bryan, were friends. Mr. Bryan's vanity was piqued by the review, and Mr. Gallagher's *purse* had suffered by his friendly act of being security for the debt contracted by Mr. F. while we were in Charlestown. Both these gentlemen sought revenge in the way I have mentioned. Alas, how poor a thing is retaliation! It is but a wretched victory to those who suffer from wrong and persecution. I have no doubt that all parties, in their more dispassionate moments of reflection, regretted these foolish and miserable proceedings.

This persecution did not stop here. The effects were felt long, long years. Attacks from all parts of the country were poured forth, until, by their effect on the mind of the poet, they had nearly destroyed him. It was at this crisis, broken in spirit, and lost to hope, that George D. Prentice, Esq., came out in the poet's behalf, in a paper he then edited at Hartford, Connecticut.

Never was there written a more consummate defense. The greatness and eloquence of these letters were proverbial. They had the effect to relieve the public mind from the painful impressions that had been made upon it by these wanton attacks, which had been so recklessly poured forth upon the poet.

Mr. Prentice, whom at that time I had never seen, was a firm and warm friend of my husband. They had been boys together, and classmates in college. They had from early youth been endeared to each other by an ardent and affectionate friendship.

Young as I was, my heart had become exhausted with life's absurdities and incongruities; but I had one happiness left me; my heart, with its affections, had become centered on my lovely boy.

Sorrow and joy are strangely blended on this earth; and though, according to the course of nature, the tie of parent and child is doomed to be severed, fortunate and happy are those who have such ties.

The mortifications my husband had endured from persecutions and trials, induced him to wish for a change.

On the opening of the coming spring, there was found a vacancy in the Newtown Academy, Bucks County, Pennsylvania. Mr. F. visited the place, and found a warm welcome by the trustees, returned, and secured his credentials from several of the most prominent men in Philadelphia. Among them were Peter A. Browne, Esq., and David Paul Brown, Esq. He soon took possession of the Academy. Already a number of scholars had been secured. Two young gentlemen from Philadelphia, by the name of Strawbridge, were to remain with us to complete their education. They were nephews of one of the trustees, Dr. Gordon, who lived about a mile distant from the town. The Academy was a beautiful building. We lived in it. It stood on an eminence, in front of which was a green lawn. In its rear were a fine garden, and a running brook, and foliage, and flowers. The poet had had no position equal, or in any way to be compared, to this. The building was furnished and made ready for our reception. The school opened prosperously. I had never passed so calm and happy a summer. The inhabitants of the village were plain, honest, and good people. My husband and myself, with our little son, in company with the young Strawbridges, after school hours, amused ourselves by pleasant walks around the village. We congratulated each other upon what we believed and felt would be a permanent support, and a safe retreat from the trials that had heretofore beset our path. Our visits were frequent to the beautiful and romantic dwelling of Dr. Gordon. In this family we found much that was congenial. The doctor had a fine library. His mind was highly cultivated. He had a sympathizing, noble, and generous heart. With the hospitality of the doctor and his excellent and lovely wife we were consoled.

My little Angelo, my beloved boy, was an attraction to all. At least, my mother's heart thought so. Some declared he was the image of his father, but with his mother's eyes — a perfect picture! My own vanity and love of admiration, I think, increased after I became a mother. Perhaps vanity, after all, is the true source of the sublime, and, in many respects, it may be of the ridiculous. Still it is our admiration of each other that has caused the accomplishment of many great events in this world. The possession of it doubtless produces emulation in talent and genius, "by it great deeds have been accomplished — great books have been written. It has congregated multitudes," and organized what we call *society*.

The season for vacation had now come. Mr. Prentice had written to request my husband to bring me with him, and come on a visit to Hartford. I was delighted at the idea of seeing my husband's endeared friend. I longed, beside, to become acquainted with one who had written me so many beautiful sonnets and flattering poems. We made ready, and set out on our journey. Our visit was a flying one. I could not remain long from my child, nor Mr. F. from his scholars.

It was like parting with my own identity to leave my child a day. On our arrival we hastily sent our cards to Mr. Prentice. It truly exhilarated my heart to see the meeting of these two poets. The spontaneous joy felt by each was really quite overwhelming. Our visit extended to a few days. In that time, how much of conversation, of visits, and introductions, had been gone through with! It was requested by many of my husband's friends, and insisted on by Mr.

Prentice, that he should have the benefit of a poetical reading. Mr. Prentice made choice for that purpose of my husband's poem, entitled "The Cities of the Plain." This poem had gained him a reputation among the clergy while in England. It drew a crowded audience of the intelligent and *élite* of Hartford.

The day after, Mr. Prentice called for us to pay a visit to Mrs. Sigourney, who, at that time, was the mistress of a beautiful residence a short distance from the town.

Whenever I visit an author, I am more than ever convinced that such have no right to the marriage tie; and I wholly believe this of authors of both sexes. No one has any right to involve another.

The life of authors is one of suffering, and if they prefer that life, they should have it alone. We need to suffer to understand the language of suffering. And who, that ever married an author, has found his or her lot to have fallen in pleasant places? Authors are wedded, heart and soul, to their productions. The society which delights others becomes wearisome to them; even their wives, husbands, and children. They blend their existence with fame and the future. Let those who love Dreamland dream on, but let them dream by themselves.

How many melancholy instances can I call up within my recollection of unfortunate literary marriages! Perhaps Byron is one of the most prominent in my mind; but there are many others. "You talk of marriage," said Byron, in a letter to Murray; "ever since my own *funeral*, the word makes me giddy, and throws me into a cold sweat." When was there any thing so absurd, in this respect, as the conduct of Bulwer and Dickens? I might trace many such, to prove that my assertions are true.

After a pleasant visit among the charming people of Hartford, which I shall long remember, we made haste to return.

On reaching home, my heart bounded with joy to find all was right with my little boy. His infant smiles cheered my heart, and made me forget all my sorrows.

Our two amiable young boarders, the brothers Strawbridge, were glad to see us returned. The eldest was nineteen years old, and quite a favorite and companion with his preceptor.

It was about a week after our return, when, on a very fine afternoon, they all three started off for a bathing amusement, of which Mr. Fairfield, as well as the young men, was very fond. They had often, during the heat of the summer, repaired to the same spot, about a mile distant from the academy, for that enjoyment.

Evening came on. We had been waiting tea an hour. We vainly looked to see them descending the hill which led to the academy. It was not long, however, before we heard the rapid tramp of a horse. I ran quickly to the door, feeling a presentiment of evil. The man on horseback had reached the academy gate. He informed me that one of the young gentlemen was drowned, and that my husband was taken out of the water, and lay on the shore, where he had left him. In a few minutes almost the entire village had assembled.

It was not long before my husband was brought home, insensible and almost lifeless. They had not been long in the water when young Strawbridge was seized with the cramp. My husband hastened to assist him, while his poor brother stood on the shore, so frightened as to be unable to render the least assistance. The cramp was so violent that, with all the efforts of Mr. Fairfield, he could not be saved; the poor fellow sank at last.

It was with much difficulty they got my husband to shore. He remained insensible during the night. The next day he awoke to his own wretched and melancholy reflections.

The body of the young man was recovered about twelve o'clock the same night, and taken to the house of his uncle, Dr. Gordon, for interment. As the carriage passed with his remains, it stopped before the academy, for us to take the last look of our young friend. The moonlight was clear, and fell gently upon the face as they uncovered it. The countenance was one of sleep instead of death, calm and mild as in life. The lateness of the hour, the quiet of the place, the stillness unbroken by a sound — all seemed to whisper to my heart — *he is at rest.* So wearied and worn had I become with these interminable changes, that a longing for death seemed at that moment to take hold of me; for in this life I felt that I was the mere plaything of fate — of subtle and malignant chance.

I never was morbid. My nature was as joyous as a

bird's, and hopeful; nor did I sigh for splendor or wealth. I took no delight in what generally comprises the happiness of women. Idle and useless visits, and small talk about little nothings, had no fascinations for me. My mind had been trained and tried by suffering. My heart craved sympathy, peace, and rest; above all, it yearned for what it now found too late to dream of—*true affection*, which is the highest, the noblest, and holiest part of our nature; for some, I really believe, life is destined to be an unfinished existence. Such I believe to be mine. But enough of this melancholy for the present.

As soon as my husband had recovered from the severe shock he had suffered, he began to talk about giving up the academy. The scholars were waiting to return to their places; they were all of them delighted with their teacher. Their parents, many of them, used every effort to induce Mr. Fairfield to continue, assuring him of their support and friendship, but all to no purpose. He loved young Strawbridge, and blamed himself for what he deemed a want of decision in so often gratifying his requests to visit this fatal spot. I made use of every argument in my power, reminding him of the scenes of want and suffering we had gone through, and that by remaining where we were we might at least be comfortable. He sallied forth into the garden, then the school room. Every spot seemed to haunt him with the loss of his young pupil. He could not bear the aspect that told of trial and death. He had not the mind which can bear trouble. He was always trying to rush from it, and therefore rushed in the face of it. He could not meet real affliction steadily, nor struggle with it patiently until the storm swept over, looking to that source on high which is never long invisible to the hopeful and trusting heart.

It was useless for me to urge or insist. His feelings once ruffled, from *any* cause, he would not rest satisfied until he had left the scenes where the unpleasantness occurred. Alas for the poor poet, he could not escape from himself!

New York, at this time, seemed, in his mind, to have more attractions than any other place. He thought of his early literary friends there. Thither we went. With what means he had, he hired a small house, and we soon became settled. I had a disposition to be content any where, provided I could live comfortably, without mortification. The *rapid change of scenes* which had heretofore affected me so sadly and tragically, now began to assume the shape of comedy. Sometimes I would laugh at them, at ourselves, and at all the world.

Mr. Fairfield had been for some time forming in his mind the plot for a new poem, entitled "The Last Night of Pompeii." He had now begun its composition. He also obtained, with his reputation as a teacher, a fine situation in a school, which had at its head a very charming and intelligent lady, a Mrs. Dunderdale. This lady, whose talents and manner had made her very popular, continued her school successfully for a number of years in New York.

Again returned to the city, after an absence of nearly two years, we were greeted by old acquaintances with warmth and kindness. Fortune for a time treated us a little more favorably. Mr. Fairfield worked with ardor at his poem, expecting little pecuniary reward. For my part, I believe that true glory — I know it well — is the reward of virtue alone. To me the noble traits of a noble heart are of far more value than all the honors that can be bestowed by either birth, talent, or genius without them.

It is somewhat singular, that through life it has been my fortune to attract and draw after me the most melancholy and unhappy.

Our house soon became the receptacle of broken-down authors and persecuted clergy. Among them was the poor poet, McDonald Clarke, with whose homeless career the New Yorkers had been long familiar. This unfortunate poet came often, during the cold, bitter nights of winter, to share our fireside and partake of our comfortable cheer. How often I have been made sad by the recital of his sufferings and woes! He was a most inoffensive person; though insane, he was always mild, always happy. He was very fond of my little Angelo; he would seat him on his knee and talk for hours in broken sentences of the "ills which flesh is heir to." He had often, he said, when he had not a shilling in the world, sought a bed between two graves in Trinity churchyard, and when hungry made his meal of a cracker and a cup of milk. Just after the site for Greenwood Cemetery was selected, he came to see me one day, assuring me he had chosen his grave. He had in his hand a small placard on a board, containing the following line: "The poet's grave."

This placard he placed on a tree in the cemetery, to mark the spot for his final repose. The trustees had kindly presented him with this foot of earth, where, in a few years after, he was peacefully laid. His death, it will long be remembered, was occasioned by the wanton sport of a few thoughtless young men.

> " There is a little lonely grave
> Which no one comes to see;
> The foxglove and red flowers wave
> Their welcome to the bee.
> There never falls the morning sun;
> It lies beneath the wall:
> But there, when weary day is done,
> The lights of sunset fall,
> Hushing the warm and crimson air,
> As life and hope were present there."

It often so happened that several of our friends would meet accidentally of an evening. It was amusing to mark their various characters. It had been our good fortune to have become acquainted with Signor Pietro Maroncelli, the friend and companion of Silvio Pellico. This interesting and accomplished gentleman and exile came to New York, and there taught school many years. He was a just man and a liberalist. My husband was always delighted with his society. His conversation was often on the bondage and suffering of his beloved country. I would listen to him as an oracle. He disputed on subjects with an inexhaustible storehouse of arguments.

This good man was for a long time imprisoned, for his noble and generous sentiments, with Silvio Pellico, at Spielberg, Germany. "I have engaged," said he, "in a war that will descend to my family after my death; an inheritance of hatreds, quarrels, and dangers, with which my country will always be agitated. The fates have ordained that order should be overthrown, and the reign one of confusion in our beautiful Italy." I should never end my eulogies, were I to speak of his fidelity, loyalty, and eloquence.

How true it is that distress softens the heart, and ties close bonds of affection between those who suffer! Among our visitors was Mrs. Stebbins, the gifted but unfortunate daughter of the great artist Gilbert Stuart. This lady had married unwisely, and, finding her sorrows too great to bear, parted from her husband, and devoted her attention to the composition of school books for a support. She did not long continue submissive to her trials. Her fortitude and health forsook her, and the irregular life she led in a short time reduced her to a most pitiable state of want. In this melancholy situation, she was taken to the hospital, and treated in the character of a menial. She grew infirm before she had reached the middle age of life. One day she was ordered to perform the work of a servant — to scour a flight of stairs, from which she fell. She sustained an injury by this fall which caused her instant death. How often, in the bitterness of anguish, I have seen her weep! When referring to her gifted father, she would say, "What would my dear father say, were he now living, to behold the wrongs and grievances of his once favorite daughter?"

Thus suffered and died the child of a great artist.

For years she lived utterly isolated. The ties of blood or of early affections were all severed. The one to whose love she had a right had forsaken her. She was too delicate to appeal for charity. Often had she talked with me on the subject of asking for assistance, but her heart would fail her. She knew the cold repulses she must meet, and felt she could not brook them. There were many gentlemen of standing and wealth, at that time, who knew of her case, who might have saved her.

> "Ah, countrymen! if, when you make your prayers,
> God should be so obdurate as yourselves,
> How would it fare with your departed souls?"

But I find myself wandering from my subject, which, unfortunately, is myself.

What a change a little prosperity creates! What an influence appearances have on the minds of those we call our friends!

I always dreaded these intervals of peace and quiet. With us they were sure indications of a coming sorrow — heralds of darker trials.

One beautiful moonlight night I sat alone in my chamber, looking on the lovely and calm face of my sweet boy, who lay sleeping beside me, feeling those strange forebodings of sorrow so common to the heart of mothers. I wrote the following lines: —

> Sleep on, my babe, till the morning breaks,
> And thy spirit shall dream of bliss;
> For my yearning heart a rapture takes
> From thy lovely smile and kiss.

Would I could know thy infant dreams,
As thou ly'st by thy mother's side;
Mind o'er thy face like a sunbow gleams,
Without its scorn or pride.
Thy spirit in joy hath gone to roam
With angels in yonder star:
O, better and brighter would be thy home,
Wert thou a dweller there.
O, the tears of thy mother fall fast and free,
As the rays of yon moon on thy face;
And the wish and the prayer of my heart for thee
Are poured in a deep embrace.
Sleep on, my boy, for thou can'st not know
How my heart doth thrill for thee,
As it looks on life and its frequent woe,
The ills that shadow the days to be.

James G. Brooks, Esq., the poet, and Mr. Losson, his most intimate friend, were often visitors at our house. They were like the Siamese twins — always together. If you saw one you were sure to see the other. Mr. Brooks married a poetess, and, with their united efforts at authorship, gained little else than a life of misfortune. Mr. Losson, being of the canny Scotch, left the literary for a more available business, and ensconced himself in Wall Street as a *real* estate broker. Surely a sensible man was this.

The Rev. Richard Varick Dye, the eloquent successor to Dr. Hooper Cummings, in the Vandewater Street Church, was another of my husband's devoted admirers. His rhetorical and classic discourses will long be remembered. We uniformly attended his church, which was an independent one. Mr. Dye often returned with us, after evening service, to our home. Then would commence the long train of anecdotes and witticisms of clerical life, than which nothing could be more amusing.

I remember, on one occasion, of a Saturday night, he came, breathless, into our house, it being quite late, to implore Mr. Fairfield to help him out with something for his sermon the next morning. He had, he said, nothing prepared. It was too late to undertake a long, serious paragraph; so, said he, "Dye, I have a couplet which I will give you, but which I think, with all your gravity in the pulpit, you will not be able to introduce." This was a challenge to his eloquence. He at once, and without knowing the character of the lines, consented. The next morning, on our way to church, we queried if it were possible for him to introduce these lines. His sermon was on the "Vanities of Life." It was near the close of the discourse, and they had, so far, been omitted, when, of a sudden, he came to a pause; after having uttered a sublime thought, he continued, —

> "For why should we foam, and fret, and fume, and fidget;
> Earth and its glories are not worth a digit."

I held my head down and shook with laughter, while Mr. Fairfield nearly pinched a piece of flesh from my arm, so fearful was he that I would disgrace myself. The gravity and eloquence with which he recited these lines made them appear sublime, and no one in the congregation could have thought else. This generous and noble-hearted gentleman was not without his trials. He was often attacked, and called to an account, by those whose religion consisted in long faces, sermons, and hypocritical cant — whose hearts, before high Heaven, could not bear the scrutiny with his own. It is but justice to him to note that he was "more sinned against than sinning." His nature was honest. If he had a fault, the world knew it.

There is no tyranny, affectation, or cant in true religion. When will the world learn to be just? to know that there is no such thing as piety without *its essence*, which is charity? that benevolence which suffereth long, and is kind and forgiving, is that which covereth a multitude of sins? The fact is, I have often commiserated the situation of some of the clergy. They are often forced into an unnatural and constrained manner, from false and erroneous impressions the world has formed of what they should be, how act, and how bear themselves. They are men tempted in all things like unto others. The same faults and worse, that we *are willing to watch for in them*, can be found in our own hearts and deeds.

The next event that had interested me was an introduction to Colonel Burr, the most extraordinary man, perhaps, of his time. At the poet's introduction of him, I was struck, old as he was, with his fine address. He took both my hands in his, and assured me that nothing could render him more happy than that presentation, adding that, in the future, I must be entitled to the honor of being made the tenth muse. I had read his history, and was acquainted with all the events of his life. His visit to Blennerhasset's Island, its fatal results and consequences, were incidents I always thought of when in his presence. I could not help my admiration of his genius. His conversation was fascinating and eloquent. He used to interest me greatly by his description of the beauties at the Court of St. James, during the time he was our minister to England. His admiration for beauty, as is the case with most men, exceeded that for mind. I never could see why it is that men should prefer the simpering of pretty silly women to the conversation of the intelligent and intellectual — for, really, it seems to me it would be a wiser plan to endeavor to raise the emulation (if possible) of the vain and ignorant by giving the preference to the best informed.

I was invited by Colonel Burr to visit a fair, which took place in the old Masonic Hall in Broadway. It was attended by the gay and fashionable of the city. As we were promenading around the hall, I saw nothing that attracted me so much as a painting of the head of Christ, said to have been done by one of the old masters. This, however, was doubtful. The painful and agonized expression, the tears that fell trickling down his sorrowful face, impressed me so mournfully, that I stopped before it, and directed the colonel's attention to it; to which he replied, "It is a fable, my child; there never was such a being." This expression had such an effect upon me, that I was quite silent the balance of our visit.

I always managed to keep in a state of content, as long as there was peace, though I can with truth assert, that I never awoke in the morning with the thought of what I had to enjoy, but of what, for the day, I had to do and to suffer. With my husband's salary we had been living for a time in tolerable comfort. Though I had had my own griefs and *fears*, I had suffered them uncomplainingly; things wore so much better an aspect than they had at the first, that I hoped time would work wonders. I consoled myself, though I knew there was an habitual animosity toward me in the heart of my husband's mother. With this, and his strange nature to contend with, none knew what I had to endure. In his temper he was fitful and moody. Sometimes, sunk in melancholy, he would seek the lonely attic, and lock himself in, seat himself by a window, and remain the greater part of the night gazing at the heavens. If I interrupted him by any inquiries, he would command me to depart. If I took no notice of these attacks or words, he would accuse me of indifference, and a want of affection. These were scenes to which I was forced to accustom myself.

In the month of May, after having exposed himself by walking some distance in a drizzling rain one evening, he took a violent cold, which gave him a long and severe attack of rheumatism, and which entirely incapacitated him for attending to the duties of his school.

This painful suffering continued during summer and autumn, and part of the winter. Having now no resource whatever for means to sustain us, we were again in a state of helplessness and need.

In the midst of this dilemma I was ill from the birth of my second child.

We were obliged to give up the house we had occupied, to remove to cheap apartments, and sell part of our furniture to obtain the comforts we needed.

Dr. John W. Francis was my husband's friend. He was kind to the poet. He admired his works, which gave him sympathy for his sufferings. It was difficult to know how to feel for one of his temperament. Under keen sufferings, his patience and mildness would make one forget the wrongs and injustice he may have suffered.

It was now by the assistance of friends that we were sustained. This was very galling to my pride. My nature was independent. I began to consider what it was possible for me to do to effect a change, so sad had our condition become.

The fatal months flew on. They had nearly reached the holidays. Fortunately, Mr. Fairfield had completed his poem. I proposed to him that, if he felt able to travel, I should accompany him to Boston, to obtain the subscribers requisite to print the poem, and sustain us through the winter. This proposal astonished him. He could not believe me sincere — much less did he think me heroic enough to undertake with him, sick as he was, such a journey. The snow was very deep, the weather intensely cold. "Beside," said he, "the journey to Boston must be by stage coach, — a very expensive one, — and we have no means; then, if all could be arranged, how can we leave our little Genevieve, who would suffer without her mother's care? Impossible," said he; "we can not go."

I had thought of all these obstacles; but something — it was *imperative* — must be done. Death was preferable to the state of life we daily endured. I said no more. The next day I arose early, made my arrangements, and went forth to visit the agent of the line which left for Boston.

A mother is always eloquent when pleading for her children.

I found the agent, told him my story, and made my appeal for a free journey. He looked at me intently for some minutes without speaking a word. I believe, for the time I was talking to him, he doubted my sanity. He asked me for my address, saying that he would visit my husband. I was not to be put off in this way. I begged him to accompany me. I feared, if I left him, the impression, if I had made any, for success might pass away.

Forth we hastened. My husband looked amazed at seeing us march in together. He had given up the project as one impossible to be accomplished.

The agent saw at a glance the situation of my family, and the ill health of my husband. He at once granted my request. The heart of my poor unhappy husband melted at this unexpected kindness.

Some writer has said, "Our destiny is our will, and our will is our nature." Words fail to trace the lot of that future, of which this was the fatal beginning.

On the third morning after the decision was made we got ready. The good agent sent a buffalo robe, by which to make us comfortable. I left my little ones in the care of my husband's mother, and off we started.

CHAPTER IX.

My husband rapidly gained strength after we left. The change of air and the excitement of travel was quite beneficial. He began to feel more cheerful at the prospect of restoration to health. Arrived safely, we were set down at a comfortable hotel, and shown to a delightful room, in which blazed a cheerful wood fire. All was as it should be. Now for the trial of my courage. A prospectus had been drawn up before we left home, and placed in a little book, in which I was to take the names of my patrons, if I got any. We came in town about ten in the morning. We took our breakfast in our room over a hot cup of coffee, and if ever I realized the comforts of an inn, I did that morning.

My first thought was now, how to begin. To succeed well, I must begin right. So I called for the Directory, to cull out the most prominent names. The Rev. Dr. Channing I placed at the head. With this preparation I started to make my *debut on the world's stage*. The cold was piercing, the snow deep. The doctor's residence was on a hill, about half a mile from the city. The path that led to it had only the print of a few feet upon it, — the snow scarcely trodden. As I turned the bleak corner in the direction which led to the doctor's house, the raw, cutting wind blew full in my face. I was thinly clad, without overshoes. At every step I sank a foot deep in the snow. I had worried half my way through, when I fell, and had some difficulty to regain my feet. After falling several times, I managed to get on, but was nearly frozen. On reaching the doctor's gate, I saw some one looking from the window. It was himself. He turned away in a state of apparent astonishment. In a moment a servant was at the gate, and assisted me in. The warm hall, as I entered, made me faint; the reaction produced by the warm atmosphere created intense suffering. It was some minutes before I was able to utter any thing but groans. As soon, however, as I was relieved, this good man invited me into his library, and on learning who I was, and my errand, he seemed intensely pained. He said, "You are young, indeed, to begin life's lessons; but you will have this consolation — the more you lose, in this life, of happiness, the less you will have to lose hereafter." After a visit of an hour, and a conversation I shall never forget, with his name on my book and a subscription for ten copies of my work, I was prepared to leave. He expressed the warmest sympathy for myself and my children, and with his blessing and wishes for my safety and success, we parted; he insisted, in the mean time, that I should accept of a pair of his India rubber overshoes. The doctor had a tiny foot, and the shoes fitted me very well. On going out, I found a sleigh and servant waiting to take me back to town. Instead of returning to the hotel, I hastened to Long Wharf; over the door of the first warehouse I came to, I saw the name of John Fairfield; in I walked, and found the gentleman in his counting room. I quickly introduced myself and my business. He seemed surprised and pleased. He added his name, and kindly offered to accompany and introduce me to the gentlemen through the wharf. My success was complete. I returned to the hotel with such a bounding heart and step, a queen might have envied me my happiness, strength of soul, and purpose. I had been out nearly the entire day. On entering my room I found my husband pacing the floor in a terrible state of agitation, fearing I had perished, or that some evil had befallen me. I placed in his hands my roll of bills, which was ninety-five dollars, the reward of my day's labor. The gratitude and tender emotions he manifested at my willingness to serve him were enough of reward.

We had left our little ones with scarcely the means to sustain them three days. Our first anxiety was to hasten a remittance by the first mail. That done, I had nothing to think of but the accomplishment of my object — to gain the means to publish my husband's poem, and as much beyond that as possible, to make my family comfortable and independent until the work was out.

We remained two weeks in Boston; each day brought me equal success with the first. Friends gathered around us. To the editors — God bless them —I am deeply indebted. My success from this visit amounted to twelve hundred dollars. With grateful hearts to the noble Bostonians, and with many and deep regrets at parting with kind friends, we hastened our return by the same route we had come.

The stage coach was crowded; the route a dangerous one. The snow was so deep, that it was impossible to discover, even for our experienced driver, the undulations of the road. Among our passengers there was one so immense that it was impossible to place even an ordinary sized man on the seat with him. As there were six of us to go, it was proposed that I should share the back seat with him. I did not like the arrangement, but it seemed one of those things which impel us to make a virtue of necessity. I had taken such a dislike to this person, that I regretted not having waited another day for our journey. I said to him, on taking my seat, "I hope, if we should have the misfortune to upset, that the stage may go over on your side." He grumbled out something in answer; he seemed too fat and indolent to be able to enunciate distinctly. We had got on very well until night came, and we were somewhere in the vicinity of New Haven. I had become exhausted, and fell asleep — when over went the coach *on my side.* We were all injured, except this fat man, who came very near crushing me to death.

This accident occurred near a small house, the occupant of which was a shoemaker, who, with his men, sat late at work. We were assisted into this place. The injury I had sustained was a severe one on my head; the shock was so great as to destroy for the time my memory. In the midst of the groans of the passengers, I was wondering at the appearance of every thing near me. On looking round I saw my husband bent over, suffering from an injury he had received on his arm. I asked him to tell me where we were; at my question he seemed annoyed. I insisted upon knowing; he petulantly answered, "We have been to Boston, going to New York." Not being able to make it out, and fearing to say any thing more, I repeated in a whisper several times what he said, still puzzled to comprehend any thing. In this state of anxiety I was placed in the coach, but at this time by the side of my husband, who was suffering much with his arm, but who sustained me as well as he could upon his shoulder. After getting on our way I soon recovered myself.

The day dawned. We stopped to breakfast, and had a merry time of it. The fat man sat opposite me. We all joined in merriment over the accident of the night, and congratulated ourselves that it was no worse. The fat man laughed immoderately, and apologized, certainly for what he could not help.

One thought alone interested me, and by its engrossing influence sustained me under all sufferings — the love I felt for my children; their helplessness, and the conviction that fate had little of good in store for them, redoubled my vigor, and added fresh inspiration to my energy.

With the blessing of Heaven my first efforts had been crowned, and I was now returned safe to my little ones, whose gentle caresses and sweet smiles would a thousand times repay me for all I had suffered. They flew into my arms. O, how their sweet prattle rejoiced my heart!

After the excitement of meeting was over, my first inquiry of my husband's mother was, how my children had fared before the remittance reached them. She replied, "Not very well; the fuel gave out, and they suffered for fire." She could, she said, think of no one who, she believed, had a kinder heart toward the family than Colonel Burr. The cold was intense, and she feared to trust the children in any one's care. She wrapped them as warmly as possible, and started with them for the residence of Colonel Burr, in Reade Street. She found him at home. On being told we had gone to Boston, and of the situation in which she was left, the old gentleman wept, and replied, "Though I am poor, and have not a dollar, the children of such a mother shall never suffer while I have a watch." He hastened on this godlike errand, and quickly returned, having pawned the article for twenty dollars, which he gave to make comfortable my precious babes. This noble and Christian-like act is recorded above.

"Inasmuch as ye have done it unto one of the least of these my brethren, ye have done it unto me," said the immaculate Saviour. I never have thought of this pious act without the tears of gratitude gushing into my eyes. Peace and repose be to his spirit!

My husband hastened to prepare his new work. The difficulty attending his own publications was the impossibility (owing to the expense) of having them stereotyped. An edition of a few hundred copies was soon exhausted, and always left him in the same emergency. His great poem, "The Last Night of Pompeii," was finished in eighteen hundred and thirty, and soon after its publication my husband sent copies to England, to Bulwer. He also wrote him a very long letter, but never received either an acknowledgment of the poem or the letter.

Bulwer's novel of a similar title appeared about two years afterward, and, it is only *justice to the poet* to say, was in *every* respect an entire and most flagrant plagiarism. The Argument, the Introduction of the Two Lovers, Converted Christians, Forebodings of the Destruction, the Picture of Pompeii in Ruins, the Forum of Pompeii, the Manners and Morals of Campania Portrayed, Diomede, the Prætor, the Night Storm, Vesuvius Threatening, Dialogue of the Christians, — the scenes of the *whole plot*, even the names of characters, *were all taken from this most grand and sublime poem.** To steal a purse is to steal trash, but to rob one of his thoughts, genius, and fame, is a greater injustice.

It is unnecessary to say that the edition was soon exhausted, and that the profits served to make our family comfortable for several months.

The love with which my husband became inspired, as a father, seemed to change his nature. I have often thought, had it not been for his temper, living

* In Bulwer's reply to the charge of plagiarism that had been made against him, he says, that "the names of persons and scenes in the novel were taken from history." But is it not very strange that in so extensive a history as the destruction of Pompeii and Herculaneum, containing, as it does, so *many* names and such a *variety* of scenes, that the two authors should have chosen *precisely* the *same scenes*, *plot*, and *names*?

with him might, at least, have been made endurable. His heart was benevolent, and susceptible of the most lively impressions ; but his temper was easily wrought upon. Fitful by nature, he was often led to commit acts of sudden violence, which were followed with bitter repentance. With the world he was always at variance. It did not comprehend him, nor he it. He was often deceived, and mistook his friends for his enemies, and *vice versa.* His soul floated in perpetual uncertainties, and knew not where to fix. It was deplorable to observe the instability of his mind and conduct.

CHAPTER X.

It was one of those soft summer nights in July. We sat with our little ones upon the porch, talking over the past, and wondering if the future had any thing of happiness in store for us. All things around seemed to assume a calm repose. The full-orbed moon in pearly beauty walked the heavens. It was one of those hours of thoughtful loneliness which sometimes steal over the heart, and bear us back, on darkened wings, to earlier passages of grief and sorrow. I held in my arms my little Genevieve. My son Angelo, who was chatting with his father, suddenly turned to me, and said, "Mamma, do you see that beautiful planet yonder, just over our heads? That planet is my home. There, mamma, I shall live in my beautiful *Orion*." His father had taught him the names of the constellations and planets. He would often point them out to me in the heavens, and while directing my attention to them, he would eloquently repeat Addison's most celebrated "Paraphrase on the Nineteenth Psalm" —

"The spacious firmament on high."

This dear child had a seraph's spirit. He had entered his fifth year, with one of those lovely natures born of heaven to return thither. His mind, naturally matured and thoughtful, by being too early forced, had produced that insidious disease in the brain so common to such children, but which we had not suspected. His memory was so remarkable that in his recitations he never blundered. At five years old he had read the Bible and many story books. The sufferings and crucifixion of the Saviour so affected him as to cause him such *excess* of weeping that we were often alarmed, and kept the volume from his presence. The last year of his life, on seeing the unhappy scenes that so often occurred in our family, he would take my hand and lead me aside, kiss me, and say, "Dear mamma, you shed so many tears, and papa is so unhappy, that I wish to go and live with the dear Saviour. Mamma, the dear Saviour says, 'Suffer little children to come unto me.' I wish to go and sit in his arms, where there will be no more trouble." He would plead with me to tell him what it was that made us so unhappy. With his sweet temper he could not understand why all were not happy; for he loved all. He would plead with me for the poor beggar. Often on his way to school he would drop my hand, and run in advance of me, at the sight of any unhappy child, man, or woman, and give them his pennies or his lunch, — to which, if I objected, he would, as he always did on such occasions, weep to excess. He would offer as an excuse for his charities, that he was not hungry — that he would wait until he got home.

Again we began to feel anxious. For myself, I

could never adopt the advice given, to "take no thought for the morrow," but was ever haunted by fears for the future. I advised my husband to fix his mind upon something permanent, that would give him stability, and insure us a support. I suggested the establishing a periodical — a quarterly work. At that time there was needed a work of this kind. He thought the idea a good one, embraced it at once, and issued his prospectus.

The better to succeed in this enterprise, I proposed to him to visit Washington.

Our president, General Jackson, had that year been inaugurated, with a new cabinet. To obtain prominent names at the beginning, I thought, would insure him success. For this purpose, he started in company with our little son, who began to show signs of ill health. A change of air, and the amusement of travel, I believed, might restore him. The following day after their arrival, my husband, with our little son, visited the president, who warmly urged the project of the work, and kindly introduced the poet to his friends. This outset, so cheering to his heart, gave him sanguine hopes of ultimate success. He returned to the hotel in fine spirits, to inform his mother of his prospects. An hour after dinner, our darling Angelo was suddenly seized with violent sickness and vomiting. Severe spasms quickly followed, with short intervals of consciousness.

On the fourth day after his illness, I received my husband's letter, breaking the news to me of his despair of the recovery of our idol.

Unaccompanied and alone, except with my little Genevieve, I set off. I reached Washington just in time to behold the dying agony of my child. He seemed to know me, and made an effort to speak to me. He lay in spasms until the closing of the day; then, with the evening twilight, his angel spirit took its flight to the home it had so much longed for.

With an agony too great for description, over the lifeless form of our child stood his poor father. He had not left his bedside day or night during his illness. He allowed no one to administer to his wants but himself. He had not slept for several nights; his reason seemed almost tottering. He would not allow the assistance of any one, but laid him in his shroud, and sat by him the livelong night, talking and sobbing to his lifeless form.

> "And he found with the dead the only rest
> That o'er his heart could creep."

A well of grief had opened in my heart, and nothing could stop its deep, still waters. I had little now to turn to for consolation.

We began to make preparations to depart with the remains of our son to New York. All the kindness that could be manifested by mortals to mortals under deep affliction was shown toward us. This calamity took place at Brown's Hotel. By its noble and hospitable keeper, Mr. Brown, nothing was omitted that could by any possible means contribute to our comfort.

It was the last of July. The weather was very warm. We started for Baltimore in a carriage that had been provided for us. We reached Philadelphia the next day, in the afternoon. Finding it impossible to proceed to New York, owing to the illness of my husband, we stopped here at a boarding house. A post mortem examination was hastily made by Dr. Horner, after which the dear form I had so much loved was laid in its dark and silent sanctuary. Dr. Horner came to me in his kind and sympathizing manner, and said, "My dear madam, be grateful that your son has gone to rest: had he lived, such was the formation and quantity of his brain, the overaction which had already begun must have continued, and probably at twelve years of age your son would have fallen into fatuity. Don't mourn; it is all right." Surely, thought I, this information ought to console me, and I tried to be resigned; not so with my husband.

We decided to remain in Philadelphia. We sent for our furniture, and hired a very small house, into which we betook ourselves. Mr. Fairfield, not caring apparently for any earthly object, entirely relinquished his project of getting up the work he had projected. He did nothing but grieve and visit St. Stephen's churchyard. He would there seat himself on the slab of marble which lay on the grave of Angelo, and weep for hours.

Want again stared us in the face. Our house rent became due, with a prospect of being ejected, and losing what we had. With these dismal trials, I again, more than ever, saw the finger of fate pointing to me as the only deliverer. One day, while taking a scanty meal with our only little one,—each was silent, and seemed to have lost courage to speak, — so desperate seemed our case, that a secret determination entered my mind. I looked upon my little one, and I vowed upon the altar of courage and energy, that she should never suffer while there remained within me the strength of a noble purpose. From that hour have I felt that the necessity which forced me to begin my exertions made it a still greater necessity to continue them.

The next morning I arose strengthened in my decision. I said not a word about my plans, opened my drawer, and took from it my prospectus, on which were the names of the president and cabinet at Washington. I bent my way into Market Street. O, how little I felt like encountering new faces, or forcing my urgent appeal! But it must be done, cost me what it might. I had vowed to be faithful to my impulse — to sacrifice all for my family.

The ancients have said that "impulse comes from the gods." In this emergency I felt that I was engaged in a good cause, which gave me confidence and courage. All were kind and exceedingly polite. I returned to my home after having obtained the number of eight signatures, amounting to forty dollars. My husband took little notice of my success for a time. I paid the house rent, and secured the comforts of a home. Each day I set apart for my visits five or six hours. In this way I soon laid aside the means sufficient to issue the first number of the "North American Quarterly Magazine." When I had accumulated the sum of seven hundred dollars, I gave it into the hands of Mr. Fairfield. He seemed amazed at my success.

He left home for the first day, on business, since the burial of Angelo, awakened to a sense of duty, to look for an office to begin business immediately. He found a dwelling to rent on Tenth, near Chestnut Street. To this pleasant abode we immediately repaired. The change was of service to us all. In a very short time the work was out, and once more my heart rejoiced.

CHAPTER XI.

The prospect of success, and the consciousness of the terrible destiny that awaited a failure, demanded of me all my energies. I lost not a moment. I began to feel certain of success, at least among gentlemen; with women it was a failure. The sympathies can only be called into play by the opposite sex. I had made a few attempts, but always found their curiosity paramount to their sympathy — that, so far from a desire to assist me, they were always ready with their limited empire to prevent, if possible, their husbands from doing so. I remember on one occasion having called several times at the residence of a very wealthy gentleman in the city, without being able to find him at home; feeling a certainty of his subscription, I was inclined not to give it up. Again I called. I discovered by the questions put to me by the girl who attended the door, that the lady of the house had felt unhappy at the anxiety I manifested to see her husband, and, refusing to see herself, I asked the girl at what hour they dined. At three, was her answer. I called precisely at that hour. I was invited in the parlor to be seated. In a moment the gentleman made his appearance through the folding doors which connected the drawing rooms, and closed them after him. I introduced myself, and the object of my visit, at which he expressed himself happy and honored. During the few moments of conversation that passed, I observed the folding doors move, and open a little. While the husband was placing his name on my list, the wife flung aside the doors with the velocity of lightning. The husband, nothing daunted, opened his purse, and took from it the five dollars, saying, "Madam, this I believe is the amount. I shall be most happy to continue a patron to the work as long as you shall have such labor to perform."

"You will — eh?" said the partner of his bosom, looking a fit subject for a lunatic asylum, instead of the home circle. "Our house is already flooded with books; beside, it's no charity to give to this woman, whose *dress* (the first object of a woman's attention) is more expensive than you can afford your wife. Her work shall not come here; if it does I'll throw it in the street."

This woman, no doubt, had a plenty of every thing she could possibly desire to make her happy; yet, like thousands of her sex, she withered in an atmosphere of unhappiness, of wretchedness, from her own irritable temper. There are many such, who, having no *real* trials, are not long in manufacturing them.

This may be taken as a specimen of my reception, whenever, in my business, I have met a woman — but, for the honor of my sex, there have been some noble exceptions.

I had been taught self-dependence from suffering more than from choice. How often have I felt a disgust for those of my sex, who, surrounded with every thing that can and ought to make them grateful and happy, instead of being cheerful, mild, and kind, fret and fume over every little contemptible nothing, taking pleasure in making their homes and *those who labor to sustain them wretched!*

These are the women who *boast* of their *affections!* who would go into hysterics were you to doubt their *love* for their husbands and families. O love! "*how many crimes are committed in thy name!*"

Our new work was fast gaining celebrity, as well as the most gifted contributors in the country. My husband's labors became intense. Mental labor is the most wearing of all. I was the sole financier, and it was astonishing to see how we got on for a time. After having obtained many patrons among the noble people of Philadelphia, my next effort was in the gay metropolis of New York.

On reaching the city, my first visit was to James Gordon Bennett, Esq., the gifted editor of the New York Herald. This gentleman received me with courtesy, and gave me, *I will not say a flattering*, but a *just* notice of my courage in projecting and *carrying out*, *unaided*, *so herculean* a task.

This notice created a desire in the minds of the people to serve me. We had not been long in the city before we were visited by many of the most distinguished and talented. The poet Halleck, our early, tried friend, came often to see us; we always found in him a convivial and delightful visitor. I admired his good sense in remaining *single*. He was a happy poet — a rare thing to be met with. He had a contempt for such as are always groaning over "the slings and arrows of outrageous fortune." He believed in the propriety of laughing at mishaps. It was truly refreshing to meet with one so gifted, who could turn tragedy into comedy with so much grace, wit, and *abandon.*

After paying my visits and respects to the noble and princely merchants of New York, I next bent my steps into Wall Street, among the bankers and brokers. It seemed a carnival week, so delighted was I with the stir and excitement. Escorts gathered round to introduce me. I felt grateful for such wishes to serve me, though I much preferred to introduce myself. It was a delightful thing to get away from stilts and ceremony. I liked to feel that every man was my friend. My business was a *carte blanche* every where.

During my stay of three weeks, though I was abundantly successful, I had left much undone. I felt anxious to return to my little girls, Genevieve and Gertrude. I left New York with regret. I had been greeted by all with feelings of interest and kindness; it had been a continued ovation. My path, indeed, seemed strewed with flowers, in contrast with what it had been.

CHAPTER XII.

WINTER had come. We returned from New York just in time to witness the debut of Fanny Kemble and her father. Mr. Fairfield, as an editor, had free access to the theatre. A portion of our Magazine was devoted to the criticism of the drama. Mr. Maywood, who was then manager of the Chestnut Street Theatre, kindly tendered to me a *carte blanche* for the season.

I was present to witness the entire range of characters performed by this great and beautiful actress. She was a radiant and gifted being. It was a delightful relief to repair for forgetfulness to witness these *great* performances.

It is the adverse circumstances that give the triumph. Toil, exertions, and obstacles had now become utterly mine — obstacles which grew out of the very nature of my energies and exertions. My business was calculated to create public sympathy in my behalf, which often became the source of domestic suffering and tyranny ; so that, in my despair I often appealed to Heaven for assistance to guide my steps, and to know which way I should turn for consolation ; but the world was before me, and I never could understand sinking under any shape adversity could take. I began to enjoy the struggle, in my strong belief of success. They who suffer, as has been my lot to suffer, have a right to speak of themselves. And if I have cause for pride or boasting, it is merely on account of my power of endurance.

Bidding adieu to our little ones, and taking letters of introduction along our route of travel through the State of New York, thence into beautiful Canada, our visits to Geneva and Canandaigua were most gratifying. It is by no means wonderful that men of eminence should seek retirement in that lovely spot. As soon as we had made ourselves comfortable at Blossom's Hotel, I started off in pursuit of patrons, having previously sent our letters of introduction to Mr. Greig and Mr. Granger. From these opulent and agreeable gentlemen I received a hearty welcome and encouragement.

The society in Canandaigua is excellent. Many invitations were sent to us, which, on account of my excessive labor and the fatigue I suffered, I was obliged to decline. This village is luxuriant with shrubberies, and beautiful foliage, and lofty trees. One incident connected with my visit I can not forget. Adjoining the hotel there lived a Scotch gentleman, a Mr. Wood, who was a bachelor, whose chief delight and happiness were in the cultivation of his flower garden. Mine host gave me some very curious anecdotes about this gentleman, and added, "He pays court to all fine women who visit this hotel, and you must not be surprised if in some way you receive a compliment from him."

The next morning, when it was scarcely light, the

chamber-maid knocked at our door with a message from Mr. Blossom. It being so early, I was startled. I opened the door in haste, fearing bad news from my family, instead of which she handed me, smiling, one of the most fragrant and beautiful bouquets I had ever seen. The dew was yet upon the flowers. A note was placed among its leaves. I opened it, and read,—

"These flowers, which represent grace, beauty, love, devotion, and suffering, are sent *from a Wood, by a Blossom, to a Fairfield.*" I was enchanted with the gift, and my husband delighted with this chaste and beautiful compliment.

We hastened on our journey to Buffalo, a point to which we had ordered our letters; on arriving there we found a letter had awaited us for several days with the information of the illness of one of our little daughters. We rapidly retraced our journey home, and my visit to Canada was made alone in after years.

Returned to Philadelphia, we found all right; our little one had recovered from what had been thought a dangerous illness.

This incident had made me nervous, and I feared to leave home again during that summer, and proposed to Mr. Fairfield to visit the environs of our city, and the "gentlemen of leisure" who had not yet seen our work.

One day, in my rambles, I accidentally called at the residence of Mr. James Brown, our Hon. Ex-Minister to France. This gentleman had been suffering from an attack of apoplexy, the effects of which confined him to his room. I informed the servant who was sent to me for my name, that I had called on business; that if Mr. Brown was too ill to see me, I would call at some future time. After delivering my message, he returned with an answer, desiring me to walk up stairs into his room. On entering, I saw a fine, intelligent-looking gentleman, his age about sixty-five; he seemed bending toward "that bourn whence no traveler returns." His manner was noble and dignified, and his conversation charmed me for a few moments, which, as I had called for patronage to a periodical work, turned upon literature.

He expressed himself surprised at my arduous undertaking; but on his discovery that the work was edited by Mr. Fairfield, his affability of manner changed so suddenly that I felt that I was transplanted to the frigid zone, somewhere in the vicinity of an iceberg. His face changed with his expressions, which were sarcastic and severe toward my husband. This vituperation had been occasioned by some misunderstanding with Mr. Fairfield during his visit to France, at the period when Mr. Brown was our minister to that nation.

I bade the gentleman good morning and left. Before I had reached the door which led to the street, the servant came running to me, saying Mr. Brown had sent him to request my return. On reëntering his apartment, he said, in a subdued tone and manner, "Madam, you had not left my presence a moment, before a feeling of regret came upon me at having ventured my opinion to you in regard to your relatives. I have been rude and harsh in my speech to a wife, for which I pray your forgiveness. Young as you are, the imprints of sorrow and suffering are already on your brow, and, Heaven knows, I would not add to these. I see how it is. Rough indeed are the chances from poverty and suffering for you, and though I can not consent to receive your work, remember that in me, if the future brings you calamities, you will find a friend. Promise me that, in any emergency that may befall you in the future, you will call on me, and this will give me some relief for the pain which I feel I have inflicted upon you during this visit." Touched by his obvious sympathy, as well as reassured by his gentle manner, I could not help weeping, and on taking my leave, promised to adhere to his request.

During that summer and autumn, I had walked many a weary mile to sustain, by my labors, our family and our work. Such had become the state of fermentation and disorder in our dwelling, that though I often faltered in strength, I preferred the out-door labor to the in-door disquiet.

> " There's nothing like the weary foot
> That betrays the weary heart."

Several months had passed away, and I had been barely able to keep down expenses.

The cost to sustain the Magazine amounted to about seven hundred dollars per quarter. This sum, together with our household expenses, required on my part great labor and travel; and though I began to think I had mastered my destiny, that the work had become so well established that my husband could get on without further aid of mine, in this, as in every thing, I was disappointed.

I forbear expatiating, but pass over five fearful months of illness and pain, to my convalescence.

I had been ill so long that our work became involved. Indeed, during my long suffering I myself had needed many of life's comforts. One morning, while making an effort to amuse my children, I heard a loud, uproarious noise in the hall below, and though I had not since my illness left my room, I walked to the head of the stairs. My husband was loudly talking with two men, who were officers, sent by our landlord to fulfill their duty, which was to remove the furniture on account of unpaid rent. Trembling with debility and nervousness, I begged these men to come to me, for I could not reach them, so faint with fright had I become. I informed them that I was Mrs. Fairfield, the lady of the house; that, though I was ill, if they would promise me to cease their unpleasant bickerings, and wait a sufficient time for me to walk as far as Washington Square and return, I would pay them the amount of rent they required.

To this request they kindly consented. They walked away, and seated themselves in their vehicles at the door. I made as hasty a toilet as my strength would permit, and walked slowly to the house of Mr. James Brown, then living in Washington Square. A thousand vague fears crossed my mind on the way. I knew in part the world. The offer this gentleman had made me, thought I, may be forgotten; if not, it was not likely that he believed I would ever, under any trial, have the presumption to call on him for any such favor as he had offered.

With these fears agitating my heart, I arrived at the door of Mr. Brown. I rang the bell. The same servant attended the door as before when I called. He asked me to be seated in the drawing room while he carried my message.

Mr. Brown came hurriedly in the parlor. He saw at a glance that I was ill and grieved. My feebleness of health made me hysterical, and I could not speak for weeping. As soon as I could do so I told him my errand. "Great God!" was his reply, "what suffering!" He then ordered John, the servant, to bring his portfolio, and filled a draft for the amount I needed. Language failed to express my gratitude, nor did I attempt to express any.

On my way to my dwelling I could not help saying to myself, 'Fool that I am, to toil, hour after hour, in giving others what they will take thanklessly and even reproachfully, full of their own petty cavilings and jealousies.' I never cared for money half as much as "golden opinions." Yet gold is better, perhaps, in reality; for what can make life endurable in this world but wealth?

Thus early had life become a burden to me almost intolerable. I paid the men and dismissed them. I then returned exhausted to my chamber.

CHAPTER XIII.

DOOMED always to a cosmopolitan life, as soon as my health was restored my husband and myself set out together to make the tour of the south. We came to Washington, where we remained a few days. We then pursued our route through South Carolina and Georgia, to New Orleans.

It had been my good fortune to secure letters from several gentlemen of Philadelphia to our eminent statesmen at Washington, Mr. Forsyth, Daniel Webster, and Henry Clay. By these honorable gentlemen I was received with marked cordiality. They each in their turn introduced my husband's work, and were the means of greatly increasing my success. Mr. Forsyth was at that time secretary of state, under General Jackson's administration. His manners were delightful. His countenance was mild, pale, penetrating, and intellectual. The abundance of curly white hair around his expansive forehead gave it a peculiar expression. He accompanied me to each of the departments, and presented me to the gentlemen comprising the cabinet. One proof of a great man is fitness for the circumstances in which he is placed. Mr. Forsyth possessed the genius of representation, and no one could be more suited to the high stations he filled in his country's service. His was a genius especially requisite among a people who require to be both excited and impressed. His character was brave, chivalric, and high-minded; above all he was sincere and faithful in his political principles and friendships.

Life's high places have many paths; and what brilliant dreams these great men had of their own and their country's future. *Webster* and *Clay* — these were names to which homage came from every quarter, and adulation from every lip.

I went for the first time to visit the Capitol. I listened, entranced, to the eloquence of each of these great statesmen. Ah, these were men who by their loyalty and genius could reunite discordant spirits, relieve their country from calamities, repair its ruins, and extinguish tyranny. How necessary were the lives of these illustrious men to our nation! They were, as all know, models and guides in political greatness; in a word, they were *the senators of senators*, who now sleep in their graves; who rest from their labors, but whose names are immortal. Their successors can do nothing better than to tread in their steps.

It will be remembered that General Jackson and his friends were the first who subscribed to our work; the general was in arrears in the sum of fifteen dollars. This afforded me an opportunity to visit him and pay my respects. I had been told that he was a very gallant admirer of ladies, and I longed for nothing more than to see the hero of the battle of New Orleans, and the man who had the courage to veto the

United States Bank. Before starting I made out my bill. It was cabinet day, which I did not know until I reached the White House. Intent, however, upon my object, I sent in my card; I was at once ushered into the presence of the president and cabinet.

The general met me at the door. He took both my hands in his, and presented me to the party, then led and seated me in his chair. Nothing could be more gentle or graceful than his manner. We chatted and passed compliments. I then presented my bill. There was a pause, and all business suspended. The general glanced at it; then straightening up his tall figure, he said, "Madam, I am sorry to speak harshly to a lady; but before this bill can be paid, your husband must recant a most foul calumny which I find in the last number of his Magazine against General Coffee — my friend, and one of the noblest specimens of God's works. Madam, I say, *by the Eternal*, that wrong shall be redressed; and unless your husband makes an apology to me through the work in which appeared his unjust and savage attack, not one dollar of my debt shall ever be paid." This, thought I, is conclusive. I replied that, though I knew nothing of the article to which he referred, I presumed that Mr. Fairfield had written what he believed to be just, and without prejudice; and that I doubted the propriety of an apology, unless he were *convinced* of an error. General Coffee had recently died, and in a paper then edited by Mr. Blair, of Washington, there appeared a eulogy, which Mr. Fairfield thought unmerited, on his life and character. General Coffee acted under General Jackson in command in the war with the Indians. Mr. Fairfield, to substantiate what he had assumed, obtained a history of the war, and, to prove his assertions, copied therefrom letters from General Coffee to General Jackson; these letters gave the information that he (General Coffee) had obeyed strictly his commands — had burned the wigwams of the Indians and exterminated their women and children.

Mr. Fairfield was a warm friend to the Indians; he believed that they were defrauded and unjustly treated by the white people.

It was the cruelty of *murdering* the *women* and *children* which gave him an unfavorable impression of the character of General Coffee. And to this day the fifteen dollars remains unpaid.

We left Washington delighted with our visit, and hastened our journey to Savannah, stopping at Richmond and the smaller places on our way. A pilgrim who is in search of hospitality and noble hearts may find them here. Even so soon on my southern journey had I fallen in love with southern manners and kindness.

It would cost me much patience to sum up and set down all my adventures, discoveries, opinions, and speculations in the new school of experience I had entered; many of which were no less farcical than those of "Gil Blas."

We hastened our journey to Savannah. On arriving there I at once called on Mr. T——t, a banker, to whom I had a letter of introduction. On my entering the bank he came hastily to me, blushing, and taking my hand he gave it a hearty shake. His face had not the celestial rosy-red, but a good positive scarlet. He most warmly said, "How glad I am to see you! When did you arrive?" He called me so familiarly by my first name that I began to wonder if I had not seen the gentleman before. "I believe, sir," said I, "that we are strangers," at the same time handing him my letter. At this information he dropped my hand, looking like a startled fawn.

The conversation turned on my business, each trying to be very grave; but it would not do. To relieve the embarrassment he seemed to feel, I said, "Never mind, sir; these accidents will sometimes happen;" at which we both enjoyed a hearty laugh. He then frankly acknowledged that he thought me an old flame of his, the resemblance was so striking.

What was most remarkable, the flame and myself both possessed the name of Jane.

My husband and myself were invited to dine at the house of this gentleman. The grace, ease, and good feeling with which his charming wife and himself performed the honors of the table, made us feel quite at home. We talked over the adventure of the morning, which made a gay scene. Indeed, I have not often met with a more agreeable family, or any who better understood the art of pleasing conversation.

I can not, nor, if I could, have I time or space to enumerate one half of the agreeable people or the happy incidents of my journey to the south; but all seemed anxious to make my stay with them as pleasant as possible; all expressed the warmest regard for me, and a desire for my success.

I can truly say, that during this journey not one unpleasant occurrence took place to mar my happiness.

Arrived at Columbus, Georgia, we took it in our heads, being so near Florida, to extend our visit to that beautiful country. We found a steamer sailing direct to Tallahassee. We immediately took passage, and found ourselves in excellent company as we glided down on this beautiful river. There happened to be on board a large party of ladies and gentlemen who were *en route* to a ball, to be given the next night at the mansion of Governor Call.

We arrived in Tallahassee early in the morning; after breakfasting we took a stroll to view the town.

In this work it is not my purpose to go into ecstasies over *scenery;* mine is the record of suffering and experience. All who travel, if they have sense enough to understand and admire the beautiful, can do so in the still worship of their own hearts. There is a great deal of cant by travelers and authors on this subject. The Supreme Being has told us to *be still*, and admire, and know that he is God.

We returned from our walk pleased with what we saw. On entering our parlor we found that Governor Call had left a note for us, with an invitation to the ball to be given at his house that night. I have seldom been present at a more elegant or delightful party. There was dancing until a late hour, in which I joined. It was a recreation in which I greatly delighted.

My husband never danced. This was an amusement, he said, belonging to women and children.

During the evening, my *vis-a-vis* was the accomplished Princess Murat. I was presented to her by the governor, and was charmed by her unaffected and lady-like demeanor. The ladies of Florida rank in beauty among the belles of our country. I have not often met with more charming women.

In the early part of my history I had forgotten to mention the fact of my friendship for Madame Murat. I allude to the wife of Prince Achille Murat, brother to the husband of the lady I met at the ball. They are sons of the Ex-King of Naples. We were about of an age, and were married nearly together.

She was a Miss Frazer. Her early history was something like my own.

This lady, during the vicissitudes and exile of her husband, was reduced to teaching a small school in Bordentown, New Jersey, where for a long time she resided, and where I sometimes visited her. She needed no title to exalt her, for she was nature's own princess and gentlewoman. I recollect on one occasion I called on her for patronage to my husband's work. I found her employed in her school. "O," said she, "this marrying princes and poets is not exactly what it should be; it does not secure happiness."

She is now living at the court of Napoleon the Third, in the enjoyment (if not of happiness) of the full honor of her title as princess.

We passed a delightful week in Florida, then hastened our journey to Columbus, and from thence as rapidly as possible to New Orleans.

CHAPTER XIV.

WE soon found ourselves in New Orleans, located at the princely St. Charles. The time for our absence had nearly expired. Mr. Fairfield's time was always limited. He must be at home to issue his work at the end of every three months.

I had but three weeks left me for business. Amusements I never thought of. Domestic uneasiness, and anxiety for my children, filled all my thoughts.

My life was that of a wanderer, up and down in the midst of toils and perils, always uncertain, never fixed, having a residence, but no home. I began to find that this manner of life procured me a great number of acquaintances — of real friends perhaps but few.

"What greater happiness can we propose," says the great Petrarch, "than to pass our lives with the *one we love*, and with a few united friends, with whom we think aloud, and who have but one will, one soul, with faces always serene, minds always agreed, and hearts always open!" Alas! this picture belongs to but few.

The New Orleans "Picayune" gave a fine review of our Magazine, and one of those notices to myself which I so constantly received from our noble-hearted and generous editors *every where*, and which aided me much in my arduous labors.

I do not wish to be thought egotistical, (autobiographies are always more or less so,) or take any undue merit to myself. I therefore exclude from my work these notices, so full of praise and good wishes, and simply mention the adulation I received from the people, the invitations to parties, balls, dinners, and the attentions with which I was every where overwhelmed. Nor do I deny that I possessed the vanity, so common to human weakness, of being enchanted by all these ovations; but I must confess, I take more pleasure in describing the scenes of my adversities, for in these there are experience and knowledge. A Greek writer has said, " What does one know who has not suffered?"

In these my sad memoirs, I address myself more to the wretched than to the gay or happy — those who like myself have passed the ordeal of suffering.

In human existence there is an infinite variety, and minds have as little resemblance as faces. To the beings who are puffed up with prosperity my life would be an enigma they could not comprehend.

The hospitality with which I was received by the citizens, natives as well as strangers from all nations, is shown by my success, which in a little more than three weeks amounted to the sum of *three thousand dollars*, independent of our expenses.

We hastened our departure from the Crescent City, from its charming scenes and people, by steamer, up the Mississippi to Wheeling, thence to our abode in the delightful, quiet, and happy city of Philadelphia.

On my return home, I found several letters from

kind friends. Among them was one from Mr. James Brown, our ex-ambassador, inclosing a letter of introduction to Captain M——z, from England, of her majesty's navy.

I called with my letter, and sent the gentleman my card. In a few moments he entered the drawing room. His appearance was very distinguished — his manner courtly.

"The circumstances," said I, "in which I am placed, sir, have induced me to call on you, as I do on others, with a work edited by my husband. Will you do me the honor to give me your signature as a subscriber?" At this request he handed me his card, and added, —

"Madam, I shall be most happy to be of service to you in any way you may mention. Perhaps I may be permitted to ask what those circumstances are."

I had by this time become accustomed to what is called "dead sets." I was generally composed on these occasions, and quite collected.

"They are, sir, pecuniary embarrassments," I said.

"Your information," added he, "does not leave a single obstacle in the way of a most perfect happiness. May I claim the privilege of being told something more of your history?"

"This would occupy too much time," said I, "and my life, such as it is, could little interest a foreigner and a stranger."

He had a singularly encouraging manner, and talked easily.

"There is nothing in marriage," he replied, "that can supply the want of affection, and you surely can not love the man who enforces on you such exposure and labor."

I inquired, "What better evidence could I give of affection than my willingness to sacrifice my life for my husband and children?"

"A weakness, madam," said he, "a weakness; but you will allow me the pleasure of calling on you with the names of some of my friends. At what hour shall I have the happiness of finding you at home?"

This was *alarming*. The idea of receiving a stranger, a visitor, unknown to my husband, was something I never dared to dream of. I informed the gentleman that my avocations absorbed the most of my time, that I had no moments set apart for visitors, but was ever occupied with business, and my duties to my family. Thanking him, I took my leave.

I could never relate any of these episodes to my husband. "Take any shape but that," was what I always felt when tempted to deal in witticisms, or relate an adventure.

My husband could not see that, though I felt keenly the inequalities of human allotment, I had my choice of every earthly advantage that fortune could bestow, and that I *preferred* to waste the best years of my life, and the deepest feelings of my heart, in anxiety and toil. Alas! how much was there of bitter lessons of which he little dreamed — lessons which come in the experience of but few!

The following day after this visit, late in the afternoon, I was preparing a salad for dinner. My husband stood near me, holding in his arms our little babe, when suddenly a carriage stopped at our door. The bell rang. In a moment more the servant handed me a note. As I was more intent on having a good dinner than on seeing the contents of the note, I handed it to my husband, saying, "See what that is." He opened it and read.

It was fearful to behold the expression of his face, it was so full of despair, wrath, and revenge. During these moments I stood horror-struck, not knowing what were the contents of the note, or by whom it was sent; nor dared I ask. In a few moments his wild frenzy turned into weeping, when he threw himself into a chair. His agony seemed so intense, that I felt the deepest sympathy and sorrow, though I remained ignorant of the cause. He asked me if I would consent to copy an answer to the note — one that he should dictate, over my signature. I answered, "Certainly," at which reply he seemed relieved. He then handed me the note, and went into his library, made his toilet, and went out. The letter was from Captain M——z.

He soon returned, and wrote the note, which I copied, the tenor of which demanded an apology, or a challenge from my husband would be the result. There seemed to be a pretty fair prospect of pistols and coffee.

The answer came with not one word in reference to my husband, who could not, however, demur at its contents. But I am dwelling too long on these trifles.

> "Great sufferings have great strength; there is a pride
> In the bold energy that braves the worst,
> And bears proud in the bearing."

I was philosophical by nature, and therefore had not to become so, with my husband's keen feelings so incompatible with happiness. It were well I was so. Alas for the child of genius! — the very word *poet* is synonymous with misfortune. Few indeed there are who comprehend such natures. In prosperity or adversity, the poor poet finds nought but discontent. His genius and ambition, the sorrows and disappointments which are his allotments, turn to poison, or to a void. "Their empire is divided between bitterness and exhaustion." If he has any happiness, it is only when he luxuriates with the aspirations and efforts which link his name to the future — the visionary of sublimest dreams.

My poor husband labored industriously with his pen. Night after night I have known him to sit late, alone and unaided, to perform the task of writing or correcting articles for his Magazine. I have seen him often — how often! retire after taking some anodyne, perhaps laudanum, to calm his nerves and fevered mind, worn by excitement and exhausting exertion. O, is it not a sad page in which the annals of the great are written? For such ought we not to exert the kindest sympathies of our nature?

During five successive years we labored together, fondly dreaming of that future which should bring us repose and independence. My husband had concentrated in his Magazine the genius and talent of the country. The clouds of adversity that had hung over us so long and so fearfully were rapidly dispersing, and cheerful gratulations came to us from many lips.

Our two lovely daughters grew in beauty and intellectual loveliness by our side. O, how entirely my every hope was centered in my children! though I looked upon them, thus early, with a dread, which haunted me with a perpetual shadow, that fate would some day exact a terrible penalty for the happiness they afforded me. Miss Landon has said, "The shadow flung from the soul is an omen;" and mine at that time must have held some mysterious communion with the future. My eldest daughter, my Genevieve, was a blonde, pale and fair, with sculptured features, soft and large blue eyes. There was an expression on her face too thoughtful for one so young. Her smile was sweet, but never glad.

My youngest daughter, Gertrude, was a brunette, with features and expression which bore a striking resemblance to her sister. They were equally intellectual, and gave early evidence of genius. In many things they partook largely of their father's nature — such as an early fondness for study. They each possessed great memory, and an ardent desire for knowledge. They were so unhappy when placed at school, that we agreed between us to educate them at home. Their father gave his time and attention, all that he could spare, to this purpose. They preferred solitude, apart from other children.

The first years of their childhood were passed in study, in their father's library, which was composed of choice selections of historical, philosophical, and literary works. Thus situated, they early learned to think, and to know the value of self-application. They read and studied much.

At this period, just as I had begun to feel secure and sheltered from actual misfortunes, those especially which spring from poverty, my husband was suddenly seized with the fearful malady of epilepsy. The frequent occurrence of these convulsions in the course of a short time so enfeebled his mind as to render him unable to perform the duties required of him for his Magazine.

An awful thing it is — the failing energies of a master mind. The poor poet, who had placed implicit confidence in his genius, now found himself utterly defeated. Slow indeed are such minds to credit that the never-failing resource can at last fail them. But so it is. Like a dried-up fountain, the perennial and bright fertility ceases, and ceases forever.

There are some natures which seem sent into this world but for a brief and bitter trial: such a nature was my husband's; he had not strength for the struggle. He had ever felt despondency steal over his highest moods from his earliest youth. The weight of an unfulfilled destiny was ever upon him, and he became fully impressed that these feelings had long been the unconscious omen of an early death. His was a hopelessly melancholy nature, and therefore much to be commiserated. It is very easy to say, *for such as have no feeling*, that such a state of misery as his was morbid and mistaken. Let such remember that before we can change our feelings we must change our natures; and a temperament of his sensitive and excitable kind is of all others the most difficult to alter and subdue. For such there is no peace until the fevered brain be calmed, and the beating heart at rest forever.

In his poem of the "Idealist," which I annex here, may be found, expressed in the sweetest language of poesy, the extreme sensitiveness and melancholy with which during life he suffered.

When the last hues of sunset fade away,
And blend in magic wreaths of light and shade,
And stillness sleeps beside the closing day,
Drinking the music of the breezy glade,
'Tis joy to wander forth alone
Through shadowy groves and solemn woods,
And muse of pleasures past and gone,
'Mid nature's holy solitudes:
For then my spirit to its God aspires,
And worships in the light of Love's ascending fires.

Where rocks hang tottering from the mountain's side,
And ancient trees in hoary grandeur wave,
I love to sit, forgetting pomp and pride,
And all the passions that the soul enslave,
And yield my heart to the sweet charm
Of Nature in her loneliness,
While soft-voiced zephyrs, breathing balm,
The perfumed flowers and shrubs caress,
And the last songbird pours her parting lay
Of love and praise to bless the brightly-closing day.

There is a loveliness in Nature's smile
Which fills the heart with heaven's own holy gladness,
Though he, whose heaven is in her charms, the while,
Feels thoughts steal o'er him of surpassing sadness.
When 'mid the perfect works of God,
He muses on the sin and folly
That make man's heart their dark abode,
O, who would not be melancholy?

How sad the thought that this fair world should be
The dwelling place of guilt and helpless misery!

Yet if his woe be unallied to crime,
And suffering not from evil conscience spring,
To Nature's bosom let him come, what time
Flowers ope the bud and birds are on the wing,
And there the fretful world forget,
And search the world of his own breast,
Where thoughts, like suns, arise and set,
And whirlwind passions rage unblest;
There let the son of song and sorrow lie,
And inspiration catch from Nature's speaking eye!

From earliest youth I loved alone to climb
The moss-wreathed rock, and from the mountain's brow
O'er sea and land, an amplitude sublime,
To gaze when sunk the sun in radiant glow,
And poured o'er quiet vales, and hills,
And groves, and meads, and gushing streams,
Such glory as creation fills,
His last full swell of golden beams.
O ye, who would adore the Eternal Power,
Go forth alone and pray at twilight's hallowed hour!

The spirit then throws off the garb of clay,
Which in the warring world 'tis doomed to wear,
And robes itself in beautiful array,
And soars and sings amid the blooming air,
Where in aerial halls of light
Meet kindred spirits pure and good,
And parted souls again unite
Where grief and pain can not intrude,
And in the radiance of soul-mingling eyes
Reveal the mystic power of heaven's high harmonies.

I ever was a melancholy child,
Unmirthful and unmingling with the crowd;

The loneliest solitude on me hath smiled
  When lightning darted from the rifted cloud;
    And I have felt a strange delight
      'Mid forests and the cavern's gloom,
    And wandered forth at dead midnight
      To muse beside the lonely tomb.
I always loved the light of that dread Eye
Which flashed upon me from eternity!

I knew not whence such unshared feelings came;
  I only knew my heart was full of deep
Emotions vivid — but without a name;
  Within my breast they would not, could not sleep,
    But swayed me, in their giant power,
      To passion's uncommuning mood,
    And drove me from the festive bower
      To ruined tower and lonely wood,
Where on my soul ideal glories came,
Fairies and Oreads bright, and coursers rapt in flame.

O, how I loved that solitary trance,
  That deep upheaving of the bosom's sea,
O'erstrewn with gems that dazzled on my glance,
  Like eyes that gleam from out eternity!
    Creatures of every form and hue,
      Lords of the earth, and angels passed
    In garbs of gold before my view,
      Like lightnings on the hurrying blast,
And voices on my inward spirit broke,
And mysteries breathed and words prophetic spoke.

The child of reverie and the son of song,
  A word could wound me or a look depress;
I saw the world was full of ill, and wrong,
  And sin, and treachery, and sad distress;
    And so, e'en in my boyhood's morn,
      I fled the haunts that others love,

That I might think why I was born,
And what below and what above
Was due from one thus sent upon the earth
To sow and reap in tears, and mourn his mortal birth.

My birthplace was the airy mountain hight,
And childhood passed 'mid nature's grandeur wild,
And still I see, by memory's magic light,
How on my soul each Alpine mountain smiled!
Though years have passed since I was there,
And many a change hath o'er me come,
There's not a scene, or wild or fair,
Around my long-forsaken home,
But I could point in darkness out, and tell
The shape and form of things I loved so well.

Trees, birds, and flowers were my familiar friends
In boyhood's days, and every leaf that grew
Whispered soft oracles of love; there blends
With budding thought a spirit from the dew,
That gems each quivering leaf and flower;
And precious to the mind mature
Are memories of that guiltless hour,
When with a worship fond and pure
The soul beheld in every thing below
A God sublime, whom we in works alone can know.

Deep in the soul rest early thoughts, and now
My spirit roams 'mid lonely hills, when Night
Her starry veil throws o'er her spotless brow,
And wraps her elfin form in fair moonlight;
Then o'er me come those thoughts again,
Which were my heaven in other years,
And I forget my bosom's pain,
And cease to feel my trickling tears.
Weird sibyls! cease of destiny to prate!
The boy creates for life, and ratifies his fate.

Here let me rest, a wanderer tired and faint,
  Dear Nature, on thy soft maternal breast,
And learn for others those fair scenes to paint,
  Which taught me wisdom and which made me blest!
    Fashion and folly still may rove
      And seek for pleasure in the throng,
    But I will live in thy sweet love,
      And blend thy praises with my song,
O holiest daughter of the Holy One,
Whose smile wafts spirits to the heavenly throne!

CHAPTER XV.

The best part of biography, that which would interest the most, perhaps, is that which is generally omitted. From this darkened period I must lock my griefs deep within my inmost heart. How many untold and buried memories lie hidden there! aye, of wasted affections, of faults as of sorrows, hopes, and fears.

It was about a year after the poet's health began to fail, that our magazine ceased its existence.

To save our home and household, for the future provision for my family, depended solely on myself. From this period commenced the decline of the poor poet. I determined to get together the poems of my husband, — his fugitive as well as his elaborate productions, — and compile them in one large volume. For this purpose, I immediately engaged a printer to commence the business, while I, with my eldest daughter, Genevieve, began our preparations as *compagnons en voyage* through Canada and the British Provinces. It required great labor for so expensive an enterprise.

Youth, health, and energy are strong consolers. With these I was abundantly blessed, so that I envied no one. It was not long after we started before we reached the charming city of Montreal. Taking our route by the Niagara, we glided down on the beautiful St. Lawrence River, with its thousand isles.

Arrived safely, we were delighted with the old aspect of the town. I called for a cab, and was taken to Rascoe's hotel — a fine house, which had just been opened. Genevieve, my little daughter, was in ecstasy with this her first journey. The day following we drove through the city to the mountain. We were delighted with the beautiful residences, and the free, fresh, invigorating air. Though Montreal lacks some of the agreeable superfluities with which some of our cities of the States abound, it contains leisure, repose, and solitude — three pleasant things, necessary to one's happiness. But as my business is more with men and manners, and books, (at least the sale of them,) than with towns or a description of rivers, with the endless variety of inlets, noble bridges, and causeways, I shall not stop to count the number of the streets and lanes, nor to describe the beauty of the public buildings, nor the numerous cottages that surround the city and form its most beautiful interest, but proceed to narrate my adventures.

The Canadian rebellion, together with the border difficulties, which had their origin as far back as the treaty of 1783, created the same state of affairs up to 1839, and obliged the government of England to put their frontier in a state of defence. For this purpose they sent over to the Canadas and the Provinces many of their bravest men. These gallant and accomplished officers, with their regiments, which were quartered in Montreal at that time, gave to the city an appearance of gayety and animation. I witnessed several of their sham battles. The discharges of their arms, and the glittering of their swords gave to the scene the appearance of a well-contested battle field. However great the glory mankind attach to war, to me, it breathes of nothing but strife and carnage, of the destruction of families, of broken hopes and hearts; so that the sight of these regiments had only the effect to make me melancholy.

In company with a friend, I often, at the close of the day, after my toils were over, visited the barracks, to listen to the tattoo and England's national air of "God save the Queen." We had visited the place several times, when one evening there came suddenly through the crowd a servant, with a chair in one hand and a silver tray in the other. On it was placed a cup of porcelain with delicious coffee, with cream and cakes, arranged in a style which would have done no discredit to a queen. As I was the only one to whom this delicate mark of attention was shown, I was very anxious to know the officer to whom I was thus indebted — for no woman thanks another for a compliment addressed to the sex in general. My introduction to the *elite* of Montreal, and their kind and hospitable manner toward me, made me in love with the people; and though I intended a stay of only a week, I extended it to three. I passed my days delightfully. *But all things that give happiness in this world pass rapidly away.* Having succeeded beyond all expectations, I bade adieu to friends, and departed for other scenes of labor to Quebec.

The order of the day with me was *en avant*. The next morning, after a pleasant journey on board the steamer, I saw the sun rise in all its majestic splendor upon the city of Quebec. We breakfasted, myself and daughter, in our own private apartments — there being no *table d'hôte* at the hotel for ladies. I liked the plan of private table much better. It gives one the agreeable feeling of being at home with one's own family. After this repast was over, we soon found ourselves in a carriage, being driven to all the remarkable places in and around the city. We visited the citadel. We then drove to the Plains of Abraham, from which we gazed upon the grand scene below, around, and above us. As we had been out several hours, and had nearly expended our stock of admiration and romance, we returned to the hotel to dine; after which we again started off to take a view of the beautiful cottages which dot the environs outside the walls. The moon, when it arose, found us still unsatiated with the beauties of the scene. My daughter Genevieve, whose mind was alive, almost by intuition, to the slightest signal of intelligence, was so far beyond her years that she never seemed a child. She had become, in my lonely wanderings, my solitary companion, my chief consolation; and whether, with her, this day had been well or ill spent, I must leave to Him to determine who reads all hearts.

"Accept, then, O supremely great! O Infinite! O God!
From this primeval altar — the green and virgin sod —
The humble homage that my soul in gratitude would pay
To thee, whose shield has guarded me through all my wandering way."

The following morning I sent out my letters, which I had brought from my noble friend and others at Montreal. During the day and evening I had many visitors; among them were the noble and gifted editors. The next day I found myself kindly mentioned and warmly received by each of these gentlemen in their several papers. The Canadian men have a peculiar, gentle manner; they are not so stiff and formal as the English. They have the chivalry and courage which we look for in men, with the delicacy and tenderness of women. During my stay I had the happiness to be introduced to Mr. Burroughs, the acting prothonotary of the city, and his charming and polite wife and daughters. We were invited to visit them at their cottage, a little distance from town, where we met several of the officers of her majesty's army, with whose unaffected manner and easy conversation I was much pleased. By this amiable family we were most kindly and hospitably entertained.

I have traveled far and long, and I have never met kinder hearts or nobler natures than in Canada. Those who exult in beautiful scenery, rich hills and fertile valleys, could not fail to enjoy a visit to this enchanting country. I passed much of my time, during my stay, in drives and pleasant walks. The Falls of Montmorenci delighted me. The distance, I think, is about ten miles from the city. Our visit was in September. The falls are pleasantly situated, with groves of trees around above them. Their breadth is narrow, though their hight is stupendous. The body of water is small, but the scene is majestic and inspiring; they fail, however, of the grandeur and awful sublimity of Niagara. The autumnal tints of the oak and maple, showing both scarlet and crimson, some yellow and red, with the birds singing so lively among the foliage, made this a most charming day's ramble. *There are a few days, and but a few, from among the many of our lives, which*, from their *happy associations, we never forget*, and this was one such to me.

Equally successful here as every where, I again took leave of friends, and departed in the beautiful steamer Unicorn for Halifax, Nova Scotia, a voyage of three days.

On our arrival, the porters from the hotels were already at the vessel, only to inform us, however, that they were crowded with people — that not a room could be had. Some new excitement had filled them to overflowing. This information was quite terrifying to me, alone as I was, in a strange land; but in these dilemmas I never lost presence of mind. Just at that moment the captain came to me, bringing with him a Mr. Bennett, a resident of Halifax, whom he politely introduced. He had come in his carriage, expecting to meet some friends. On being told by the captain that a lady was on board, with her daughter, from the United States, he came at once to offer me the hospitality of his home, until I should be able to find hotel accommodations. This invitation I gladly accepted; nor shall I ever forget, or ever cease to feel grateful to, this amiable and intelligent family, to whom I was so much indebted. Kind acts should be communicated;

and I have felt chagrined at not having it in my power heretofore to speak of this noble family. I fear with us in the States you would scarcely find such an instance on record; for in these days the *stranger* is eyed *askance*, and not received, as of old, with magnanimous and irreproachable benevolence.

As soon as we were comfortably fixed at our lodgings at the hotel, I sent out my credentials, which were addressed to the Hon. Judge Uniacke and the Hon. Leander Starr, including the editors. The following notice appeared of me the next morning: —

"MRS. SUMNER LINCOLN FAIRFIELD. — This intrepid and accomplished lady arrived in our city in the steamer Unicorn a few mornings since. She is a resident of Philadelphia, in the United States. She brings letters of introduction from eminent gentlemen in Canada, where, from our contemporaries, we learn she has been highly appreciated, and amply rewarded by her success in her arduous undertaking, in her holy errand of love for her family. The work she proposes to publish is the poems of her husband, who at present is suffering from the loss of health, and whose genius entitles him to patronage every where. We ask for this lady what we feel quite sure she must obtain — a kind and warm reception from the citizens of Halifax."

Judge Uniacke, in company with his excellent wife, came immediately to pay their respects, and to request my attendance at a social party of friends, to be given at their residence the next evening. I was introduced to several fine-looking women; but really it is impossible to see every thing and remember every body; and beside I must confess that I prefer to talk with men than with women — simply, for the best reason in the world, they are natural and unaffected. From them one can generally derive solid information. My attention was drawn to the judge; his manner was grave, his person was tall and stately, his conversation remarkably intelligent.

I passed a pleasant evening, and left impressed that, if the people were generally as agreeable, I should have a delightful visit at Halifax.

At that period Colonel Starr filled a high place as member of the House of Parliament. He was also *aide-de-camp* to the governor, who at that time was his excellency Sir Colin Campbell. Colonel Starr lived on an equality with the governor. At his house all foreigners of distinction were nobly entertained. This gentleman married a lady from the United States, a Miss Throgmorton, a most lovely and graceful woman. Several of our statesmen about that time visited Halifax, and were entertained by this charming family: among them were Daniel Webster, and John Quincy Adams. At their residence, during my stay, I had the happiness to meet with many persons of distinction and talent; among them was Mr. Villiars of England, a gentleman universally admired for his genius and urbanity. I am deeply indebted to Colonel and Mrs. Starr for the warm interest they felt in my success, which was shown, not in idle compliments or good wishes, but in *actual noble acts and deeds.*

Mrs. Uniacke kindly urged upon me her carriage,

12 *

for the purpose of making my visits to the citizens. With this kindness extended to me, my labors were exceedingly lightened.

During my stay, Mr. Howe, the accomplished editor of one of the principal papers, called in his carriage to take me to his country seat, where were gathered a pleasant party to meet me. Among the guests were Mr. McNab and family. I love the study of men and manners, and I must say that the people in these Provinces charmed and delighted me. Say what you will, in England, Canada, and the Provinces, the aristocracy of wealth is altogether subordinate to the aristocracy of intellect — *intellect always first.* Even with the best informed Americans, there is a mania to trace their pedigree to families of the mother countries, which have been famous for talent and genius.

I left Halifax with regret; but I had this consolation — that I should be making my way onward, and soon find myself among the same class of people I had left. On the morning of my departure, Colonel Starr brought me a letter of introduction to his friend Sir John Harvey, who was then the lieutenant governor of New Brunswick, residing at Fredericton. This letter was a *carte blanche* into the best society. I hastened my journey, stopping for a few days in the delightful city of St. John. I began to feel anxious concerning my family, and to hasten my journey, *my sorrow for them always preying heavily at my heart.*

We took a steamer at St. John, and arrived at Fredericton. The good captain escorted us to the best hotel, the name of which I have forgotten; names

I seldom remember. As soon as my name was entered on the books there arose an excitement. I was believed to be the wife of Governor Fairfield, of Maine, and suspected to have come to Fredericton as a spy. This excitement was kept up until the object of my mission appeared in the newspapers. About that time there existed a feeling of dislike toward Governor Fairfield, owing to the stern attitude he had taken on the subject of the agitated border question; so that had I really been his wife, I fear my reception might not have been as agreeable.

On the second day after my arrival I sent my letter to Sir John Harvey. Captain Tryon, of the British army, who married Sir John's only daughter, called on me in his name, to express his regret at not being able to pay his respects in person, owing to the deep grief he had suffered at the loss of his eldest son. He had been for several months confined to his house, during which time he had received none, except his personal friends. Captain Tryon assured me of Sir John's desire to see me, and that in a few days I should hear from him.

I began business at once, and occupied my time very advantageously; when one morning, about a week after my arrival, I was agreeably surprised, on my return from my morning's walk, to find Captain Tryon awaiting me, with an invitation from Sir John to dine with the family at six o'clock on that day; with the information also, that Colonel Shore and his wife would call in their carriage for me at half past five. Colonel Shore belonged to the army, and was on intimate terms of friendship with the governor. On entering Government House, after unrobing ourselves, we were met by Captain Tryon, who offered me his arm, led us into a spacious drawing room, and presented me to his excellency, who, placing my arm in his, introduced me to Lady Harvey and their lovely daughter, Mrs. Tryon, and the company present. We had only a few moments for conversation, when dinner was announced. Sir John and Mrs. Shore led the way; Lady Harvey and Colonel Shore followed; myself and Sir John's youngest son; Mrs. Tryon in company with an officer, and Captain Tryon. The fine appearance of the party, and the remarkable and noble elegance of his excellency, filled me with admiration. With Lady Harvey's sweet smile, her mild, calm, and matronly manner, I was enchanted. There was but little merriment at table, in consequence of the late death of their son, which had greatly afflicted both parents. All things were tastefully arranged, with every luxury that could be desired. A neatly-dressed servant stood at the chair of each guest. Silver urns, with the most beautiful and fragrant flowers, graced the table, with the best wines to cheer the best hearts. Dinner being over, the ladies left, as is the custom in English society. The gentlemen remained to enjoy their cigars and wine.

During the evening we had an animated conversation. Sir John's spirits seemed to rally, and I found him possessed of much wit and *naïveté* of manner. He related several anecdotes, which referred to the scenes of the war of eighteen hundred and twelve.

In our last American war, Sir John Harvey was the commander-in-chief in opposition to our General Winfield Scott. "Sir John's noble bearing and gallant disregard of danger attracted the notice of his adversary, and General Scott gave orders to his riflemen not to draw a trigger against so fine a fellow." From this circumstance commenced a warm and unbroken attachment between these two gallant generals. Of their friendship his excellency spoke to me in very affectionate terms.

Before taking our leave, Sir John informed me that there was stationed at the garrison, at that time, the thirty-sixth regiment, commanded by the brave and gallant Colonel Maxwell. He added, "I think, with your Scotch natures, you will be mutually pleased. With your permission I shall be happy to introduce him."

The evening grew late, and we parted; I in sadness, with the impression that I had enjoyed, for a few brief hours, the society and conversation of an illustrious and noble gentleman and family, whose voices and faces I should hear and behold no more.

A day or two had elapsed, when, during the morning, Colonel Maxwell called, and sent me his card, along with a letter from Sir John Harvey. We both expressed ourselves grateful to his excellency for the pleasure we derived from this introduction, and commenced an animated *tête à tête*, which lasted for an hour. The colonel informed me that he was hastily making preparations for his departure to visit the United States, and that, though his stay must be short, he expected to find a great deal of enjoyment in going to a country of which he had heard so much. I gave him a letter to our poet Halleck, who afterward told me how fascinated he was with this valiant and noble Scotch officer.

Before taking leave of me, the colonel inquired at what hour, the next day, I should be at leisure — that he wished to bring out his regiment. I assured him that nothing would delight me more than to see him on parade with those brave men, over whom I had heard Sir John so proudly exult. Three o'clock was the hour set for this display. The next day, at that hour, myself and daughter took possession of the drawing room. We had not sat a moment before we heard the beating of the drums and the marching on of the regiment. A moment more, they halted in front of the hotel. The sight of this graceful and splendid regiment, with their long, black, waving plumes, with the brave colonel at their head, reminded me of the golden days of the feudal ages and of the crusades — when the traits of the heart were of moral courage, and deathless deeds, and of self-sacrificing chivalry. The gallant colonel gracefully turned toward our window, then to the regiment, and gave orders to proceed through the exercise. This done, they presented arms ; they then marched a little distance above the hotel, turned, and marched to their quarters. For this honor paid me by one of Scotia's bravest sons I felt happy and proud.

Many years have passed away since then ; and all that is great, and brave, and noble in this world passes away. Sir John Harvey, and Lady Harvey, and Colonel Archibald Montgomery Maxwell have long since slept in their graves.

> "We die with every friend that parts from earth,
> But live again with every soul whose home
> Is the blue ether. From our hour of birth
> Lost loved ones are around us, and they come
> Into our thoughts like moonlight, when we roam
> In silvery silence 'neath the starlight sky;
> They charm in grief, irradiate in gloom,
> Impart meek gladness to the brow and eye,
> And teach our weary hearts that spirits never die."
>
> S. L. F.

Having completed my visit through the Provinces, I hastened my journey to Windsor, Nova Scotia, to meet the steamer which sailed from St. John to Boston. On arriving there, I found several persons already at the hotel waiting to leave. The tide had been so low for several days that no steamer could come near enough to take in passengers. Luckily for me, I had brought a letter from Judge Uniacke to Judge Haliburton, the famous "Sam Slick." His residence was beautifully picturesque; his family a very agreeable one. He had two fine, robust, English-looking daughters growing up, very much resembling their father. From the grave appearance of the judge, one would never have suspected him to have been the author of any thing so humorous as the "Yankee Clock-maker." In appearance he was very stout, with a fine head, with rather a dull and heavy physiognomy. We enjoyed our stay, as regards the agreeable party at the hotel and the citizens we met.

We visited the college, which is a fine, spacious building. In these halls of learning many have been educated who fill high places of rank in the Provinces and in the Canadas.

The steamer was suddenly announced to have arrived. Each one rushed for his luggage in great confusion, and away we started. None ever left these pleasant shores with deeper regret than myself.

CHAPTER XVI.

OUR voyage being rough, with much seasickness on board, we had nothing to boast of on our journey. On entering Boston, I was happy to find myself safely arrived on *terra firma*, and among old and dear friends. I stopped a day at the Tremont, only for the purpose of paying my respects to the poet Longfellow, whom I had never seen. In company with Genevieve, I took a carriage and drove to Cambridge. I had long wished to see the poet, as well as the venerable head quarters of the immortal Washington. I was invited into his library, which occupied a large front room in the second story. Nothing can console a poet and a *littérateur* for the absence of his books ; they are his friends and his society. With his appearance, genius, and pleasant humor I was highly pleased. The poet was young — he seemed almost boyish ; being single and untrammeled, he was quite happy. I envied him his retirement, leisure, and liberty. My visit was late in the fall. How my fancy kindled as the autumnal winds came sighing through the lattices of the old mansion ! The windows shook and trembled. I could almost figure to myself, while conversing with the poet, the spirit of Washington hovering over the place which was once his residence on earth — the meadows around where he walked, the trees under which he sought the cooling shade, the woods which were his asylum against the heat, and the green banks on which he rested.

On taking my leave of the poet, I informed him that my daughter was in the carriage at the gate. She preferred to remain rather than alight. At this information he expressed himself anxious to see her, and walked with me to the carriage. Her sweet face lighted up with joyousness, as it always did at making the acquaintance of the great and intellectual. The poet expressed himself charmed with her grace and address, and congratulated me on having so lovely a daughter.

Again on our journey, we did not stop until we had reached our home in Philadelphia.

I wish that here I could lift the curtain on a beautiful perspective, instead of the dark and dismal scenes where the light is lost and memory can no longer look on the form of hope. My husband had changed. The frequent attacks of epilepsy he had suffered had so shattered his nervous system that both mind and body showed rapid symptoms of decay. He was deeply affected at seeing me, and quite overwhelmed. My daughter Gertrude ran to me, and, throwing herself into my arms, wept bitterly. Child as she was, on her tender and impassioned heart had been written the pages of suffering, of grief and sorrow. She loved her father. His sufferings, genius, and misfortunes won from her her deepest sympathy and untiring attentions. She was like him in some things; she possessed his genius in a remarkable degree.

My youngest boy, my little Eugene, about three years old, expressed his joy by running to me, and talking with his large, expressive eyes. He could not enunciate. From his birth he had inherited the same convulsions his father had suffered, which deprived him of speech until he had attained his seventh year. I feared he had forgotten me; whereas, on my return, his infant memory kindled with as much joyousness as any of them.

I found my home altered. Many of the little heirlooms and ornaments I had treasured had gone, and I looked at their vacant places with a deep sigh, without uttering a word. I had sent hundreds of dollars to my family in my absence, but it failed of the amount my husband desired. What grieved me most was the absence of my silver, and pictures, and many of the most valuable volumes from the library. These I wished preserved for the future benefit and instruction of my children. Some of the articles I found and redeemed, only, however, to see them eventually disappear.

My heart was sad, but I did not falter. I immediately devoted all my time during the coming months to the publication of the work then in press by Mr. John H. Guion, of Philadelphia; and I found the best stimulus to its completion to be a round sum of money, which I paid in advance. The work thrived, and in the early part of the year 1841 was issued from the press, and boxed up and sent to my patrons every where. During this summer my mind was seriously exercised about my children. I did all I could to soothe their little hearts.

I had been able to save a few thousand dollars, which I invested in a small property in Baltimore, in the names of my children. Through the kind aid of Judge Glenn the purchase was effected, and thereby made safe, entirely out of the power or the reach of any one.

It was about the beginning of June of that summer that I began to see that something new must be attempted, some new enterprise, to sustain my children, now five in number. While I queried to myself what this should be, a sudden thought came to me of going to England — to visit England for the purpose of republishing my husband's works, and renewing the copyright in that country. I laid large plans for success. I felt so sanguine on this subject, and talked so confidently of my ability to effect what I had planned, that my parents, whom I visited at that period, thought that I had lost my senses. I forgot my losses and crosses in the belief that by carrying out my project I should ship home a golden fortune. I consulted many of my friends, some of whom expressed a belief in my success; others doubted. But I was not to be discouraged. I collected letters from the poet Halleck and Mr. Wikoff to our consul in London, to Sheridan Knowles, and to the poet Rogers.

With these letters, I made hasty preparations to sail the following September. I chose the new and splendid ship Stephen Whitney, which was to make her second voyage on the 20th of that month. Past misfortunes had instructed me, together with my philosophical nature, to trust and hope. I provided every thing to leave my children comfortable, with their father, and grandmother, and servant. On the 18th, in company with Genevieve, I set off on my voyage.

On the morning of the 20th my kind brother accompanied us to the steamer at the Battery, which was waiting to convey the passengers to the ship, that lay out at the Narrows. I dislike leave-takings, for they always make scenes; I therefore waved a good by to my brother, who did not come on board the ship, but returned with the steamer. A stiff breeze soon sent us off on our voyage. As our vessel was careering in her onward course, I was filled with enthusiasm at what I believed would be the result of this journey. In these delightful dreams I had already obtained my thousands, and fancied myself sending heavy drafts to my family.

"Like the foam on the billow
 As it heaves o'er the deep,
Like a tear on the pillow
 When we sigh in our sleep,
Like the siren that sings,
 We can not tell where,
Is the Hope that hath wings,
 The phantom of air."

S. L. F.

I leave descriptions of scenery and sea voyages to those who travel for that purpose. Sea voyages are pretty much alike. Sometimes there is a calm, and sometimes a storm. To me such subjects have but little interest; beside, they have become fatiguing and hackneyed. Suffice it to say, our Captain Thompson was clever enough in his vocation, and performed his duty; he kept a good table, and carried us safe to Liverpool. We had been out about four weeks when we had the happiness to reach her docks in safety.

We arrived too late for the morning train for London, and stopped for the day at the Adelphi. We took the train at eight o'clock that evening, and arrived about six in the morning. A cab was provided me; my luggage was placed on it, and brought to me as if by magic. I ordered the cabman to take me to Morley's Hotel, Trafalgar Square, Charing Cross. Here we found every comfort we desired. We remained only a few days at Morley's, when we sought lodgings in Regent Street, decidedly the most cheerful (if the word may be applied here) part of London for strangers. We occupied a very comfortable suit of apartments facing the street, which gave us a never-failing source for observation and amusement; for here the tide of life seemed like the ever-rolling ocean, never at rest. It rained incessantly, and with all the movement and stir of the crowd, there seemed nothing like the stillness of London; it is intense. The very wind has no voice here. There is a depth of grayish hue in the sky, in winter, unbroken by either sun or stars, and all sound seems to mingle in one low, deep murmur. There is no solitude like that one feels amid a wilderness of human beings. This feeling took possession of me, and I saw at a glance the great difficulty I must have in the attempt to prosecute my plans. I saw that *England was not. America* — that from the queen to the poor beggar, the *ensemble* had no resemblance. The sight of royalty, with all its pomp and parade, had no attractions for me, for my heart was made sad at the contrast of splendor with the numberless perishing poor I daily met of the unfortunate people; and for the first time in my life I felt the moral rottenness of aristocracy, and the greatness of our own *glorious republic. O America! America!* how my heart bowed in thankfulness when I reflected that I was a daughter of thy land, liberty, and affections. I never could feel elated at the paraphernalia of the queen, the trappings of royalty, the gems that are set in diadems, or worn in abundance by the nobles, when I reflected there were *starving thousands* within sight of their equipages.

The obstructions I saw in my path made me put off the commencement of my enterprise; in this way days passed away, waiting for *to-morrow.*

> "To-morrow! 'tis the changing dream of hope,
> The vision of the weary-hearted in the depth
> Of solitary suffering, and the crown
> Of many a proudly imaged enterprise,
> That never was accomplished." S. L. F.

I did not immediately deliver my letters; my anxiety rendered me unfit for society, and I concluded to wait the decision of my success. Early one morning I took a cab for the purpose of calling on the editors. I drove to the "Times" office, and inquired if the editor was within, saying that I had called on business, and desired to see him. I was surprised to find the editor *incognito*, but was informed that "any communication I might wish to make, must be made by letter, addressed to the editor of the 'Times,' Times office." I began to see how it was that in England there was no such thing *as favors by the press*. I returned to my lodgings dispirited, for I had no means to spare for any exorbitant demands that might be made on me from that source. Though I met with this difficulty in the outset, I could not think of relinquishing my efforts without further trial. I wrote a note to the editor of the "Times," to which the following is a reply: —

To Mrs. Sumner Lincoln Fairfield,
165 Regent Street.

The Times Office.

The Editor of the Times presents his compliments to Mrs. Fairfield, and regrets that his numerous avocations will prevent him from having the pleasure of waiting personally upon her. Any communication with which she will honor him, however, shall receive his best attention.

London, Nov. 29, 1841.

I gave up every hope of success, and decided to pass the winter as happily as possible in visiting and sight seeing. The following letter I received from Lady Blessington: —

Mrs. Sumner Lincoln Fairfield,
165 Regent Street.

Lady Blessington presents her best compliments to Mrs. Fairfield. She begs to express her warmest thanks for the very beautiful volume of Poems Mrs. Fairfield has been so kind as to present to her. In them she has found much to admire. The poems to Clara, Westminster Abbey, Pere le Chaise, and the Last Night of Pompeii are sublime and lofty conceptions. She will read them all with great interest.

Unfortunately, most unfortunately for Mrs. Fairfield, Lady Blessington fears she may meet with many difficulties in the attempt to republish the Poems of her husband at this time in England.

The friends of the late Mrs. Hemans have been making great exertions to get a subscription for a volume of unpublished manuscript, but have entirely failed.

Mrs. Fairfield will pray accept Lady Blessington's kindest wishes for her success and happiness.

London, Gore House, Dec. 2, 1841.

My imagination had been warmed by descriptions of travelers and visitors to the residence of the poet Rogers, whose poems I had so often read, and whose "Italy" enchanted me.

On entering his dwelling in St. James Place, the servant led me up a flight of winding stairs, into a large, square anteroom, where I stopped for a few moments to admire the works of art in painting and statuary that adorned the walls and recesses. After having satisfied my eyes for some time with those delightful objects which elevate the mind and inspire it with a love for the beautiful, I was led into another large room, which was adorned in the same manner. I seated myself by the lattice window which overlooked St. James Park, to await the poet's entrance; here my eyes feasted. Every piece of art here seemed perfect, like the poet's own beautiful poems, almost too perfect; they always put me in mind of a clean cultivated garden, so precise that one longs for a little careless spot on which to rest. The mind wearies with too prolonged scenes of beauty, too much finish.

On the poet's entrance I found him to be almost entirely the same in appearance and manner that I had pictured to myself. Our conversation led, for a few moments, to the subject of my enterprise, which seemed to surprise him. "Even," said he, "were it possible for such an object to be accomplished, the labor and fatigue attending it would place it beyond your power." I then handed him my husband's Poems, and begged his acceptance of the volume. I told him that during the fifteen years of my married life I had published, by subscription, by individual labor, two editions of those Poems, in detached parts, and lastly, during the past year, I had brought out my husband's works entire in the volume I presented him. Beside, during that period, I had established and sustained a periodical work for five years. The poet looked at me, I thought, with an expression as though he either doubted my sanity or my words. "Impossible, impossible," he repeated. I informed him that my husband's works had never been brought out by the publishers — that they had never been in the trade, and that my noble countrymen had done much for me, but that I had come to England expecting to make a *fortune*. At this last information the poet laughed heartily, and replied, "Such energy and devotion deserve every thing. I wish in my heart it might be so. He asked many questions about America, its authors and artists. I told him, what he must often have heard before, that he was one among a few of the poets on whom our country had placed its favoritism. He replied, "I am happy and proud to be a favorite in America."

The poet said it was a misfortune with authors that they wrote too much; that if all authors should lay aside their productions for six months, and review them carefully at the end of that time, they would cut them down at least one half before placing them in print. He assured me that he never wrote more than *four lines* a day during the period of his authorship.

In this *method* of writing I could only conceive taste and judgment, for true genius is not slow and measured, but it is rapid and impulsive. We are rarely wrong when we write, or even act, from impulse. (I speak of good natures.) Genius must be allowed its natural course, which is the *first* warm and generous thought that springs up in the heart. Second thoughts are almost always cold and calculating.

The poet informed me that at that time he was *eighty-four* years of age. I might have thought him seventy, but not beyond it. His complexion was fair, with mild, soft blue eyes. His fair, broad forehead bore little trace of care, and less of sorrow. I passed almost the entire afternoon with the poet, and left him, charmed and delighted with my visit.

The following day I paid my respects to the great Henry Hallam, the author of "Middle Ages." I had long wished to see this great man. I made my way alone to Crescent Row, his place of residence, with no other introduction than my card. I was invited immediately into his study, which was also his library. It was a large, long room; little, however, of the wall was seen, for it was nearly hidden by the arched bookcases, and the ponderous tomes, some bound in black, some in vellum, grown dingy with age. In the center of the room stood a large oval table, with elaborately carved lions' feet; near it, in an antique arm chair, sat this venerable author.

The classic and poetic seclusion in which he lived, the grace and refinement which surrounded him, made this a visit of no ordinary happiness to me. He had that repose, and that superb self-reliance of manner, which always characterize the truly great man or woman. He talked of England, its character, its prejudices, its past greatness, which, he said, "shed its own sanctity on the atmosphere." When I ventured to speak of my motive for visiting England, he smiled, and said, "I have spoken of her prejudices, of which this is one. No work can succeed in England outside the usual means of publication."

I took my leave of this great man (whose genius I had so often heard my husband admire) deeply impressed with the force and greatness of intellect. He invited me to visit him frequently during my stay in London.

How often since, in my wanderings over earth, has my mind reverted to those *scenes, those pleasant scenes*, when with the sympathy of the good and great I was consoled.

There is something awfully sublime in the solitary life of a great intellect.

> "Such spirits fill the universe — they live
> In the blue ether, and their dwelling place
> Is the immensity above; they sit
> Upon the thrones of seraphs in the stars,

And hold converse with them, when night with stars
Canopies earth, and holy Nature folds
Her moonlight drapery round her, and lies down
By bright Hyperion's side to bridal sleep.
This world of peril they in thought forget,
And all its crimes and woes, and they become
Associates with the blest in pure desires
And feelings holy; and they love to tread
The verge of Paradise, though mortal yet,
Seeking to know the loves that blossom there,
The joys that never fade in those bright fields,
The thoughts of bliss expanding ever through
The pauseless ages of undying love.
Such spirits find no thoughts reciprocal
In earthly beings. *Few* can estimate
Their greatness rightly; *few* can feel the same
Dissolving and absorption of all powers
In soft Elysian visionry. *They live*
Alone, starbeams round the sun-throne of God!
The sovereign eagle ever dwells alone
In solitary majesty, and waves
His mighty wings in air unbreathed by things
Of lowlier nature; and the lion walks
His monarch path untended and alone;
So the proud spirit lives in loneliness,
All uncommuning, and its solitude
Becomes its empire, where it reigns fore'er
In might and majesty."

S. L. F.

CHAPTER XVII.

I HAD not been long in London before I had the happiness of meeting with several Americans. Among them was a gentleman of fortune and leisure I had long known, who had left his home for a travel of two years on the continent. This was a fortunate circumstance for me; for without an escort, Genevieve and myself must have failed of seeing many of the most interesting scenes in England — scenes in which, when once entered, is found much to subdue the troubled present with the mighty past.

We sailed on the Thames, with its shores haunted by a thousand fearful events. Passing the dark old Tower, the whole history of England, with its bright and glorious deeds, and its *dark* and *fiendish* acts, is called up at a glance.

We next went to the Abbey — this magnificent world of tombs and mausoleums. In this vast abode where Death sits enthroned over kings, amid its lonely passages and aisles, its antique shrines, we gaze and gaze, until the mind becomes overpowered and confused amid its wonders and cenotaphs. I found no spot in England that interested me as much as a visit to the Abbey, " this great assembly of the dead — the pride and glory of the earth, of almost countless generations — of kings and queens, bards and warriors, and statesmen and orators." They lie here "who once shook thrones and sundered monarchies." Next to the Poets' Corner, I was interested at beholding the tombs of the haughty Elizabeth, and her rival, the lovely and beautiful Queen Mary, whose effigy in cold marble brought to my mind the cruel suspicions and wrongs she endured, and her long and painful captivity and execution.

"Why burns thine eye with such triumphant light,
O proud Elizabeth? Lo! there the shrine
Where worship now the people of the earth
Scotia's lost Mary, — beauty's loveliest queen, —
A sacrifice, if innocent, and thrice
A sacrifice if guilt confirmed her doom.
Leman of Essex! Tyrant Henry's child,
Meet daughter of thy sire! bend that proud head,
And look beneath thy foot, O haughty Bess!
Thy broken sceptre lies by Mary's tomb!*
Grandeur, thou hadst thy crown. *Misfortune now*
Hath her reward — the tears of half the world."

S. L. F.

Scenes of pomp around the dead always impressed me with deep melancholy. Far happier were the dying thought that I should lay my weary head to rest on earth's green bosom, beneath the smile of heaven, where the sunlight and storms, the stars and the gentle light of the moon, and showers and dews would come, — where birds would sing and flowers

* During Cromwell's time, the mob broke into the Abbey and defaced many of its monuments. The hand of Elizabeth containing the sceptre was broken off, which fell at the foot of Queen Mary's tomb.

bloom, — than that my form should molder in melancholy vaults or sepulchers of grandeur.

I left the Abbey sadly impressed. Byron's beautiful lines came forcibly to my mind: —

> "The pictured forms of other times,
> 'Twas all they left of virtues or of crimes,
> Save vague tradition and the gloomy vaults
> That hid their dust, their foibles, and their faults."

Walks and drives in the magnificent parks occupied much of our time, which we divided, from breakfast, usually at ten, into three parts for the day. All writing and business were attended to from eleven to two; walking or driving, from three to five; dining at six; and the evening spent at the opera or theater, otherwise at our cheerful fireside in reading or conversation. I often saw the queen, and Prince Albert, the Duchess of Kent, and the Duchess of Sutherland, with many of the distinguished English nobles. The queen I thought a very good woman. She was very young, without the regal appearance, however, we look for in a queen. The prince I thought handsome, stately, and amiable. Neither the queen nor prince possessed those remarkable lineaments we look for in the intellectual.

During the winter of 1841 the Prince of Wales was born, which created an intense hubbub. The whole city was in a state of commotion at this event; even the poor beggar was shouting lustily, "God save the queen!" For the soul of me, I could get up no other feeling than that of indifference upon this occasion. As I have said, royalty has no other attraction for me than as a moral. It is a subject for sad reflection. The extreme contrasts it brings of luxury, pomp, and poverty admit of no feelings of happiness. When we look upon the numberless poor, unfortunate people who throng the streets, the alleys, and the lanes of London, we know and feel that there must be an injustice in the formation and existence of a government that affords all the power and wealth of the earth to one portion; to the other, penury, houselessness, and starvation.

Some writer has said, "America is the child of the earth's old age," on whose youth Heaven has bestowed a double portion of its blessings. In our cities and towns there is labor enough and a home for all. Our wharves closely swarm with multitudes busy in all the various toils of daily subsistence, ministering to a commerce whose home is the world. In our noble America none need starve, none need suffer.

We next visited the British Museum, and Madame Tussaud's rooms in Portland Square, where, after having viewed the exquisite grouping of kings and queens, emperors, and statesmen, and nobles, we were led into the room of *horrors*. Here we saw the shirt worn by Henry IV. of France, when stabbed by Ravaillac, with the blood-stains still distinct — a relic for which Charles X. offered two hundred guineas; the imperial carriage of Napoleon I., taken from the field of Waterloo, and the carriage used by the emperor at St. Helena; the original guillotine blade used in the decapitation of the beautiful Marie Antoinette and her husband, Louis XVI., the Duke of Orleans, and Robespierre; the coat worn by Nelson at the battle of the Nile, and a piece of the Cloth of Gold from the field of that name.

On entering these magnificently lighted rooms the effect is startling. You feel really in the presence of living, breathing beings, so perfect are the characters and the groupings. Queen Victoria and Prince Albert are there in their marriage attire. What struck me most was Queen Mary Stuart, sitting on an elevation, a sort of throne, attired in black velvet. Standing near her is the inveterate reformer, John Knox, exerting his influence with the queen, and urging the relinquishment of her faith in Catholicism. A little distance from the entrance stands the immortal Malibran; nothing can be more striking than this figure, with her large, dark, impassioned eyes, as I had seen her in life.

February had come. I began to feel those longings for home that a child suffers when it perceives on a sudden that it has overstaid its time. I began to make preparations to sail in the ship Quebec, which left for New York on the 22d of that month. I had one regret at leaving — that I was obliged to return to America without seeing the continent.

Many of my friends tried to dissuade me from my voyage, and offered as an impediment the stormy season I had chosen. Genevieve was in love with London. She could not bear to leave the parks, and the beautiful Serpentine, where she had daily amused herself with her loaf of bread feeding the swans, which came sweeping over the bright lake at her approach; for she was loved by every thing beautiful, fair, and pure.

The 22d had come, and, late that night, we were hurried on board the ship Quebec, which was to leave at four in the morning. The sails were unfurled, and we were off, once more wending our way toward dear America. The captain had gone by railroad in advance of the ship, which was taken around by the mate to Portsmouth. Unfortunately, on our arrival we found no prospect for sailing, owing to the strong head winds, which lasted for a week.

The weather was fine, however, and we concluded we would make the best of our delay; and as there were a number of vessels in the Channel in the same predicament with ourselves, we would pass our time in exchanging visits. After breakfasting, our party set off. We met several parties, who, like ourselves, were in search of something for pastime. Captain Paget, an officer of rank in her majesty's navy, who was sailing alone with the oarsmen, left his boat, and joined us on a visit to the Queen's yacht. This graceful vessel was built by one of the Georges; though it was old, it was still beautiful. Captain Paget introduced us to Captain Fitz-Clarence, of the yacht, who was the son of William IV. and Mrs. Jordan; a most charming and courteous gentleman, who gave me a history of the vessel, with many anecdotes connected with the royal personages of its time, but which I now forget. He showed me the state room, where the king was dangerously ill from seasickness, on a voyage he was making to Germany. It was a most comfortable room, with a richly bound library; the bed was such as crowned heads usually lie on.

After viewing the vessel throughout, the captain invited us to lunch with him. We had a delightful conversation during this pleasant repast; and, after drinking a glass of the best wine, we took our leave, much delighted with our visit. But how true it is that in this world there is always a bitter mixed with the sweet! While on board the yacht, my mind, instead of being present with the scenes around me, was carried back, far back, to the scenes in the life of that noble, self-sacrificing woman, the mother of Captain Fitz-Clarence, Mrs. Jordan, in whose life, and wrongs, and sorrows I had felt so deep an interest. Her exile in France, and the prohibition, by the king, of all communication with her children during her last hours, is a deep and *everlasting* stain upon his memory. This great and distinguished woman died of outraged affections and a broken heart.

O, is it not a painful thing to think how the purest and dearest ties that can exist, that bind *heart* to *heart*, and parent to child, are doomed to be severed! And yet so inextricably blended are happiness and sorrow on our earth.

Once more on our voyage, with fair wind and prospects of a speedy return, our spirits revived. Myself and daughter were the only ladies on board; there were two unfortunate females, who were steerage passengers, an aged mother, with her daughter, who had left England to seek their home in our new world. The Quebec was a fine vessel, small, compact, and well built. For two weeks we passed our time on deck, looking out on the broad expanse of the ocean, charmed with the speed of our little ship. Genevieve amused herself, often, with talking to the sailors, and asking questions. She would often take them something nice to eat — fruit or cakes, which they seldom saw. Her kind nature sympathized when she saw them partaking of their coarse meat and bread; and in her sweet manner she would often beg the captain to share with them the good things of the table. They named her the *little flower*, and at her approach their hard and worn features would always lighten up.

Just as our hopes were at the highest, the wind changed, and we found ourselves suddenly overtaken by a fearful storm, which lasted during three weeks. So terrific were these gales, that during that time not a sail was unfurled. The poor sailors, with their arms folded, crouched in the forecastle, almost in despair of making further headway. During this period we were left at the mercy of the waves; the ship at every lurch creaked as if its heavy planks were about to separate; the noise was deafening. We could not keep our hold any where; the safest place seemed our berths; even there it did not prove very safe to me. I placed my daughter in the lower berth, while I took the upper one. The door of our state room was fastened back, and opened into the outer saloon. About midnight I was thrown violently from my berth, my head striking the hard floor of the saloon. The stewardess, whose room was opposite, heard me fall, and came to me. Near where I lay was a sofa, on which she managed to place me. I was seriously injured, and for a time almost lifeless. This blow produced congestion of the brain, and for two weeks rendered my case almost a hopeless one. The kind captain and stewardess were unremitting in their attentions to me. During this period the aged mother, of whom I have spoken as a steerage passenger in company with her daughter, was taken suddenly ill, and died of lockjaw. She was too old and feeble to bear so rough a voyage, and sank under it. The pitiful wailings of her poor solitary child were enough to rend the heart, as they lowered the corpse of her mother into its watery grave. I prevailed upon the captain, who was naturally kind-hearted, to take her in our part of the vessel.

At the end of the third week, the elements were merciful to us, and it was indeed cheering to hear the sailors once more at work aloft, unfurling the sails to the breeze. The ship was soon making her way in a steady course.

Nothing occurred to mar our progress for the balance of the voyage. I was too ill, however, to take any interest in any thing, and remained in my berth until the ship neared New York.

After having passed seven long, painful weeks at sea, we arrived safely.

If ever the heart has cause for gratitude, it is when

Providence has granted to us a safe return from an ocean voyage. Let him praise the Lord who goeth down to the sea in ships, for there we learn the awful majesty and power of the Supreme. "He layeth the beams of his chambers in the waters; he maketh the clouds his chariot; he walketh upon the wings of the wind."

CHAPTER XVIII.

I TOOK a hack, and soon found myself at the home of my brother, where I remained a few days. I then left New York for my father's residence in New Brunswick.

My health continued broken, which gave my parents and friends much anxiety — too much broken to permit of a return to my family — to *former scenes*. I remained with my parents, who did all they could to console me for the loss of health and happiness. I grew attenuated and lost strength daily. I remained in New Jersey during that summer and the autumn without any apparent change. Before winter set in, it was thought advisable that I should go to Cuba. My home was no longer home to me. That home for which I had toiled with the might of my energy, had gone like a sweet vain dream, which it is useless to remember; yet, O, yet there are some offenses which it is an unworthy weakness to forget. Hush, my heart, and let thy sorrows lie hid in the charnel house of happiness, amid the secrets of life's sufferings.

Again alone, save with my darling Genevieve, my solitary companion, and sharer and soother of my sorrows, I set off for Cuba. It was the last of October when we landed at Havana. We were taken to delightful and comfortable lodgings kept by Mr. Fulton. Perhaps there is no part of the world that, on first entering, produces the same magic effect upon an invalid, as the climate of Cuba. Beside, the novelty is greater than even that of Europe, to a stranger.

My dear Genevieve left nothing undone her heart could suggest to make me comfortable and happy.

Far away from the scenes of wretchedness I had suffered, I felt better. It is better to forget one's misfortunes than to talk of them — to escape is a woman's only refuge. The climate, the scenery, and the fruit of Cuba were delightful to me. The Paséo is like an Eden to the invalid as you glide along in the noiseless volante, passing the long rows of beautiful palms, with flowers springing up on all sides, and vehicles filled with fairy-like looking women in their gossamer attire, radiant with many colors. The grace and ease with which they move along adds to the enchantment of the scene. The women of Cuba are amiable and kind. They have sweet smiles and soft words, and no doubt many of them are by nature gifted; but the usages and customs of their country have hitherto rendered them almost strangers to cultivation, especially as regards social life and the sacred family ties. In these there is an unnatural separation and want of confidence, which have exposed to the world the barbarous and immoral state in which they have lived — bound by none of those sweet affections which grow up unconsciously, swayed by no early sacred remembrances which bind the brother and the sister together far more than the fancied force of blood. But these things are gradually changing, and Cuba now is not what it was at that time. The Cubans themselves, — those of them who travel, and who are educated abroad, — when they mix with other nations, perceive this at once, and I have often heard them express their regret at the mistake they have made in their ideas of right and wrong.

No ladies are seen walking the streets of Cuba; the intense heat would prevent, if nothing else. Opposite our hotel there lived a family whose daughter had become insane in consequence of being debarred the sight of her lover, who from his appearance seemed an estimable young man. He was in the habit of visiting our hotel, and remaining there for hours, to obtain through the half-closed shutters a sight of his unfortunate lady love. He sought every opportunity he could to escape with her, which, with the constant surveillance in that country, and iron bars and bolts, was impossible. I had often seen him weep, while listening to her cries, and her incoherent singing and playing on the piano. It was really touching to witness these scenes of despair on one side, and the mind's distraction on the other. The parents of this young girl were relentless, and would not allow their marriage. The young man kept a very beautiful volante, and a fine horse, which he politely offered to myself and Genevieve whenever we felt disposed to take a drive. It generally stood ready in the court-yard of the hotel. One day, as we were anxious to see the city, we took the volante, and after a drive on the Paséo, we returned within the walls, and began our visit of exploration. It was about six o'clock. Our desire was mostly to see the churches and nunneries. Neither myself nor child understood one word of Spanish. But Mr. Fulton, on our starting from the hotel, gave me the words *a casa*, which, interpreted, mean "go home." He also informed the *calesinero*, that when we wished to return, we would repeat that word. He added, one stamp of the foot signified to the right; two to the left; three to turn a corner. We had been out some time, and were delighted with the novelty and the lighted city. We drove around and around, passing the captain general's palace, and the same scenes several times. It grew quite late, but I had forgotten the words *a casa*, and I attempted to call the negro's attention by stamping my feet, and telling him to go home; at which he spurred the poor animal, and turning corner after corner, to the right and to the left, for at least two hours, until my head grew dizzy, and Genevieve became alarmed and wept, and wrung her hands in despair, when suddenly she recollected the name of the street and of our hotel, which she shouted out to the poor negro, promising him a chastisement on our arrival. We ceased stamping, or I believe we should not have got home that night, and the *calesinero* made haste to our quarters. I will venture to say the race of "John Gilpin" was nothing to this.

It was ten o'clock when we arrived. Our evening's adventure was a subject of amusement to the people in the hotel for at least a week.

Every way one turns in Cuba one meets with victims of disease and death ; but really death loses much of its gloom in sunny climes, such as Cuba. I saw a number of poor consumptives fall, one after the other, like autumn leaves — just at the moment, too, when they were most sanguine of recovery. It is a misfortune that these poor people resort to that country *too late*. In this case the climate enervates them, and they die almost as soon as they reach its shores.

We remained on the island, visiting different parts of it, until February, when I took it in my head I should like to see Jamaica.

We took a steamer to Trinidad, where we staid for a week. I brought letters here to Count Brunet and Dr. Cantero. Both were gentlemen of great wealth and position in Cuba. We happened to reach Trinidad just in time to attend the balls that were given during the *fête* days of Queen Isabella. The splendid theater, which at that time was the property of Count Brunet, was thrown open and illuminated. In this place the grand balls were given. The pit and stage, being thrown into one, formed a magnificent ball room. Around the tiers of boxes was hung scarlet cloth festooned with flowers, the floor covered with scarlet ; and the many thousand lights that gleamed upon the beautiful faces and diamonds made a gay and brilliant scene. One week passed pleasantly enough. Had my health been established, and my heart free from sadness, I might have enjoyed these bright scenes.

From Trinidad we again took a steamer to St. Jago de Cuba. On our arrival we were taken to dismal lodgings, though they were the best to be found. St. Jago is so far distant that few strangers visit it, and it is seldom one hears the English language spoken there. We, however, had the good fortune to meet with a Mr. Armstrong, an Englishman, whom we had met at Mr. Fulton's, in Havana. He was a merchant living at Kingston. He had been waiting a week for a conveyance thither. There were no regular lines of travel on that route to Jamaica. We waited as patiently as possible another week, when, hopeless of a conveyance, we decided to retrace our journey to Havana, and were actually packing up for that purpose, when Mr. Armstrong came to us with a polite invitation from the commodore of a Spanish man-of-war to accept a passage in his ship. This vessel was the Creolia. The government of Cuba had ordered her (for the first time) to get ready to convey the mails to Kingston. We gladly accepted the opportunity, and immediately set sail.

The heavens were bright and clear, the wind was fair, and for three days every thing seemed auspicious. On the third night the commodore lay at anchor, fearful of encountering the reefs at Morant Bay, extending far out from the shore. These reefs in former years had occasioned many wrecks and great loss of life.

About one o'clock that night I was awakened by the noise of the ship rocking to and fro, striking violently the rocks on each side. Then I heard the loud language of the officers to the sailors, which I could not understand. I arose quickly, and awakened Genevieve. We hastened to dress ourselves, and went on deck. Here was a fearful but a grand scene. Above us all was serene and calm; the moon shone in all its beauty; there was not a cloud in the sky. Around and beneath us the sea was dashing against the ship; the waves were making over us.

The minute guns — the signal of distress — shook the little ship to its foundation. They were pulling at the ropes for the purpose of righting her, but all in vain. The noise was deafening. Hope was lost; all was confusion and despair. We were closed in by an immense mountain that rose before us, forming a sort of crescent, in which the ship lay. A lantern was hoisted mast-high, which the mountain entirely concealed.

Mr. Armstrong assured us that the morning would bring us relief, as soon, he said, as the pilots came out. Alas! the poor pilots were out during the night, and heard and saw all; but negroes are always timid. They came near enough to hear a strange language, and in their fright retreated. They could not suppose a wreck on so clear a night, and believed an enemy had come to besiege them. As soon, in the morning, as they heard the English language spoken by Mr. Armstrong, who hallooed to them to come near, they used their oars with great velocity, and came to our rescue. Our luggage was placed in the hold of the ship, which we gave up for lost. Mr. Armstrong said "he was glad to get off with his life; he did not think of his luggage." I might have felt so too, had I not been going among strangers, with neither money, nor letters, nor clothing, save what I had in my trunks. Losing these, I thought, I might as well remain and share the fate of the ship. Upon this thought, I offered the negroes a guinea if they would bring up the trunks. At this offer they rushed and entered the hold, and in a minute or two they brought out our trunks, which had been immersed in water, and threw them over the side of the ship into their boat. The unfortunate commodore came to me, looking sad enough at the fate he knew awaited him. He threw a mattress into the boat to make it less dangerous for us. The vessel lay very high on the rocks, and there was no way but to leap into the boat. This done, we took leave of our unfortunate party, — the kind commodore and officers, — selfish, like all the world, and glad to find ourselves rescued, though we had left them behind us in trouble.

The sun rose in its usual burning heat in the tropics. We left the ship about five in the morning, and we reached the landing at nine o'clock. The wharfinger's family resided near — the only house within several miles of the landing. This, indeed, was providential, for we were exhausted with the scenes of the night, and with the boat sail in the burning sun that morning. During all these scenes and dangers not one word of complaint was heard from my dear Genevieve. She looked like a sweet angel amidst the wreck, so submissive she seemed to the will of Heaven.

We remained with the wharfinger's family for several days. They were plain, good people, honest, upright, and sincere. They lived in a simple and comfortable way, and they were happy. The climate I found more conducive to health than even Cuba, especially in that mountainous part of it. Here Genevieve for the first time attempted riding on horseback. In this way we amused ourselves riding over the beautiful hills, through the rich palm-groves and the enchanting scenery. We passed a few pleasant days.

Mr. Armstrong hastened his journey on horseback, — there being *no other* conveyance, — through a rough route to Kingston. In the mean time, I took a private conveyance to Port Morant, a small town, distant only a few miles from Morant Bay. In this place we were to remain until I should hear from the governor-general at Kingston, who at that time was the accomplished Lord Elgin. Mr. Armstrong communicated our misfortune to this kind nobleman, who immediately ordered a coaster manned for our convenience. In this little vessel we were comfortably taken to the long-wished-for city of Kingston. We soon learned by the newspapers the sequel to this misfortune. The commodore and officers were summoned to Havana, to appear before the captain-general, to await the decision of the law. The commodore was tried and cashiered, and sent to Spain. The beautiful little craft, the Creolia, was a total loss — shattered to pieces on the rocks.

They honored me by taking rooms for my accommodation at *Date Tree Hall*, at the *West End* — places for which I care but little; they belong to the small, the petty, and the present.

The city of Kingston compared badly with the luxuriant, picturesque scenery I had left. Since the emancipation of the negroes it has declined — gone among the things that were. The negro race, collectively or individually, when manumitted, are like swine who "return to their wallowing in the mire." Ladies or gentlemen can no longer dwell in comfort in Jamaica. There are among them at this time *but few* pure white people; the African stamp prevails. The place abounds with poverty, indolence, and filth. For the sacrifice of this once beautiful garden spot of the world, we are indebted to fanaticism and a *Wilberforce*. Let the abolitionists of our day take but the history of this once beautiful island, and its decline, and it ought to satisfy them (even the most ultra among them) that they are misled and mistaken.

Much as we deplore the system of slavery as it there existed, — deprived of all rights to humanity, shut out from every Christian influence and family tie, which are in general strictly regarded in our own country, — let the blackened cloud surrounding this once beautiful island reflect its own darkened shadow, and as a watchful monitor, remind philanthropists of the present day, that to be *free* is something more than to sever the bonds of servant and master.

Our stay was short. The detention we had suffered by the wreck brought us into April. The weather was intensely hot, and the fever had already broken out among the shipping. I found little here to interest me, save a few friends, travelers who, like myself, were in search of health; beside, the wretchedness of the place made me anxious to leave almost as soon as I came. I never could endure an existence where exclusive authority and power are given to negroes. I found this to be a little too much for my nerves. The *lady* that kept the house where I stopped was a *colored* one, and talked of her majesty the queen as if they were on familiar terms. Her children, she said, were in England, being educated. Really the airs put on by these blacks were most impudent. I always thought myself to be philosophical until now. To have remained long here, I believe, would have fretted me to death.

I examined the papers daily to find a vessel sailing to any part of the United States, but in vain; when on a Sunday afternoon, two gentlemen called to pay their respects to me. One of them was a Mr. Hawthorne, from New Orleans, the other a Mr. Williams, from England, *compagnons en voyage*. They informed me they were to leave that evening for New Orleans; that the vessel lay out, and was to sail at ten o'clock. I caught at this opportunity with as much eagerness as a drowning man at a straw. I begged them to hasten to bring the captain to me, that I might secure my passage. They did not encourage me, on account of the wretched absence of every comfort, it being only a coal vessel, which, as they said, had been sent over from England to convey coals along the coast. The ship had come to Jamaica to get freight, but failed of doing so, and the captain, who was a rough Irishman, had decided to go to New Orleans, to try his luck there. So determined was I to go, that the gentlemen started in search of the captain, whom they brought to me. He frankly told me the situation of his ship, which he said was so old and inferior, that he felt ashamed to take a lady passenger on board, but assured me he would do all he could to make us comfortable. This was enough. I got ready, and in less than an hour from my decision, we found ourselves safely on board, and were off on our voyage at ten that evening.

We found it comfortless enough, but I determined to make the best of it. My philosophy returned, which I found had only been obscured by the presence of the negroes.

The old, worn-out ship was top-heavy. She had no ballast, and with every breeze that came, I expected to see her upset.

Genevieve amused herself by reading some books that were loaned her by Mr. Williams, and playing with a little pet lamb that belonged to the cook. We got on very well. We amused ourselves telling stories and anecdotes, in all of which I joined with a hearty good will — "the ruling passion strong in death." I pity the poor mortal that is incapable of rallying under a racy anecdote or a good joke. I love to laugh, and amid the worst of life's evils — and few have had greater — I am glad to find an opportunity of doing so.

Mr. Hawthorne related to me a singular adventure connected with the fortune of his young friend, which occurred a short time before he left England. He was the son of poor but respectable parentage; he was educated for the law; but ill health had interfered to prevent his success. His home was at Windsor. One day, while walking in the park, his attention was attracted by the appearance of a very old man, bent over with age, accompanied by his dog. Walking slowly, leaning on his staff, which he accidentally let fall, he seemed too infirm to take it up; at seeing which, the young man hastened to replace it. This little incident led to a conversation, which, with the kind attentive manner of the youth, so pleased the aged man, that he invited him home to dine. He lived sequestered and solitary, without a being near him but an old servant and his dog. Dinner was waiting. The fare was frugal and plain.

The youth was pleased with his visit, for he too was a misanthrope, and they became mutually attracted. A few days passed and they met again. The old gentleman invited him, as before, to dine with him. He questioned him about his business and prospects, and added, that he was lonely and old, and had but a short time to live — that if he would remain with him as his friend and companion during the remainder of his life, and would take his name, he would make him heir to all he had. The young man gladly accepted the offer, though he could hardly suppose the old gentleman to be wealthy.

In less than a year he died. In his will he bequeathed to his adopted son a fortune of *ten millions of dollars*. *Williams* was his adopted name.

After an absence of nearly six months' travel and mishaps, with health unrestored and heart unblest, we arrived safely in New Orleans.

CHAPTER XIX.

The morning after my arrival, I took up a newspaper. The first notice on which my eyes rested was the following: "The widow and daughter of the late poet Fairfield arrived here last night in the ship Ambassador, from Jamaica." I sent immediately for the proprietor of the hotel. He informed me that my husband had died in New Orleans on the 6th of March, and that the papers had reported myself and daughter to have been lost on the wreck of the Creolia. He informed me also, that my children were at the same place where their father had died. I hastened with Genevieve to meet them. On our approach they heard our voices, and ran into our arms. Their tears, and grief, and joy were overwhelming. After having believed us dead, to find us returned and safely restored to them, was a happiness they had not expected. But there was an absent one, whom I *no more* found. One of my beautiful boys, a child about seven years old, had gone to his last peaceful rest. This bereavement, and the circumstances of his sufferings and death, rent my heart. He was a beautiful, promising child. But I tried to check my grief for the sake of those that remained, and to console and heal, as best I could, their young, afflicted hearts.

Thus, at scarcely the middle age of life, ended the days of the poor poet.

Whatever of thought, of feeling, or of faculties we may possess, we must look to the tomb as to an altar; from whence let us hope they will arise purified and exalted into the presence of the Creator.

The following pathetic and beautiful poem, by my husband, was addressed to me a few days before he died, and was *the last* breathings of his poetic spirit before it took its flight.

"Dove of the Deluge! wearied are thy wings,
   Winnowing the void air on thy flight with me;
Yet every sunbow o'er thy beauty flings
   The heart's bloom, born of God's infinity.
Lone, faint, o'ercast by huddled worlds of gloom,
   Wronged by the heartless, wrecked in reach of bliss,
O'er life's Sahara, *on to unknown tomb,*
   Alone I wander — hopeless but for this —
This beauty of the blossom, breathing heaven
   O'er earth's dark, withering woes — o'er tempest Time —
Stumbling on Doubt's wild mountains! yet 'tis given
   Despair to know Love makes its own sweet clime,
O'er crashing wreck and smoldering ruin flies,
   Its cherub pinions flashing glory back,
The holy smile of Eden in its eyes,
   And angel hosts triumphing in its track.

"O, but for this — for thee — divinest child
   Of sorrowing, sinning Earth! Time had not now
Hurled howling tempests o'er my spirit wild,
   And left its lightnings on my blasted brow.
Supremest GOOD bequeathed thee to impart,
   E'en to dim Earth, the blooming light of Love,
And, though the footsteps falter, still the heart
   Seeks thee, its ark, lone wandering, deluge dove!

"Through fleckered clouds the molten moonlight streams,
As o'er my spirit floats thy smile of youth;
Visions of Arcady and Argolic dreams
Wear, to my yearning gaze, the garb of Truth;
And all that Nature, through its myriad spheres,
Could frame, in thy sweet bosom hath its home;
Yet o'er the Past swirls a dark sea of tears,
And sighing Sorrow dims the days to come.

"What but blest knowledge of thy sweetest spirit
Hath Time vouchsafed through all its years of woe?
What its sad eras given me to inherit?
Bereavement, want, and malady, that grow
By needing nutriment; 'mid vivid flame
Doomed e'er to dwell, yet destined ne'er to die,
The martyr mind, through lingering years the same,
Still from the *burning bush* glares on the blackened sky,
And finds no fellowship in any world;
Or avalanche, or earthquake, maelstrom, ocean,
In the dread wrath of Ruin — each hath hurled
Its maniac vengeance, 'mid the mad commotion
Of anarch Woe — Time's tyrant reigns alone!
With giant strides he treads the voiceless waste;
Without a smile mounts empire's gory throne;
Onward looks hopeless — darkly on the Past!

"Bride of my bosom! though denied on earth,
Blend thy blest spirit with my saddened thought,
And breathe the blessing of love's holiest birth
Around life's pathways; what deep skill hath wrought,
Refine thou and exalt; be with me, Love!
In trial, toil, temptation — guide and guard
My erring steps — and O, my prophet dove,
Hail to heaven's shore thine own lamenting bard!"

My husband had often appealed to me, if I survived him, to defend his reputation. The following little poem I have treasured, and will now add, as corresponding with the remarks I have made. It was written in an hour of deep domestic suffering.

"Wilt thou espouse my memory, love,
When I no more can brand the base,
And true in thy devotion prove,
'Mid scorned despair and shunned disgrace?

"Speak to my heart while thus it pants,
While thus it yearns o'er future hours,
Ere, dead to all its woes and wants,
It slumbers in oblivion's bowers.

"O, for a name, when I am dead,
To live till life doth cease on earth;
For deeply hath my bosom bled
Since the quick peril of my birth!

"Turn not away with that wrought brow,
As I had craved a lawless boon,
But let thine eyes of beauty now
Beam like sweet stars at night's still noon!

"And tell me that thy smile shall be
The sun of fame's undying flowers,
And Life's will henceforth be to me
Far happier, brighter, better hours."

In a few days, after having provided all things for the comfort of my children, I left New Orleans with them for New York. Arrived there in safety, it was not long before I found and leased a small, comfortable house for the space of four years, into which, with grateful hearts, we at once betook ourselves.

My dear Genevieve, who was the oldest, and was but a

child in years, felt the bitter cares of life coming upon her thus early. She had acquired the experience within a few weeks.

Brought up only to the exercise of graceful accomplishments — accustomed to attendance and indulgence — occupied with her books and studies — she had suddenly found the necessity of care and exertion. The two sisters, however, found much happiness in assisting each other in their studies and daily avocations.

My whole heart became absorbed in the future of my children — their education and happiness. Alone with them, I began to feel more repose and contentment, with all my care upon me, than I had felt before, during the sixteen years of my married life.

The year following the poet's demise, I wrote a short biography of his life; the sale of which, with what I had, was sufficient to sustain my family, and continue to my daughters the opportunities they had of education. They were never sent to school.

No mother was ever blessed with two more lovely or gifted daughters. But for these, Heaven only knows the desolation I must have felt. My great hope was their happiness. Here, in my little box, I lived isolated, as I wished, and would have felt happy; but the trials and sufferings I had endured had so destroyed my health, that I no longer delighted in employment for the mere pleasure of it. Where can one be found whose heart and energies would not have faltered sometimes under such misfortunes? How vain seemed much that I had passionately desired! And yet I could not help looking forward with an enduring belief that my ardent nature and energies had not poured themselves forth wholly in vain.

> "It is the past that maketh my despair —
> The dark, the sad, the irrevocable past!"

But the melancholy records of life belong to many of us. There is also a charm in suffering when it idealizes our natures; this it is which gives the interest to the poet's page, and sorrow is made musical.

Four years had passed away. Genevieve had grown a woman. The time of my lease had expired, and I concluded to remove further south, for two reasons: first, my health; then, I had observed a nervousness at times in my eldest daughter's manner, which I attributed to too much mental labor. She was ever at work, with no desire for recreation. She was now in her sixteenth year. She had read hundreds of volumes. There was nothing in history or literature with which she was not familiar. To remove to Washington, to introduce her into gay scenes, I believed would create a healthful change — would draw her mind from the monotony of study in which she had so long indulged.

On the eve of my leaving with my family for Washington, the news reached me of the death of my father. I hastened to New Brunswick, to perform the last solemn duty to my parent, and to look for the last time upon his face, now pale and set in the rigidity of death — the eyes were closed forever that had so often wept over the sorrows of an unfortunate child.

Shortly after the death of my father the old homestead was sold. My mother found a home with my youngest brother, whose opulence afforded her every comfort. My poor afflicted sister, Caroline, whose mind had long since gone into fatuity, was removed to the new asylum at Trenton, which had been built by the instrumentality of that genuine, noble, and philanthropic woman, Miss Dix. The family gone, the home of my parents was closed forever.

I returned to New York, and was sadly impressed with the wise man's words, "Man dieth and goeth to his long home, and the mourners go about the streets."

What strange, inconsistent beings we become, even after we know the world! Society was a thing I loathed. Its baseness I despised; yet, like most mothers, I wished to introduce into it my two daughters. I was convinced that nothing in it is really what it appears to be — that it begets mean envyings and jealousies. In it we never know what we may trust, and are often misled by that which only seems from that which really is.

After we became settled in Washington, I began to make preparations for the gay scenes of the coming winter. It was during Mr. Polk's administration. The season opened gayly — more so than usual. In Washington one is always sure to meet acquaintances, if one has any. Our house we kept open for our friends, which rapidly increased in number. My daughters were both musical, as well as conversationists. These are gifts which always attract. Gertrude differed from her sister. She was more hopeful.

She united with her genius an acute knowledge of character, and withal was very philosophical. Her manner was fascinating, kind, and gentle. Her benevolence was too great to admit of wounding, by sarcasm, the feelings of another. We had not been long in Washington before Genevieve's reputation for beauty, wit, and fashion was firmly established. Even her caprices were pronounced charming. But with all these, there was a perpetual fever of her mind, which broke out sometimes in sarcasm, and often it was painful to witness her really misanthropic nature. I have often seen her return from a ball, or a levee, where she had been the bright particular star, so sad, that she would declare to me it should be the last night she would ever pass so vainly and foolishly. All these things added to my secret sorrow, for I early saw that hers was not a mind fitted for the cold and glittering life of society. On a New Year's night there was a large assemblage met at a grand ball at Carusi's saloon, where she with her sister had gone. On her return I had retired for the night. She hurried into my chamber, and in a state of nervous excitement, she said, "Mamma, during the dance to-night, I could not help the strange feeling that came over me, from which, with all my efforts, I could not rid myself—that I was a corpse dancing with corpses." More than once she spoke of these feelings, which came often upon her, even while surrounded with gayety and festivity. Though unnoticed by others, these were sealed-up sorrows that lay heavily at my heart. I saw and felt the dark future that awaited her. She was very fond of art, and had made some progress in painting before we left New York. She often found amusement in visiting the studio of Mr. Charles King, who had known her from a child. He discovered in her mind great genius for the art, and was often surprised at her judgment and criticisms. She anxiously desired me to allow her to continue her lessons in painting, to which I acceded. I thought it would be better than so much study, reading, and writing. She continued assiduously for a year with Mr. King, daily working from eight in the morning until sunset. During that year she copied several paintings, large and small, from the gallery, — two very elaborate ones, — copies from the great Claude. These she disposed of for the sums of fifty and eighty dollars. In every thing she did she aimed to excel.

During the year she remained with the artist, she formed in her mind a plot for a novel. The following year she excluded herself entirely from all her friends, to write her book. Day and night she toiled; nothing of amusement could for a moment draw her mind from this object. She often assured me that she was wedded to authorship. "I shall never marry," she would say, "but live with you, mamma, and become famous, which is enough of happiness for me." Her desire was for a name — to be known as great, and not as fashionable. She longed for wealth, not for the purpose of display, or outrivaling others in grandeur, but as she often said, "to build houses of refuge for poor, unfortunate children, to educate them, and elevate their neglected minds, and to make them comfortable."

In little less than a year she completed her novel, entitled "Genevra, or the History of a Portrait." The difficulty with authors is to get their first work accepted. Her patience had become nearly exhausted with the effort when it was accepted by T. B. Peterson, Esq., of Philadelphia. She gave to the novel her own name. She had both the following, Genevieve Genevra. She preferred Genevra, on account of its easy pronunciation.

"Genevra" had not been out long before letters of eulogy came to her from high sources. She continued to write and paint alternately. Her next productions were several stories of length. Her *last* were "The Vice-President's Daughter," and "The Wife of Two Husbands." After the completion of these works she wrote a letter to Eugene Sue, and sent him a copy of "Genevra." She admired his genius, and to him she dedicated her last works.

The following letter is his reply: —

MADEMOISELLE:

Je serais très heureux et très flatté d'accepter la dédicace du livre que vous me faites l'honneur de me proposer; ce sera, croyez le bien, une des plus précieuses récompenses de mes travaux qui ont eu le bonheur de mériter votre intérêt et celui de vos honorables compatriotes des Etats-Unis.

Veuillez agréer, mademoiselle, l'assurance de
Mon respectueux dévouement,
EUGENE SUE.

PARIS, 27 Juillet, 1851.

The annexed letters are from our friends.

BOSTON, December 12, 1855.

I owe you many apologies, my dear Miss Fairfield, for having so long delayed to thank you for the pretty volume, entitled "Genevra," which you were so kind as to send me last week. But to thank the writer for a book before one has read it is no great compliment, and I have waited, therefore, until I could tell you how much I was pleased with it.

I have listened to it with great pleasure. The style is elegant and unaffected; and the story, which increases in interest as we advance, has many striking scenes in it to arrest the attention. Altogether, it is a remarkable production for the first effort of a young authoress. And though one may criticise some details in the structure of the plot and in the delineations of character, yet these blemishes will be cured by greater familiarity with the art of composition, while the original power shown in the book will be more fully developed by practice.

With my best wishes that you may have all the success to which your genius and industry entitle you,

I remain, my dear Miss Fairfield,

Very truly yours,

WILLIAM H. PRESCOTT.

NAHANT, July 18.

DEAR MRS. FAIRFIELD:

Absence from Cambridge prevented me from receiving your note and your daughter's novel till last evening, which will account for my not thanking you sooner.

I well remember your *beautiful* daughter, though she was but a child when I saw her last. It seems to me almost impossible that she should be already eighteen, and an authoress.

I have not yet had time to cut the leaves of "Genevra," but have peeped between them, and see that it is written with great spirit and very easy flow of style. May success attend it, and happiness its author. I beg you to thank her for me, and to say that I shall read her book with great interest, and hail her success with much sympathy.

Yours, very truly,

HENRY W. LONGFELLOW.

U. S. HOTEL, WASHINGTON, July 2.

MY DEAR MISS FAIRFIELD:

When I was informed you were the author of "Genevra," I felt deeply interested; and though I read but few novels, and hardly any of the novels of the day, I resolved to read it, and say a word in its favor for the sake of the writer.

After reading it, I published in last Monday's "Intelligencer," which I send you, a brief notice, not a review or critique, of its merits. I shall feel much gratified should this trifling performance contribute in the least to your interest.

Though I have not the honor to be acquainted with you, which I feel a misfortune, I know you are too sensible to deem me obtrusive. You will neither misunderstand my feelings nor misinterpret my motives. I have frequently seen you in Washington, and once had the pleasure of speaking with you at your door. I admired you. There is something so uncommon, so *distingué*, in your exquisitely formed features and figure, and in your *tout ensemble*, that I was anxious to know and anxious to be acquainted with you. To my regret I heard you had left the city.

And now will you permit me to speak freely of your work — to give you a word of advice? I shall do so, however, under some apprehension that I may merit the fate of Gil Blas, who criticised the Archbishop's sermon; only there will be this difference against me — that his advice was solicited, while mine is gratuitous. You have more poetry than invention; more philosophy than experience. Your style is superior to the plot. But, with such a poetic nature and philosophic mind, and such a pure, natural, and concise style, what can not you do with experience and application? Write, write, write, — let this be your motto. The subject of the age — the mighty problem to solve — is the social composition of society; and this subject absorbs all the literature of the day, not only in politics and theology, but in novels. The most successful works are those — as "Alton Locke," or the works of George Sand (Madame Dudevant), of Sue, and others — which are imbued with the spirit of the times. It is not the age of counts and countesses; it is essentially the age of the people. Subjects within the reach of every one, — at our very doors, — matters of every-day life, which all feel, — should occupy your pen. That which is the most familiar, faithfully and graphically described, forms the most striking and engaging picture.

Pardon me, and permit me to say how happy I shall be to hear of your success, and assuredly

I am, my dear Miss Fairfield,

Yours always,

W. B. PHILLIPS.

U. S. HOTEL, WASHINGTON, July 26.

MY DEAR MISS FAIRFIELD:

I have just received your letter of the 11th, acknowledging the receipt of mine and the newspaper. The amiable manner in which you are pleased to express your gratification at what you kindly call my "compliment," and the gratifying expression, mutually with myself, of regret at not having had an opportunity of becoming better acquainted, and the hope that such an opportunity may hereafter present itself, are so flattering, afford me so much pleasure, that I cannot resist the temptation of expressing my feelings.

You have, my dear lady, the full flow of my sympathy. So young, so lovely; with a mind to perceive and appreciate the beautiful in art and nature; with an ardent disposition to acquire knowledge, and a thirst for literary honor; and with the application and perseverance necessary to secure success, — who would not admire and sympathize with you? Would to God I were rich! With what pride and pleasure I would foster your young genius! Be not, however, discouraged; difficulties may develop your faculties. The noblest tree of the forest attains its highest excellence in a severe climate. I wish I was near you, to give you the benefit of my experience. I have sounded the depths of misfortune and misery, I have soared the hights of luxury and refinements, —

from the association with savages and cannibals in the far islands of Southern Polynesia, to the gay life of the most elegant Parisian society, — more romantic than romance, and more varied and astonishing than fiction. I could mark the shoals and the hidden rocks on the chart by which you should navigate on your literary voyage.

There is one thing I would point out to you. Be rather afraid, at first, of writing too much than too little. Go through your productions with the severest and most critical examinations. Read none but the best authors; hold communion with none but the greatest minds. Read the reviews and best magazines from the old world, (our periodical literature is very poor,) and so perfect yourself in a good style, elevate your mind to great thoughts and arguments, and you will soon perceive that, with wings, it is as easy to fly in the air as to walk or crawl on the earth. How much more I could say to you!

Do not think I would assume to be your Mentor. They are but the observations of a friend, who is

Yours always,

W. B. Phillips.

My dear Miss Fairfield:

I had the pleasure to receive your note of the 10th. The very gentle reproof you have administered for my presumption in dictating to you, who are so superior, is at once a cause of pain and gratification. To say any thing which might induce the inference that I thought you were not well read or sufficiently intellectual to appreciate the best authors, was furthest from my thoughts. On the contrary, I know, from your work, that you are both well read and highly intellectual. It has given me pain to know that I have written in a manner to be misunderstood; but I am gratified at the opportunity it gives me of corresponding with you. The pleasure of confessing and being reconciled to one in whom we feel interested is almost worth producing the cause. Our differences, when not real, but which arise from some misconception, make the explanation quite agreeable. This is my case.

Certainly I never meant to recommend you to imitate any

writers, French, English, or any other, either in their style or subjects; for originality is the first characteristic of a great author. But I wished to draw your attention to the fact, that as every age has its literature, — a literature which is the faithful exponent of its ideas and habits, — so whoever has the faculty to perceive and express this must succeed. To illustrate this I instanced George Sand and others. I did not express my approval or disapproval of the moral quality and tendency of their works, but I said they were the mirror of the age. If George Sand be sensual and have socialist tendencies, does she not represent Paris, or even France? And if we deem her extravagant and unnatural, it is because the habits and dispositions of foreign society are so different from ours — are not familiar to us. The same observation will apply more or less to the writers of other countries. I hope to have, some day, the extreme pleasure of discussing the relative merits of the authors you speak of, and of your preferences of the English school, which, with some exceptions, I approve. But at present, in the limits of this letter, I must confine myself to my first position, and I will take George Sand again as an illustration, not only because you have spoken more freely of her than of others, but because she is a writer of the first order. Chateaubriand (I translate from his Memoirs) says, "She is a woman of omnipotent intellect; her descriptions have the truth of those of Rousseau and of Bernardin de St. Pierre, and her works are born of the age." Beyond all question, her language is the most elegant, her composition the best of any of the present French writers. Though we may be disgusted with her unfeminine manners, we must admire her masculine mind. Her success is great, for she unveils the present. There are few who can revivify the past; besides, the spirit of the age is directness. Facts, living facts, such as come home to the hearts and experience of all, are the subjects for popularity. You want no better evidence than that which Dickens's career presents.

This was the purport of my observations in my last letter, and it is my advice in this; for you have an analytical and philosophic mind, with great powers of description, to study every-day life and make your pictures as familiar as those of Hogarth, for they always please.

Be assured, my dear lady, that whatever I have said, or may say, from which by any possibility an inference might be made contrary to the high regard I have for your character and talents, is a fault in the language, and not my real sentiments.

I shall be very happy to hear from you as often as you will do me the honor to write; and if it be in my power to serve you, I beg you will command me; and I am, my dear lady,

Yours always,

W. B. PHILLIPS.

U. S. HOTEL, WASHINGTON, August 22.

MRS. CARVALLO presents her compliments to Miss Fairfield. She feels grateful and honored by her intention of dedicating a novel to her. She congratulates Miss Fairfield on the variety and brilliancy of her talents, which she hopes will be properly appreciated and encouraged, and anticipates the pleasure of one day seeing her name enrolled among those of the most distinguished authors and artists of her country.

WASHINGTON, Saturday, January 2.

RAVENSWOOD, N. Y., January 16.

MY DEAR MADAM:

I beg to acknowledge your note of January 4, and to offer you my thanks for the accompanying volumes. The mother of two daughters, and both of them so gifted! You are indeed blessed. I could not have believed that "Genevra" was the production of a girl of eighteen, without your assurance. It gives evidence of very decided talents. I am equally surprised that "Irene," by your second daughter, was produced at eighteen; nor is its promise less rich than that manifested in "Genevra."

You ask my opinion concerning the amount of dramatic interest which "Genevra" possesses. I hardly know how to give one, for the manner in which a story is thrown into dramatic form has often more to do with its stage success than the incidents themselves. *The plot* of "Genevra" is certainly *sufficient* for a drama; but how it should be dealt with — there is the *question*, and there the *difficulty*. For the numberless *failures* made by persons of great talent who succeeded in all other kinds of writing, when they attempted to write for the stage, proves that a peculiar turn of mind is required for the dramatist.

Wishing you continued prosperity, and much happiness through your gifted children,

I am, dear madam,

Yours sincerely,

ANNA CORA MOWATT.

Mrs. Jane Fairfield.

NEW YORK, May 8.

MY DEAR MRS. FAIRFIELD:

Please accept my best thanks for your kind courtesy in sending me a copy of your daughter's imperishable memorial of genius and talent. We have all derived the highest pleasure from its perusal, and shall ever cherish it as an invaluable keepsake.

Very sincerely, your friend,

S. S. RANDALL.

MOBILE, August 5.

I have delayed answering, my dear Miss Fairfield, your note, more from a press of business than any thing else. I had commenced several times my letter to you, and as often was forced to leave it unfinished. I got the picture a week after you advised me of having sent it. Mrs. Levert was greatly pleased with it, as well as several lady friends who know you through your reputation as a writer. One young gentleman, a kinsman of my sister's husband, declared it "the most dreamy, intellectual, heavenly face" he had almost ever seen.

I heard, a few days since, from your mother, dated Girard House, Philadelphia. In two months she thinks she will be south again. Her letter was a very charming and *spirituelle* one, and repaid amply many times being re-read. What think you of Thackeray's "Esmond"? I have read a fourth of it, and find it very quaint and purely written as to style. His occasional philosophical touchings are very fine and very true.

If you will permit me, I will keep the picture until I see your mother, as there are several friends to whom I would like to show it; but, should you desire it, will return it immediately when knowing your wishes. Have you ever been in Cuba? A lady told me she was almost certain of having seen the original of the picture there. Eugene Sue begged Colonel Starr to thank you very much for your book, and to express to you his admiration. Colonel Starr requested Mme. Levert to say this to you.

In haste,

Very truly yours,

A. Waugh.

To Miss Fairfield, New Orleans.

Boston, June 8, 1855.

To Mrs. S. L. Fairfield:

I need not assure you, my dear friend, that your letter dated the Prescott House, June 4, gave me much pleasure. I was glad to hear from you once more, though grieved to find you still unhappy, longing for that which is not to be found on earth — perfect satisfaction.

Two classes of persons are sure to find themselves in sharp antagonism with the world — the obstinate and self-willed, the shrinking and delicate. The one is like the porcupine, bristling all over with sharp-pointed quills; the other is like the sensitive plant, which shrinks when touched. I need not say to which class you belong; yet, with all your sensitiveness, what energy, what perseverance has your *mother heart* enabled you to make! God grant that these may ultimately be repaid, and your declining years made bright and cheerful, relieved from care and anxiety by the assiduity of your children.

Truly,

S. K. Lothrop.

Guilford, Ct., February 1, 1856.

My dear Miss Fairfield:

I have received a package addressed to me, containing a beautifully draperied volume, as becomes one of your writings, and I have flattered myself into the belief that it is indirectly a present from you. I hope that when you do me the honor to acknowledge the receipt of this, you will not disappoint me by any explanation. Pray do me the kindness to present my best compliments to your good mother and your family, and believe me, my dear Miss Fairfield,

Most respectfully yours,

FITZ-GREENE HALLECK.

CAMBRIDGE, September 8.

DEAR MRS. FAIRFIELD:

Absence from town has prevented me from replying sooner to your friendly note. We have just returned from Nahant, where we have been passing the summer.

As soon as I can, — probably on Saturday, — I shall do myself the pleasure of calling on you and your daughter, whose acquaintance I shall be very happy to make. Be so kind as to present her my regards, and believe me

Yours truly,

HENRY W. LONGFELLOW.

TRENTON, August 18, 1844.

DEAR MADAM:

I acknowledge the receipt of "The Life of Fairfield," your beautiful little volume. It is beautifully written, and a perfect gem of biography.

Yours truly,

STACY G. POTTS.

Mrs. Fairfield.

The following letter refers to an unfortunate event alluded to in the next chapter: —

BOSTON, Court Street,
Friday Morning, January 24.

I am grieved, my dear Mrs. Fairfield, to hear of your severe loss by the fire in New Orleans. How misfortunes accumulate upon you! What a life of trial! God give you strength to bear your heavy burden! Perhaps you may hear that some of your property was saved. I trust it may prove so.

With sincere sympathy in this new trouble,

I am truly yours,

S. K. Lothrop.

CHAPTER XX.

Even thus early, Genevieve, after having acquired what she had fondly desired, celebrity and appreciation, no longer cared for them. Her frank heart would never permit her to dissemble, or even to smile on those she disliked. She was a reader of faces and character, and would never seek to say the agreeable instead of the true. She was gentle, but she was cold.

Her soul was filled with the love of art and literature. In music, she would often say, she found a record of all the lively and sad emotions of her heart. Her voice had a tender melancholy, unearthly and beautiful. She sang portions from all the operas. Her touch on the piano had something so mystic, and so sad, it seemed to vibrate the melody and melancholy of her own sweet spiritual nature. Her admirers were among all classes. Mrs. Polk, who was then our charming Presidentess, and Madame Carvallo, the wife of the Chilian Minister, were among the ladies in Washington who were her warm admirers. Among the gentlemen were the Hon. Sam Houston, the present Judge James Thompson of Philadelphia, and the Hon. Alfred Iverson and Alexander Bullett, the Hon. Henry Clay, and the Hon. Thomas Corwin. To those of her friends who survive, her misfortune will come in sadness, like the tones of her own sweet voice, and the notes of her music, they have so often heard.

One evening while promenading with her at a ball, she was attracted and amused at the sight of two elderly ladies, to whose dress, airs, and graces she directed my attention. "These ladies," said she, "somewhere in the vicinity of seventy, of whatever else they may doubt, seem convinced of their own irresistibility, and fondly fancy themselves the crowning glory of the evening." At this satire, the gentlemen accompanying us were highly amused, and could not restrain their laughter. For myself, though the ridicule was just, I feared she might have been overheard, and her expressions repeated. Sad enough that age should, by its frivolity, beget disgust in youth, instead of, by its gravity, calling forth veneration and honor. Age is *not* graceful, but it is grave, or ought to be so. It is foolish in a woman to wish to seem young when the blood is sluggish, and can no more rush to the heart; when feeling is gone, and all is gone but the breath, to simper, put on airs, and lisp love; to dress low, with bare *scrawny* neck and arms: a japonica fastened in front of the low bodice, resting on a withered bosom, to my mind greatly resembles a sheep in lamb's attire. Juvenal, in his famous satire relating to the laws and customs of the Greeks and Romans, has the following, which may be as appropriately applied in these times as then: —

"There are some faults in a wife of no great account, but yet insupportable to a husband; for what is more fulsome than for a woman to think that no one can pretend to beauty unless she has renounced her native language, and from a Tuscan prattles Greek! — from a plain Fulmonite becomes a mere Athenian! — every thing must be lisped out in Greek: whereas it is a trifling sort of ignorance with such to know nothing of their mother tongue. In this dialect they expressed their fears, their anger, their joys, their cares, and all the secrets of their very souls. What would you have more? You may pardon these fooleries in girls; but for you, whose pulse beats eighty-six, to be still mumbling of Greek! This way of speaking is impudent in an old woman. When she is languishing with these words in her mouth, 'My life, my soul,' they must be delivered in Greek. Though you lisp your fond words with a softer air than Æmus or Carpophorus, the famous players, you make no impression — still your age is written in your forehead."

My beloved daughter Gertrude, who was three years the junior of her sister, applied herself with great assiduity to her studies. She had beauty, ambition, and genius. During the last year of our stay in Washington, she produced her first novel, entitled "Irene." This work I concluded to publish myself in connection with Genevieve's two last, "The Vice President's Daughter," and "The Wife of Two Husbands." It became actually imperative to take some step for the mental health of my child. I gladly availed myself of the labor to get out the work, since it afforded me the only means I had of travel. She loved the south.

The climate and the people suited her, and my heart yearned to make any sacrifice for her happiness. A dark shadow was thrown over her future. The heaviest deprivation to which humanity is liable had come upon her.

My eldest son I placed in a law office in New York. Gertrude accompanied her brother, and remained with a friend I had in that city, where, during my absence, she continued her studies in music and Spanish.

From this time I set off to journey. I dreaded the breaking up and separation of my family. My health continued wretched. Heaven only knows how I was sustained. All I had heretofore suffered, I counted as nothing to the trials I felt sure awaited me.

As the malady of my daughter increased, she suffered from dangerous attacks of congestion on the brain. During the intervals of relief, she would describe minutely to me all the phases of the disease. But I can not dwell on this subject; it is too painful. During my travels I often became exhausted with the efforts I made to conceal the state of her mind from others. At intervals she would appear so well that I could not be persuaded that she would again relapse. For years I was kept alternately hoping and despairing. She was compelled to relinquish all her pursuits, and resign herself to her unhappy lot. Words fail to express either her sufferings or my grief. Poets are prophets. Her father wrote the following poem when she was an infant one year old.

TO MY DAUGHTER GENEVIEVE.

"Star of my being's early night!
Tender but most triumphant flower!
Frail form of dust and heavenly light!
Rainbow of storms that round me lower!
Of tested love the pledge renewed,
The milder luminary given
To guide me through earth's solitude,
To Love's own home of bliss in heaven.

"Heiress of Fate! thy soft blue eye
Throws o'er the earth its brightness now,
As sunlight gushes from the sky
In glory o'er the far hill's brow;
And light from thine ethereal home
On every sinless moment lingers,
As hope, o'er happier days to come,
Thrills the heart's harp with viewless fingers.

"For, from the fount of Godhead, thou,
A ray 'midst myriads wandering down,
Still wear'st upon that stainless brow
The seraph's pure and glorious crown;
Still, from thy Maker's bosom taken
To bear thy trial time below,
Like sunlight flowers, by winds unshaken,
The dews of heaven around thee glow.

"Hours o'er thy placid spirit pass
Like forest streams that glide and sing,
As through the fresh and fragrant grass
Breathes the immortal soul of spring;
And through the realms of thy blest dreams,
Thy high mysterious thoughts of time,
Heaven's watchers roam by Eden streams,
And hail thee, Love! in hymns sublime.

"But these bright days will vanish, Love!
And thou wilt learn to weep o'er truth,
And with a saddened spirit prove
That bliss abides alone with youth.
Cares may corrode that lovely cheek
And fears convulse that gentle heart,
And agonies thou dar'st not speak
Deepen as childhood's hours depart.

"And thou, fair child! as years descend
In darkness on thy desert track,
Mayst tread thy path without a friend,
Gaze on through tears, through shadows back,
And sigh unheard by all who stood
Around thee on a happier day,
And struggle with the torrent flood,
That sweeps thy last pale hope away.

"O'er the soft light of that blue eye
Clouds of wild gloom may quickly gather,
As, ere the sunburst of his sky,
The tempest fell around thy father;
And 'mid the cold world's wealth and pride,
The chill of crowds, life's restless stir,
Thou mayst unknown with grief abide,
Lone as the sea of Anadir.

"And thou wilt grow in beauty, Love!
While I am moldering in the gloom,
And like the summer rill and grove,
Sigh a brief sorrow o'er my tomb;
And thou wilt tread the same wild path
Of mirth and madness all have trod
Since time gave birth to sin and wrath—
Till from the dust thou soar to GOD!

"Doubt may assail thy soul, and woes
Gather into a burning chain,

And round thy darkened spirit close,
'Mid loneliness, disease, and pain,
When I no more can watch and guard
Thy daily steps, thy nightly rest,
Nor, with the strength of sorrow, ward
Earth's evil from thy spotless breast.

"Fed by the dust that gave thee breath,
Wild flowers may bloom above my grave,
And sigh in every night breeze, *Death*,
When thou shalt shriek for me to save!
The bosom, from whose fount thy lips
The nectar drew of bliss below,
May molder in the soul's eclipse,
And leave thee to thy friendless woe.

"E'en in the dawn of time, thy heart
Hath felt bereavement's chill and blight;
For thou hast seen the soul depart
That would have clothed thy path with light;
And now, my beautiful — my blest!
Where on earth's desert wilt thou find
A guide — a friend — a home of rest
For the bruised heart and troubled mind?

"Dark wiles, and snares, and sorceries
Will spread beneath thy feet, and stain
Thy spirit with their glittering lies,
Till phantom bliss doth end in pain;
And thou must feel, and fear, and hide
The doubts that gloom, the pangs that gnaw,
And o'er a wrecked heart wear the pride
That by its gloom doth guilt o'erawe.

"Yet dread not thou, my Genevieve,
The ills, allowed, allotted here,
Nor waste thy soul in thoughts that grieve —
The trembling sigh, the burning tear!

Mind builds its empire on the waste,
And virtue triumphs in despair —
The guiltless woe of being past
Is future glory's deathless heir.

"Beware the soil of thoughts profane,
The fluent speech of skilled design,
Passion that ends in nameless pain,
And fiction drawn from fashion's mine!
He, who so wildly shadows out
The darkest passions of our sin,
Draws the dark bane, he strews about,
From the deep fount of guilt within.

"THE ANOINTED keep thee, sinless child!
Be on thy path the PARACLETE!
Through dreary wold and desert wild
THE GIVER guide thy little feet!
Like buds that bloom as blown flowers fall,
New hopes wave o'er thee angel pinions,
Till thou with them who loved thee — all —
Blend round the smile of God in glory's high dominions."

Our journey extended west to New Orleans. It was in the fall of the year, as late as October, when we arrived. At Genevieve's desire, I rented a small cottage, and newly furnished it. Taking with me her beautiful paintings, with some family portraits, our little home was quite ornamented. Here we dwelt alone, with a servant during the winter. I rented a piano for her. To sing and play was her only consolation.

What time I had, apart from business, I devoted to her. To walk, and talk, and commune with her was my greatest happiness. Her intellect, at intervals, seemed to brighten up more than ever. She loved to dwell on the history of great and distinguished women — women of the past. She constantly regretted the weakness and inability of her sex — their useless and miserable lives. No woman had any attractions for her merely on account of wealth, beauty, or position. The intellectual and sterner qualities could only interest her. Neither Laura, nor Heloise, nor Cleopatra, nor Sappho, nor Aspasia, was a woman of her heart. Such women as Joan of Arc, Margaret of Anjou, Isabella of Castile, Madame Roland, Madame de Stael — these were the types of women who were her models — the stern, the brave, and the useful.

The winter passed anxiously enough with me, in toil and care. The weather became exceedingly hot by April, and I found it was time for me to repair to Boston, to make arrangements for the printing of my daughters' joint works. I promised Genevieve I would return south with her the following winter. She loved New Orleans, and left reluctantly. I stored my furniture, together with her paintings and my portraits, in the warehouse belonging to Mr. Bergen, from whom I had purchased it. I believed all would be safe, and thought I would save myself the expense of the insurance. I left feeling little anxiety concerning their safety.

We had scarcely reached Boston when the fever broke out in New Orleans, and raged during that summer and autumn, carrying off its victims by hundreds. My business detained me in Boston. "Irene" was in press, which could not be published before the coming spring, and required my presence. One evening during the winter, in looking over the "New York Herald," I saw a notice of the loss by fire of Mr. Bergen's warehouse in New Orleans. By that notice I learned that all I had on earth had gone to ashes. Genevieve had gone that evening with a friend to hear Sontag. It was her last singing in Boston before leaving for Mexico.

I cared for nothing so much as the loss of the pictures. How should I inform her of this ruin? It recalled to me all her former labor in painting them; there were about twenty beautiful landscapes; how bitterly she would suffer at their loss! For myself, I regretted my portraits. A woman takes pleasure in pointing to her picture, even after she has faded. To say, "This picture was myself in my palmy days," is a pleasure to most women. One of my portraits was painted by Conarroe of Philadelphia; the other by Charles King of Washington. They were losses to me I could never replace.

The following spring "Irene" was published, after which myself and daughter visited New York.

The papers in Boston, New York, and Philadelphia were unanimous in their praise of "Irene," and we were all of us, myself and daughters, compensated for our labors by the great success of the work.

The following is from the pen of the editor of the "Philadelphia Press:" —

"A very beautifully printed volume of prose fiction, written by the daughters of the gifted and ill-fated poet, S. Lincoln Fairfield, has so greatly interested us that we have great satisfaction in earnestly and warmly recommending it to our readers — more particularly as we have reason to believe that its sale will confer a benefit upon the family of Mr. Fairfield. This volume contains three stories: 'Irene — the Autobiography of an Artist's Daughter,' written by Gertrude F. Fairfield, and 'The Vice President's Daughter,' and 'Wife of Two Husbands,' by Genevieve Genevra Fairfield, who has previously published a popular volume entitled 'Genevra, or the History of a Portrait.'

"This last-named authoress unhappily suffers under the heaviest deprivation to which humanity is liable, and therefore we should write tenderly of her, even if she had not written well. But, indeed, her writings show great knowledge of the human heart, familiar intimacy with refined society, and no small skill in composition. 'Irene' almost painfully interested us, so touching are many of its scenes. They have evidently been drawn from life, and relate, we believe, sorrows and trials which the writer herself has sadly suffered."

Before leaving Boston, in company with Genevieve, we paid a visit to Nahant. My daughter had long wished to see the place. I can no better describe it than to introduce the following beautiful and truthful paragraph: —

"I never saw a coast before that suggested more thoroughly an eternal despair than this coast of Nahant. The cliffs are not lofty; the surfs are not so grand as some that I have seen; but there is an indefinable expression of loneliness and sorrow in the lineaments of the rocks. Nature here seems to have lost all hope. The coast is furrowed and distorted, like a human face torn by some immemorial misery. Black and shattered crags shelve out into the ocean, bearing with the heedlessness of ruin the ceaseless buffets of the waves. It is this lost aspect that has made Nahant more interesting to me than any sea coast I have ever visited. Vaguely it seems to tell some story of immortal woe. When walking through the streets of cities we pass, unnoting, a thousand happy faces, wreathed in commonplace smiles, and ruddy with inexpressive health. But sometimes in our path we behold a countenance pale, and haggard, and wild, that causes us to stop, and turn, and look after it, — for it tells us an unsyllabled story of passion, and struggle, and ruin, that interests beyond all the chubby cheeks and white teeth that ever bloomed and glistened. So with Nahant. I have a sympathy with its melancholy shores that all the laughing slopes of French vineyards or English hill-sides could not awaken."

I passed a few "good by's" to my Boston friends, to save me the trouble of what I dislike, — personal partings, — not, however, without regret. Through the rough paths of my life, my busy and excitable pilgrimage, nowhere have I met with kinder hearts or deeper sympathy than among Bostonians. They very much resemble their English ancestors. They are distant and cold until their hearts are warmed up and interested. They have no petty caprices. Their friendships once formed are faithful and reliable.

On our arrival in New York, we found the following letters awaited us:—

SENATE CHAMBER, WASHINGTON, April 5, 1855.

DEAR MADAM:

I owe you an apology for not responding sooner to your letter accompanying the beautiful and interesting books of your two gifted daughters. I have been so much occupied that I have scarcely had time to devote any thing to correspondence. I now acknowledge the personal favor of your kind remembrance of me, and beg to assure you of my regret that I am not able to respond in a manner suitable to this distinguished favor, and the high regards which I entertain for the authoress of "Genevra." You will be pleased, madam, to assure her, as well as Gertrude, of my continued admiration for the brilliant talents and personal charms which so much attracted me in former days. I wish each of them, as well as yourself, many happy days, and a most successful career in whatever path they may select for themselves.

I am, dear madam,

Your obedient servant,

ALFRED IVERSON.

OFFICE DAILY ARGUS, March 24, 1855.

MY DEAR MISS FAIRFIELD:

I dispatched a few copies of the Argus, containing the "notice," to Boston, but I suppose they went astray. If I can lay my hands upon an extra copy or so, you shall have them. If not, when our file of papers is bound, I will have it copied — that will be in a few weeks.

I am truly delighted that you are on journey near the city. The next remove will, I trust, see you in the Quaker City. Dull as it is, there are still those within its borders who will be glad to apply the spur to old Father Time, and make him gallop when you are once here. When shall that be?

I am about tempted to take a run over to New York to see you. Another such a letter as your last, — so full of poetry, all gems, —

and you may regret it. The music, the theaters, the gay sights, the gaudy things, all have their attractions for those who can look at them rightly; but they are doubly enchanting when we have those by us with whom we can sympathize, with whose natures ours beat in time and unison. There are but few golden spirits in the world, and these we seldom meet, whence they seem like birds astray from Paradise. No wonder our feelings are tuned and our hearts enchanted.

I should like to see you and give you a description of my last interview with poor Lippard. Dressed in your imagery it would make a most touching chapter for one of your choicest stories. He was ever wild and excitable; all that wit did not leave him. I have the last autograph he ever penned. It is valuable.

Let me hear from you at all times; your letters are like a stray sunbeam in an editor's sanctum. I am about well enough to say I will ever be — but of that definitely in my next. With kind regards to your mother,

I am truly yours,

S. D. Anderson.

Washington, August 11.

Dear Mrs. Fairfield:

On the 3d of July I heard that you and daughter had left Washington. I did think your daughter would have called; *but all things change.* I write without knowing your address, because I am so anxious about my pupil. I hope you have left New Orleans. I think of her constantly. She has so much courage, that I think she may be tempted to remain in spite of the fever.

If this comes to hand, write me at once. I do not know the name of Gertrude's husband, or I would write to him.

Your friend,

C. B. King.

It was with a mournful happiness that I was once more returned to greet my three children, the youngest of whom I had not seen for some time.

His sufferings in childhood gave me the tenderest feelings toward him. The convulsions he had suffered had left him, and he had grown so tall and handsome I scarcely knew him. But, in the place of his former illness, a greater had succeeded: *he, too, was rapidly hastening into the distemper of a fevered brain.* The hand of God seemed to lie heavily upon me. The heart of his sister Gertrude, who tenderly loved him, was broken at this new sorrow. She was constantly with him; his grandmother, too, who, it must be confessed, was unswerving in her attachment, was devoted to this child. "Our feelings are as little in our power as the bodily structure they animate." Thus it is with our love and our hate; neither is born of our own will. It is an error to suppose that we shall be loved by those to whom we are not attached, and an injustice to exact from them more than we can give. Nothing is freer than the heart. It will bear no yoke; it knows no master but love. And, although their grandmother, from the first, was my enemy, she had her favorites among my children, and Eugene was one.

We suffer or enjoy according to our capacity of feeling; and none ever had a tenderer heart or a nobler and more sympathizing nature than my daughter Gertrude. Her grief was overwhelming at the misfortunes of her family. What sadder or deeper sufferings could come upon humanity than had come upon me? Death has its sting and its bitterness, which the hope of a hereafter may soothe; but for sorrows, living sorrows, like mine, there is no hope.

Still it was mine to grapple for bread and life; for, if I faltered, I should sink, and where could I turn for aid? In the midday summer's heat and the winter's cold there was no end to toil, for me. Added to this, my dear Genevieve grew thin and attenuated, and required my constant care. The physician's aid seemed to be useless. Night, which brings rest to the weary and solace to the sad, brought nothing to me but wretchedness, and watching, and despair.

During the year I remained in New York my daughter Gertrude was affianced and married to a Cuban gentleman of learning, worth, and distinction. He was the Spanish professor in the New York University — Senor Francesco Xavier de Vingut. What a strange, inconsistent life is this, that we should urge upon our children a contract the same which brings to many of us all our sorrows! Yet so it is; and happiness is ever remote, and we must look forward to it and hope. " 'Tis a dark labyrinth — the human heart."

"O Hope! creator of a fairy heaven!
Manna of angels! rainbow of the heart,
That, throned in heaven, doth ever rest on earth!
From our first sigh unto our latest groan,
From the first throb until the heart is cold,
Thou art a gladness and a mockery,
A glory and a vision — thou sweet child
Of the immortal spirit! In our days
Of sorrow, with thy bland hypocrisies
Thou dost delude us, and we love and trust
Thy beautiful illusions, though the soil
Of disappointment yet is on our souls.
Thou El Dorado of the poor man's dream!

Sire of repentance! child of vain desires!
The bleeding heart clings to thee when all hope
Is madness; o'er our thoughts thou ever hold'st
Eternal empire; and thou dost console
The felon in his cell, the galley slave,
The exile and the wanderer o'er the earth,
And pour'st the balm of transitory peace
E'en on the heart that sighs o'er kindred guilt."

S. L. F.

My daughter Gertrude was married and gone, and I was left alone with my dear Genevieve.

As I have said, it has always been my misfortune to draw after me the most unhappy and unfortunate. I am reminded of an incident which occurred some years ago in New York. I was walking, in company with the poet Halleck, down Broadway; we were hastily going to see a painting of Fanny Elssler done by Inman. On the way we met with an editor, an acquaintance. He came to us laughing, and said, "I never meet you but you are with a poet. Of all the women I have ever known, you are the most extraordinary. Your monomania for poets is extreme. Your ill luck will never cease until you cut their acquaintance." This remark seemed amusing and ridiculously true.

The poet William North arrived, during our stay in New York, from London. He had not been long in this country before fate threw myself and daughter in the way of his acquaintance. He was one of the most unhappy and unfortunate of the fraternity of poets. He was educated at Bonn, in Germany. His family misfortunes drove him to our shores in search of prosperity and happiness. His nature and genius were very similar to my husband's. I never saw two beings resemble each other as much in their misanthropy. He came often to see us. Genevieve sympathized with him, as she always did with genius when suffering under misfortune. But love, with her, was out of the question ; so that when he declared his affection for her, she dismissed him from her presence. She liked his conversation, for it was truly fascinating ; but when he ventured on the subject of love he forfeited what little he had gained in her esteem. Packages of letters were sent, none of which she ever opened. He then sought to unburden his mind to me. He pleaded with me to use my influence in his behalf. Sorry indeed would I have been to have aided in so forlorn a hope.

> "It matters not its history — Love has wings,
> Like lightning, swift and fatal ; and it springs,
> Like a wild flower, where it is least expected ;
> Existing, whether cherished or rejected."

This unfriended poet often talked to me of suicide. He had frequently set the time for this act, and bade adieu to his friends. None of them, however, believed him sincere. He formed as an excuse for the postponement of the act, the coolness of the weather. "Death," he said, "is chilly enough to afford us a warm day for its journey."

It was only the day before the dreadful deed I saw him on the opposite corner of our hotel, looking intently toward the window of our room. He seemed the picture of wretchedness and woe. He stood like a statue fixed to the spot, until he saw me approach the window; he then turned and walked slowly away. The next day, the news of his suicide was brought me by a friend. It was about ten o'clock in the morning that he committed the fatal act. He made his toilet in black summer cloth — a suit, it appears, he had had made for the purpose. He was found with his feet resting on the floor, his head thrown back on the bed; the vial that had contained the poison was lying on the floor with the cork in it.

The following is taken from the "New York Times." The editor of the "Times" was a warm friend to the poet North.

THE SLAVE OF THE LAMP. By William North. New York: Long & Brothers.

The publication of this volume is attended with more than ordinary interest, from the circumstances, yet fresh in the public mind, of the author's sad death. The last pages of the manuscript of this work were found in his chamber beside the corpse of the unfortunate author. His work and his life were finished with equal deliberation. When the work-worn fingers could lay aside the pen, the willing hand of the suicide closed on death. It was horrible, it was sad, that a young man of so much genius, of such genial susceptibility, of such keen perceptions of the true and beautiful, should plunge thus despairingly into an untimely grave! But it was not remarkable. It has been, and always will be, a condition of certain melancholy, impressible temperaments to contemplate death as a desirable solution of all worldly troubles. The perplexities of life, conflicting with poetic meditations on human destiny, are calculated to produce this effect, even where common sense, or worldly wisdom, has some foothold.

Mr. North possessed very little worldly wisdom. He lived

within himself thoroughly, and looked at things not as they are, but as they should be. Acutely sensitive to praise, — and it was his honest ambition to deserve it, — he was morbidly affected by indifference. Every thing that life failed to afford him was perverted to the world's indifference, and to brood on this theme in chilly isolation was at once his solitary and maddening consolation. Throughout all his writings there is a gloomy indifference to life, and a bitter contempt for a world of which he knew nothing; yet Mr. North was capable of lasting, genuine friendship. A little genial appreciation was all he asked; he felt he deserved it, for he had worked hard for the boon. It was when this was disputed — and in his forays among strangers who had never heard his name it was apt to be — that he became most gloomy, and retired bitterly within himself to fresh contemplation of human destiny and woe. Pecuniary embarrassments and family difficulties of no ordinary kind filled the cup to overflowing. Life became a question of endurance. He bore it as long as he could, finished what work he had in hand, wrote to his friends tenderly and affectionately, and died.

"The Slave of the Lamp" is a remarkable work. It is brilliant, original, well devised, and powerfully written. A dozen essays might be extracted from it evidencing these facts. But the philosophy of the book is erroneous, and the advanced social doctrines all moonshine. The author is to a great extent the hero. An autobiography in the latter portion of the volume, founded on fact, will account for all his eccentricities, all his heart-wretchedness. It unfolds a sad tale of family wrong and misspent energy. The literary merits of the novel are unusually attractive in this section of the work. The story is one of passionate love, unfortunate and unrequited. The heroine is a beautiful blue-eyed blonde, a type which at all times fascinated Mr. North. Every thing he did was under the inspiration of beauty. How much might he have done had he been domestically happy!

In the summer of last year Mr. North wrote an exceedingly clever tragedy, founded on the Scandinavian mythology, and called "Odin." This was also written under the inspiration of beauty, and dedicated to the lady who is, we believe, the original of *Colum-*

bia in the "Slave of the Lamp." The following note addressed to the lady, and the two poems which accompany it, have never been published.

"MY DEAR MISS ———:

"Read 'Odin.' You will find that you have *helped to write it.* You will also find my soul in its pages. Were 'Odin' a *failure,* I should have no wish left but to die speedily.

Yours sadly, ever devotedly,

W. NORTH.

"P. S. — This copy I shall require to show some people to-morrow. I have therefore left the *name* in the dedication a blank, for obvious reasons. N."

ODIN.

COMPLETED JUNE 17, 1854.

Dedication.

To thee, GENEVRA, my eternal queen,
I dedicate a work at length complete,
Since well thou knowest that in every scene
Thy beauty's mirrored shape each eye will meet!
To me, alas! denied is *Odin's* sword,
But *Freya's* graces all to thee accord.

It may be that some skald of future times
Will speak of him who sought thy priceless love,
As one who had accomplished more than rhymes
Against dark, selfish vice our race to move.
It *must* be that the coming bard will tell
Whose genius and whose beauty wove the spell!

Be this a dream or prophecy, I ask
But one reward, though fleeting be my fame;
'Tis that whoever nobly scans my task,
Soul of my soul! may link it with thy name,
That all may say — whate'er they say beside —
He loved GENEVRA — *and her lover died!*

N.

THE SPIRIT'S COMMADE.

A FANTASY WRITTEN AFTER MIDNIGHT, JUNE 7, 1854.

Alone? — O, no, I am not *now* alone;
Forever with me is a shape divine,
Which my fierce soul pursued from zone to zone,
Till knowledge of its *living* truth were mine;
Till of my heart
Its image formed a part,
Immortal as yon stars, which silent shine!

Silent they are, and yet to me they tell
A thousand stories of the mystic past —
Of life's eternal contest, heaven to hell
Opposed forever! "Hope," they say, "at last
Hope, and be brave;
Thy knightly banner wave,
And stake the future on one battle's cast!"

And, to my fancy, the fair comrade smiles,
And sweetly whispers dreams of coming bliss,
Whilst dimly-visioned fame my thought beguiles,
And on the pearl-like brow I breathe one kiss,
Love's viewless crown,
Before which shall bow down
The world that shall be, and the race that is!

O beauteous comrade! shadow, which I call
From thy more beauteous substance, at my will!
Brief is the spell, and yet to me 'tis all
That gives me strength stern duties to fulfill!
Herself in vain
My worship would disdain;
Her charm is mine, although her scorn might kill!

Dear comrade! by an honor yet unstained!
Sweet comrade! by a poet's prophet-sight!

By all that has thy gentle nature pained,
Or given to thy noble heart delight!
Thou art to me,
On life's tempestuous sea,
The long-sought star that pierces sorrow's night!
W. North.

The name of a great poet is as rare as it is splendid. The ancients called poets holy; and no doubt they are, in some sort, inspired with a divine spirit, for which reason they were crowned, as were the Cæsars and heroes who triumphed in ancient Rome. Both are immortalized by heroism; one by their actions, the other by their verse. I pity the mind which has no respect for the Muses. Poetry as well as novel-writing is called fiction; but what is termed fiction is, in fact, reality. Novels, like poetry, contain truths, the experience of the darker shades of life, which many of us suffer, but to which few of us have the moral courage to attach our names; hence it is that novel-writers in all ages have been the most successful. To censure a work that shows up vice, as the strongest incentive to the commission of crime, betrays an ignorance and narrowness of mind which I think deserves no answer.

CHAPTER XXI.

My daughter's state of mind demanded of me a constant change of scene. We left New York and journeyed west. Any where, it mattered not where I went, all places were alike to me. Such was the state of Genevieve's mind, that no sooner were we arrived at a hotel, than her question would be, "Why stop here? I do not like this place." I was often impressed with the necessity of placing her for a time in one of our institutions, but failed of courage to do so. I often asked her what she thought of these places. "She had no doubt," she said, "they were necessary institutions." But when I questioned her in regard to herself — how she would like to be placed in one of them, as a trial of her health, she would always object, and seemed to shudder at the thought. She was conscious of her state of mind, and talked to me much about it. Wherever she was known, she elicited from all the kindest attentions. Often — how often have I seen the tear of sympathy fall from stranger eyes, at hearing her sing and play her pensive songs!

With her sufferings she became more and more misanthropic. After a long and weary journey to Wisconsin, we returned and passed some time in Chicago, Illinois. Here she became dangerously ill from an attack of congestion on the brain, which lasted for several long, painful weeks. This detention brought us into April. We returned from our journey as hopeless of her health and happiness as when we left. To go through with the painful details year after year, for the last four years, and of the incidents of travel alone with her during that time, would cause me too much pain, and would fill volumes. During the winter of 1859, her illness had become so severe as to oblige me to remove her to an asylum. This was the crowning point of sorrow. She was taken to the West Philadelphia Asylum, under the care of Dr. Kirkbridge. I was left alone — parted at last from this earnest child of thought, genius, and meditation. So have they perished, the aims to which I have aspired — one and all, the dreams in which I have indulged.

> "O heart, hold thee on in courage of soul
> Through the stormy shades of thy worldly way."

O, how I missed her! She had never since her birth been absent from me. I had been for years accustomed to hear her talk, often through the livelong watches of the night, sometimes to herself, sometimes to the heavens, the moon and stars, and wonder at the sublimity of those glorious orbs she could not comprehend. She would often say, "I have no doubt, mamma, that they are peopled by the beings we dream of in youth — the children of our brain with whom we people earth, but which in reality we never find."

Moonlight, unto her, had often been her sole companion, when, with watching and fatigue, I had fallen asleep, and her tossing thoughts, like stormy waters, rolled through the darkened boundlessness of her mind.

There was nothing for me, it seemed, either in heaven or on earth. "Great God!" I cried, in my loneliness and sorrow, "thou hast willed all my bereavements. Father of mercies, forgive the sorrow that questions thy righteous pleasure. Forgive the human and sinful nature that murmurs. Pardon the prayer that asks — how humbly, how fervently — for her, for my child's happiness and restoration."

Months passed away before I could form any resolution to visit her. I knew my strength of purpose in all except what appertained to her.

Accompanied by some of my friends one pleasant day, I went over to see her. She seemed better, and overjoyed to see me. She walked with me over the grounds. She spoke kindly of the people, and of the institution; but she said, "I am lonely here, and beg you to take me with you to town." She seemed so mild, and so much better, that I at once acceded to her wishes, as I knew I should before I left to visit her.

It was our dinner hour when we came to the door of our lodgings. "Now," said she, "mamma, don't wait dinner for me. I must take a walk to view the town. I have been shut up so long that all things look so joyous. I will return soon." She returned delighted, and appeared quite well.

Weeks passed away and left her so much better that I began to hope that happiness had returned once more to bless me.

She often amused me by the descriptions she gave of the antics of the poor patients in the hospital, many of which were very ludicrous, over which she herself would heartily laugh. A few months only had passed when she relapsed, and the disorder returned with more violence than ever. This interval of happiness seemed to have been given me only to plunge me into irremediable despair. Thus do the lights and shadows of human existence mingle together.

Again, through the aid of friends, I replaced her in the institution from whence I had taken her.

On the evening of the day she left me, I sat down alone in my room, only to gaze at her vacant chair and bed, feeling she had now left me for the last time. Her books lay open upon the table. I took up one of her favorite authors. It was Miss Landon. Before going to my bed I ran over its pages, on which I found many of her pencil marks.

In "Francesca Carrara" were the following passages, with penciled hands pointing to them.

"I returned to my lodgings — all was dreary, all was void — was emblematic of that change and barrenness which passes away from nature, but never from the heart."

"I went back broken in health and spirits, and vainly seeking relief in change of place. Alas, I was myself my own world. Nothing without availed to alter that within."

"O weary heart that must within itself close all its deepest leaves."

"Over how many things now does my regret take

its last and deepest tone — despondency! I regret not the pleasures that have passed, but that I have no longer any relish for them. The society which once excited is now wearisome. The book which would have been a fairy gift to my solitude, I can scarcely read."

"I neither ordered my own mind, nor made my own fate."

"My world is in the far off, and the hereafter."

"'Tis written in thy large blue eyes,
Filled with unbidden tears;
The passionate paleness on thy cheek,
Belying thy few years.
A child, yet not the less thou art
One of the gifted hand and heart,
Whose deepest hopes and fears
Are omen-like; the poet's dower
Is even as the prophet's power."

O, how my tears fell over these passages of grief so applicable to her wasted heart!

Thus, after twenty years of toil, and of perils by land and sea, have I returned to Philadelphia, to the scenes of former years.

To retrace what I have written has been of melancholy remembrance, mixed with bitterness and tears. Since the strongest cord of my life has been broken, and the years have drawn nigh when I feel that I have no pleasure in them — by the grace of God, I shall easily renounce a world where my cares have been deceitful, and my hopes vain and perishing.

"There is an evening twilight of the heart,
When its wild passion-waves are sunk to rest,
And the eye sees life's brightest dreams depart
As fades the sunbeams in the rosy west."

POEMS.

OLYMPIADS.

MARRIED LOVE AND MARRED LOVE.

I WEDDED the Beloved — the Beautiful!
She had an eye like Spring's first flowers, or stars
At summer twilight, and a high, pale brow
Of tender beauty, where the wandering veins,
Like hidden rivulets, revealed the gift
Of Mind; while Thought upon her Grecian face
Sat like a Seraph on his throne when all
The angelic princedoms bow before their God.
Pure as the May-morn breeze, or beaded dews
That diadem the rose — in every thought
The creature of a blest humanity
And purified affection — she became,
E'en to my earliest glance, the evening star,
(The holy light that hushes all to peace,)
Of a lone heart, that lingered o'er past hours,
And basked in vain though glorious imagery.
I looked and loved, and o'er my spirit came
The rush of solemn feelings (golden clouds,
Though dim and fading, on the wings of years)
And all the idol memories of life
Went by like music on a summer eve.

Love! 'tis the dream of every young, pure heart,
A fairy vision of a better sphere,
A rainbow, resting on a world of woe,
But leading unto heaven; a charm in hope
To all, though unto few the holiest bliss
Of earth — the earnest of eternal heaven.

Passion's young pilgrim, I had roamed afar
O'er foreign lands, where unfamiliar tongues
And aspects strange saluted me; my ear
Had ceased to hear the tender voice of love,
And never trusted words that knew no heart.
I long had roamed the world in utter scorn
Of all man toils to gain and cast away;
And lingering Time hung o'er me like a sky
Of deep, dull, chilling clouds, without or light
Or darkness, and all human things to me
Brought neither love nor hate, but one dead waste
Of life and all its passions, hopes and fears.

I trod my Native Land again, unchanged
In the deep love my spirit bears to thee,
Divinest Liberty! but hopeless else
Of all the common happiness of man.
Forecast not fate, nor to thyself appoint
Thy destiny! for, over all supreme,
A Power directs our days and their events
Unseen, all prescient and inscrutable;
And, in the world, full oft a single word,
Uttered unwarily, will more avail
Thy welfare, than long years of vain pursuit,

Passion and tempest, and unslackened toil.
I long had deemed that earth held many hearts
Deep, proud, and high like mine; but what I sought
With martyr-like devotion — vainly sought —
Came in an hour when Hope had passed away,
And Chance assumed her empire o'er my fate.
Deep streams will mingle, though their fountains rise
A thousand leagues asunder: so will hearts,
Whose feelings ever blend, though far apart
Born, and in fancy for another fate.
We met, — we loved, — and she became to me
A solace and the hope of better days.

I had looked forward to this sacred hour
As look the weary mariners for land,
As captives for the day that sets them free,
As desert pilgrims for Zahara's wells,
As saints for paradise. Love was to me
My sainted father's only dying gift
Not clutched away from a young orphan's grasp;
And the o'ergushing heart will spread o'er earth
A paradise of bloom, or on the waste
Of an unthankful world pour out its life.
Affections unbestowed, in the deep spring
Of o'erfraught bosoms dwelling, like pent streams,
Stagnant in their large affluence; but unlocked,
Bear wealth and beauty in their silent flow.
To throw one's self upon a kindred heart;
To love as angels do; to know one's hopes
And fears are shared by a devoted bride;
To cling through good and evil to the shrine

Whence bridal vows ascended to the skies;
This to my bosom had been paradise;—
But ever had I felt 'twas to search
For what my spirit, in its lonely moods,
Had imaged out; for, O, too well I knew
Such high revealings had no earthly type!

In other days, when earth, and air, and sea
Glowed with the glory of Ambition's dreams,
Passion awoke, and worshiped at the shrine
Of a pure heart with all the earnest love,
The wild adoring of a soul that cast
The world away to win a heaven below.
But evil came; a blight was on my love;
The storm rushed o'er the sunbeam; and, amid
The darkness of a deep, unnatural night,
Rude hands bore off the idol of my youth!
— Ten years have died! To linger on the days,
And mark their thoughts and deeds, long ages pass
Like endless shadows o'er me; but to fly
To Housatonic's stream and Derby's hills,
And that old mansion, whose great balcony
Hung o'er the waters — brief as Hope appears
The Olympiad of my first unhappy love.
Through the dark night I saw the glimmering sail
Resting upon the wave; I saw the bark,
And heard the dash of oars that bore away
My heart's best hope. Despair hath dreadful strength!
I saw the vessel glide away, and heard
Voices upon the deep until they came
O'er me like the far sounds of dreams! And then —

Then I went forth, a man, 'mid other men,
Not to lament — the proselyte of fools —
Nor rail, like girls hysteric, nor arraign
The doom of evil; but to feel and bear,
To think and keep deep silence, and to love
Too sacredly for earth to know my love.
I sought not dim forgetfulness, but nursed
Memory, and loved the blissful pangs she brought.

Years passed; but I remembered her, and then
My heart grew milder than in other times;
And when I thought of the loved one, 'twas not
With bitterness, but tender melancholy,
Shadowed and softened by the lapse of years
And many changes. Like the gushing forth
Of twilight waters, or the whispering stir
Of dewy leaves, or breath of fading flowers,
The memory of our young and blighted love
Came o'er me, and 'twas blessedness to think
How I had loved her; — though my bosom bled
O'er my lone grief and her dark sacrifice.
O'er the wild surges of the ocean oft
My spirit wandered back when far away,
But with a settled grief serene; none knew
From outward mildness, and smooth courtesy,
And mannerly respect of customs old,
That Passion's flood had left my heart a waste.
Lost to my arms, but not my love, I knew
Her days could not be blest in this wrong world,
And never would I, by remotest word,
Waken a scorpion in her wedded heart.

She was a thing of holiness — high throned
As among cherubims, beheld far off,
And worshiped unapproached ; and oft I wept
And prayed that she might calmly bear the task,
The bitter task, that was her portion here,
Without repining o'er the fatal hours
That fled like morning stars ; and 'twas my trust
That he — her unknown wedded lord — might prove
Gentle and faithful to the blighted flower !
And never — never would I see her more,
Though, sometimes, tidings of her lot would come,
Like desert blasts or storms at equinox,
To darken the bright stream of wandering thought.
So all my deep affections mellowed down
Into a sorrow gentle as the sigh
Of the low evening wind through autumn woods.

As I have said, I wedded the Beloved !
'Twas when the sweet autumnal days came on,
And earth was full of beauty, and the heavens
Of glory, and the heart of man of praise.
I gave her all the deep love of a heart
Long tried and faithful unto worse than death,
And she did love me more that I had loved
With a fidelity and strength alike
Unconquered by repulse, and woe, and time.
Her smiles went o'er my bosom like the air
O'er flowering shrubs and honeysuckle bowers,
And she, at times, was mirthful as the birds
In the sweet month of May ; and then again
Quietly sad as any nightingale.

Playful, yet full of feeling, innocent,
Without suspecting guile, in smiles and tears
Pleasant as stars when fancy images
The thrones of angels there, she gently taught
Forgetfulness of many an irking ill,
Lost in the beauty of her winsome smile,
And did become, first in herself, and then
In the blest offerings of love, a world
Where peril, calumny, and pain are lost
In this revealment of restoring Heaven.

SONNET.

What are the Past and Future? Shadows, lit
By the mind's twilight bloom, and all too dim
For clear perception; far and faint they swim
Before the visionary's eye, and flit
Away in dusky folds, whose outskirts wear
A mellow glow a while, and then resume
Oblivion's sable tinges. In the gloom
Of the o'ershadowed Past, with pensive air,
Pale Memory sits beside a sculptured urn,
Chanting the requiem of joys long fled;
And flickering tapers, for the parted dead,
Around her wasted form forever burn;
But Hope, on sunlight pinions, soars on high,
And hath her throne and glory in the sky.

PERE LA CHAISE.*

Beautiful City of the Dead! thou stand'st
Ever amid the bloom of sunny skies
And blush of odors, and the stars of heaven
Look, with a mild and holy eloquence,
Upon thee, realm of Silence! Diamond dew,
And vernal rain, and sunlight, and sweet airs
Forever visit thee; and morn and eve
Dawn first, and linger longest on thy tombs
Crowned with their wreaths of love, and rendering back
From their wrought columns all the glorious beams
That herald morn, or bathe in trembling light
The calm and holy brow of shadowy eve.
Empire of pallid shades! though thou art near
The noisy traffic and thronged intercourse
Of man, yet stillness sleeps, with drooping eyes
And meditative brow, forever round
Thy bright and sunny borders; and the trees
That shadow thy fair monuments, are green,
Like Hope that watches o'er the dead, or love
That crowns their memories; and lonely birds
Lift up their simple songs amid the boughs,
And with a gentle voice wail o'er the lost,
The gifted, and the beautiful, as they

* The Cemetery of Paris.

Were parted spirits hovering o'er dead forms
Till judgment summons earth to its account.

Here 'tis a bliss to wander when the clouds
Paint the pale azure, scattering o'er the scene
Sunlight and shadow, mingled, yet distinct,
And the broad olive leaves, like human sighs,
Answer the whispering zephyr, and soft buds
Unfold their hearts to the sweet west wind's kiss,
And Nature dwells in solitude, like all
Who sleep in silence here, their names and deeds
Living in Sorrow's verdant memory.
Let me forsake the cold and crushing world,
And hold communion with the dead! then thought,
The silent angel language Heaven doth hear,
Pervades the universe of things, and gives
To earth the deathless hues of happier climes.

All, who repose undreaming here, were laid
In their last rest with many prayers and tears;
The humblest as the proudest was bewailed,
Though few were near to give the burial pomp.
Lone watchings have been here, and sighs have risen
Oft o'er the grave of love, and many hearts
Gone forth to meet the world's smile desolate.

The saint, with scrip and staff, and scallop shell,
And crucifix, hath closed his wanderings here;
The subtle schoolman, weighing thistle-down
In the great balance of the universe,
Sleeps in the oblivion which his folios earned;
The sage, to whom the earth, the sea, and sky

Revealed their sacred secrets, in the dust,
Unknown unto himself, lies cold and still;
The dark eyes and the rosy lips of love,
That basked in Passion's blaze till madness came,
Have moldered in the darkness of the ground;
The lover, and the soldier, and the bard,
The brightness, and the beauty, and the pride
Have vanished, — and the Grave's great heart is still!

Alas! that sculptured pyramid outlives
The name it should perpetuate; alas!
That obelisk and temple should but mock
With effigies the form that breathes no more.
The cypress, the acăcia, and the yew
Mourn with a deep, low sigh o'er buried power;
And moldered loveliness, and soaring mind
Yet whisper, "Faith surmounts the storm of death."

Beautiful City of the Dead! to sleep
Amid thy shadowed solitudes, thy flowers,
Thy greenness and thy beauty, where the voice,
Alone heard, whispers love, and greenwood choirs
Sing 'mid the stirring leaves, were very bliss
Unto the weary heart and wasted mind,
Broken in the world's warfare, yet still doomed
To bear a brow undaunted! O, it were
A tranquil and a holy dwelling-place
To those who deeply love but love in vain —
To disappointed hopes, and baffled aims,
And persecuted youth. How sweet the sleep
Of such as dream not, wake not, feel not, here,
Beneath the starlight skies and flowery earth,
'Mid the green solitudes of Pere La Chaise!

THE DIRGE.

Weep not thou for the dead!
Sweet are their dreamless slumbers in the tomb —
Their eyelids move not in the morning's light,
No sun breaks on the solitary gloom,
No sound disturbs the silence of their night —
Soft seems their lowly bed!

Grieve not for them, whose days
Of earthly durance have so quickly passed, —
Who feel no more Affliction's iron chain!
Sigh not for them who long since sighed their last,
Never to taste of sin and woe again
In realms of joy and praise!

What they were once to thee
It nought avails to think, save thou canst draw
Pure thoughts of piety, and peace, and love,
And reverent faith in Heaven's eternal law,
From their soft teachings, ere they soared above,
Lost in Eternity!

When o'er the pallid brow
Death flings his shadow — and the pale, cold cheek
Quivers, and light forsakes the upturned eye,
And the voice fails ere faltering lips can speak
The last farewell — be not dismayed — to die
Is man's last lot below!

Death o'er the world hath passed
Oft, and the charnel closed in silence o'er
Unnumbered generations — past and gone!
And he will reign till Earth can hold no more;
Till Time shall sink beneath the Eternal Throne,
And Heaven receive its last.

Death enters at our birth
The molded form we idolize so much,
And hour by hour some subtle thread dissolves,
That links the web of life; at his cold touch
Power after power decays as time revolves,
Till earth is blent with earth.

The soul can not abide
In the dark dreariness of flesh and sin;
Its powers are chained and trampled on by clay,
And paralyzed and crushed; 'twould enter in
Its own pure Heaven, where Passion's disarray
Comes not, nor hate, nor pride.

Come, widowed one! with me,
And we will wander through the shades of death!
Look now upon those sheeted forms that soar
Amid the still and rosy air; their breath
Wafts the rich fragrance of Heaven's flowery shore,
Amid the light of Deity!

Wouldst thou wail o'er their flight,
Or curb their pinions with the chains of Time?
Art thou or canst thou be so happy here,

Thy spirit pants not for a fairer clime?
O, sorrowing child of sin, and doubt, and fear!
        Thy heart knows no delight.

        Wouldst thou roll back the waves
Of the unfathomed ocean of the Past,
And from soft slumbers wake the undreaming Dead,
Again to shiver in the bleak, cold blast,
Again the desert of despair to tread,
        And mourn their peaceful graves?

        Ah, no! — forget them not!
Thoughts of the dead incite to worthy deeds,
Or from the paths of lawless ill deter;
When the lone heart in silent sorrow bleeds,
Or sin entices — to the past recur —
        Trust Heaven, thou wilt not be forgot!

        Weep not for them who leave
In childhood's sinless hours the haunts of vice!
Mourn not the Lovely in their bloom restored
To the bright bowers of their own paradise!
Mourn not the Good who meet their honored Lord
        Where they no more can grieve!

        But rather weep and mourn
That thou art yet a sinning child of dust,
Changeful as April skies or Fortune's brow;
And, while thy grief prevails, be wise, and just,
And kind, so thou shalt die like flowers that blow,
        And into rose-air turn.

THE HOUR OF DEATH.

When, wrapt in dreams that throng the twilight hour,
I roam alone o'er Nature's fair domain,
'Mid the hushed shadows of the wildwood bower,
Or o'er the shell-strewn margin of the main,
    Or upland green, or lovely lawn,
    Where dewdrops kiss the breathing flowers,
    And Summer smiles, at rosy dawn,
    Like Memory o'er unsinning hours,
I think that soon — how soon! the Night will come
When I shall leave this bright world for the tomb.

I think — and frailty dims the drooping eye —
That Spring will perfume all the inspiring air,
And Summer's smile illume earth, sea, and sky,
And Autumn, Heaven's own robe of glory wear;
    That silvery voices, low and sweet,
    Will breathe the heart's own music forth,
    And plighted youth 'trothed maidens meet,
    Where now I roam o'er darkening earth;
But when all seasons with their treasures teem,
Where shall I wander? victim of a dream!

Through thousand years the glorious sun shall rise,
And myriad song-birds thrilling anthems sing:

Soft shall the moonbeams fall from midnight skies,
And groves breathe music o'er the gushing spring;
    But where will be the lonely one
    Who swept his lyre in wayward mood,
    And dreamed, sung, wept o'er charms unwon,
    In holy Nature's solitude?
In what far realm of shoreless space shall roam
The soul that e'en on earth made Heaven its home?

The paths I wear the stranger's foot will tread;
The trees I plant will yield no fruit to me;
The flowers I cherish bloom not for the dead;
The name I nourish — what is that to thee,
    Fame, phantom of the wildered brain?
    Love's tears should hallow life's last hour,
    For pomp, and praise, and crowns are vain —
    Death is the spirit's only dower!
Alone, the hermit of a broken heart,
My Mind hath dwelt — even so let it depart.

To think — alas! to feel and know that we,
Sons of the sun, the heirs of thought and light,
Must perish sooner than the wind-tossed tree
Our hands have planted, and unending night
    Close o'er our buried memories!
    Our sphere of starry thought, our sun
    Of glory quenched in morning skies;
    Our sceptre broken, empire gone,
The voice, that bade creation spring to birth
Too weak to awe the worm from human earth!

I know not where this heart will sigh its last,
I cannot tell what shaft will lay me low,
Nor, when the mortal agony hath passed,
Whither my spirit through the heavens will go.
    It will not sleep, it can not die ;
    It is too proud to grovel here ;
    For even now it mounts the sky,
    And leaves behind earth's hope and fear!
O, may it dwell, when cleansed from sin and blight,
Shrined in God's temple of eternal light!

Where'er the spirit roams, howe'er it lives,
I can not doubt it sometimes looks below,
And from the scenes of mortal love derives
Much to enhance its rapture or its woe ;
    And when I muse on death and gloom,
    And all that saints or sages tell,
    I pause not at the midnight tomb,
    Nor listen to the funeral knell ;
But think how dear the scenes I loved will be
When I gaze on them from eternity!

GRAVE WATCHING.

Bring flowers and strew them here,
The loveliest of the year,
Withered, yet fragrant as her virgin fame,
Who slumbers in this sunny spot,
Yet to Love's voice awaketh not,
Nor hears in dreams her lover sigh her name.

Where woods o'er waters wave
She hath her early grave,
And summer breathes lone music o'er the scene;
It is a green and bloomy place,
And smiling like her living face,
Whom memory weeps o'er, sighing, "She hath been!"

How sacred Silence lies,
With dreamy, heart-filled eyes,
Shedding its spirit o'er the wanderer's heart,
Beside the mound of dust,
Where, throned, sit Hope and Trust,
Serenely watching awful Death depart.

In sooth, 'twere bliss to rest
On Nature's rosy breast
'Mid all this sweetness, quiet, faith, and love,
While Heaven's soft airs flit round
The still and hallowed ground,
And the blue skies lift the pure soul above.

Albeit, I can but grieve
That thou, pale girl! didst leave
Thy lover lone in such a world as this;
Yet tender is my heart's regret
As the last beam of suns that set
To rise again, like thee, my love, in bliss!

Then let me linger here,
Where none of earth appear,
Save gentle spirits, kindred of the skies,
And muse beside the gushing spring,
Where wild birds carol on the wing,
And live as thou didst, love, on harmonies!

O'er this green bank of flowers
Hover the dew-eyed hours,
Blending the incense breath of earth and heaven;
As thou didst hallow time
By thoughts and deeds sublime,
And seal eternal bliss by wrongs forgiven.

Inspire me with thy soul;
And, while the seasons roll,
No evil passion shall corrode my spirit!
I can forgive my fiercest foes,
And think not o'er inflicted woes,
While I thy gentle soul, lost love, inherit!

What holy joy attends
Such commerce with lost friends —
Lost to our eyes but living in our minds!

Their memories breathe elysian bliss
Around e'en such a world as this,
Like Yemen's odors borne on genial winds,

Bring flowers and strew them here,
The loveliest of the year,
And I will watch their spirits as they part;
For in a place so green and still,
'Mid wood and water, vale and hill,
My lost love dwells forever in my heart!

SONNET.

WELCOME, Angelo, to a world of care!
Fair firstborn of my youth, thou'rt welcome here!
Thy smile can charm away the world's despair,
And light a rainbow in the heart's wild tear.
Thy quick intelligence, thy winning ways,
Thy deep affection in life's first hours shown,
Thy father's spirit, like a mantle, thrown
About thee, studded by the pearly rays
That float like music round the fairy soul
Of thy mild cheerful mother, with her smiles
Beaming like starlight o'er the ocean's isles,
That oft deep sorrow from my heart have stole—
These blend, my boy, in thy dark, ardent eyes,
Like zodiacs in the depth of heaven's blue skies!

THE POET'S NIGHT SOLITUDE.

Would that I were the spirit of yon star,
That seems a diamond on the throne of heaven!
Would that my holiest thought could ever dwell
'Mid the unsearchable vastness of the sky!
For 'tis deep midnight; and bland stillness sleeps
On dewy grove and waveless stream, and airs,
Floating about like heavenly visitants,
Breathe o'er the slumbering flowers and leafy woods,
Such holy music as the tired heart loves —
Low, murmuring, melancholy strains — so soft
The ear scarce catches sound, though deeply feels
The hushed, communing heart the influence
Of their lone oracles! Departed hours
Of mingled bane and bliss, of hope and fear,
Of faithless friendship, unrequited love,
Unshared misfortune, undeserved reproach,
And humble pride, and dark despondency,
Hours of high thought and silent intercourse
With the old seers and sages, when the soul
Walked solemnly beside departed bards
And lion-hearted martyrs; and o'erveiled
Forest, and hill, and vale, and rivulet,
With the deep, glorious majesty of mind!

Shadowing, with a most dainty fantasy,
The cold and harsh realities of things,
With the divine undying dawn of heaven,
Whose beauty blossoms and whose glory burns!

At such a time of thoughtful loneliness
Ye come like seraph shades, and bear me back
On darkened wings, to earlier passages
Scarce less unblest than present years of grief
I grope through now! But woes, once borne, become
Strange pleasures to our memory; the Past
Hath its romance — its mellow lights and shades,
Soothing deep sadness like the brightest hope
That bursts upon the future. While we gaze
Down the dark vista, where in bitter pain,
And weariness, and solitude of soul,
We long have roamed forsaken — all the scene
Assumes a calm repose, a verdure mild
As midnight music, and our hearts o'ergush
With tearful tenderness. O, there is bliss
E'en in the darkest memory — a depth
Of passion that now slumbers, and of thought,
Though voiceless, eloquent and full of power,
Which leaves all common hope, in life's routine,
Dim and delusive as the fire-fly's light.

Full orbed in pearly beauty walks the moon,
Flinging on fleecy clouds soft gleams of light,
That silver every fair and floating fold
'Mid the blue ether, while her beams below,
On slumbering vale and cliff, and haunted wood,

And broad deep stream, an awful wilderness,
Fall at the outskirts of vast shadowings,
Like heaven's great light on wings of angels thrown.
And now the breeze, in Music's fitful gush,
Harps 'mid the osiers and wide harvest lakes
Of grass and grain, and then the voices rise
Of fays and fairies in the fir-wood near.

Now sleepless bard — who never is alone —
May mingle with the harmony of Heaven,
Triumphant o'er the evil of the world;
His heart may banquet on each gentle scene
Of loveliness, and shrink not back aghast
As from the mock and scoff malign of men.
To voices soft as sighs of sleeping flowers,
And tender as a fair young mother's kiss,
His spirit listens in its joy. On him
The beauty of the old Astrology,
The silent hymn of heaven, in starlight falls;
And Alchemy bestows its choicest lore,
And Poetry, with all its holiness,
Sinks gently o'er him like the early dew
On the fair foliage of the Hesperides.

The cricket sings, the aspen twinkles quick
Beneath the moonbeam, and the waters purl
O'er shining pebbles and by wildwood banks,
As if blest life in every drop prevailed.
The deep enchanted forests seem to bend,
And make no sound through their vast solitudes,
As if they deeply listened to THE VOICE,

Whose whisper fills the universe. O'er all,
Waters and woods, mountains and valleys deep,
A spirit reigns whose secret counsel heals
The goaded mind and wasted heart, and guides
Ill-fortuned dwellers of the earth to peace;
And he is wise, who, in his budding youth,
Casting aside the paltry pride of praise,
In the night season leaveth strife, and care,
And vain ambition, to go forth and drink
The music and the blessedness of earth,
While man forgets the God he scorns by day.
Reclining on the moonlight rocks, he sees
The proud Orion, the soft Pleiades,
And every glorious constellation move
With light and hymn of worship, and his soul
O'erleaps the feuds and falsehoods of the world,
The trembling and the triumph of an hour,
And mingles with the universal Deity.
The warring passions of the human heart
Sink, then, to rest; bright angel forms repose
By piny woods and shady waterfalls,
And seraph voices sing of heaven and love
In every leaf stirred by the vesper airs.
And this communion of upsoaring thought,
This conscious inspiration (holier far
Than Delphic oracles or hermit's dream)
Becomes our earthly paradise, when gleams
Of worlds inscrutable flash through the gloom
Of this our sinning nature, body-bowed,
And the accepted words of ancient men,
Gifted beyond their age and station here,

Become assured revealings of that life
All hope to gain, but few dare think upon,
As Wisdom thinks, who dwells not with the vain,
The greedy, and the proud, but hath her throne
In the pure heart, whose ever-living hope
Glows like a lone star in the depth of Heaven.

SONNET.

How like Divinity this soft, still eve!
The sun of Autumn, like a god, is setting,
And, O, the beauty tempts me to forgetting
Those giant ills that long have made me grieve.
Bright angels seem reposing on yon verge
Of billowy light, and from their airy wings,
Fanning infinity, a perfume springs,
Like cherub breathings. The low, lulling surge,
Breaking far o'er the shelly beach; the deep,
Soft music of the groves; the whirl and rush
Of dropping sear leaves, and the trickling gush
Of rivulets that from the brown cliffs leap,—
This dying loveliness melts all my woes,
And hallows sorrows Death alone can close!

THE FATHER'S LEGACY.

By Hudson's glorious stream, in death's cold rest,
Thy head lies low, my great and gallant sire!
Pillowed in peace on Earth's eternal breast,
No more thy bosom pants with Hope's desire.
Now, more than ever, doth thy name inspire,
For lingering years have wept above thy grave,
And shed their cold dews o'er my lonely lyre,
But to enhance the grief that could not save,
The settled woe that sighs o'er Hudson's midnight wave.

In the first gush and glory of my years,
Ere Reason glowed, or Memory held her power,
Thy pale, proud brow was wet with infant tears,
And wild cries rose in thy deserted bower!
O, how the dim remembrance of that hour
Crowds on my brain like night's most shadowy dream,
When winds wail loud, and o'erfraught tempests lower!
A glimpse of glory in a meteor's gleam,
Sunlight in storms, — a flower upon the rushing stream.

The budding boughs, the limpid light of spring,
The mirrored beauty of the brimming rills,
The greenness and the gentle airs that bring
Life's golden hours again, when heavenly hills
And vales bore witness to the soul that thrills
The heart of youth ere passion riots there —
Shed o'er me now the loveliness which fills,
At parted seasons, such as wed despair
When Being's day-spring breaks and all but life is fair.

Yet from this scene of most surpassing love,
Not unrefreshed, I turn to happier years,
Quick in their flight, when through the highland grove
I ran to meet thee with ecstatic tears,
And in thine arms forgot my deepest fears!
O, then thou wert to me what I am now*
To one blest boy — my sorrow's bliss — who wears
The very majesty of thy high brow,
The pride, the thought, the power, that in thine eye did glow.

No proud sarcophagus thy corse enshrines,
No mausoleum mocks thy moldering dust,
But there the rose, amid its mazy vines,
Blooms like thy spirit with the pure and just;
And — image of earth's high and holy trust —
Deep verdure smiles and wafts its breath to heaven,

* What, alas! I *was*.

And, holier far than antique print or bust,
Lives in my heart the portrait thou hast given, —
The worship of pure love, — the faith of Autumn's even.

Thy legacy was not the gold of men,
The slave of pomp, the vassal of the mine,
But an o'ermastering intellect, that, when
The world reviled and trampled, soared divine,
And stood o'erpanoplied on God's own shrine!
This didst thou leave me, Father! and my mind
Hath been my realm of glory — as 'twas thine —
Though much it irks me to have cast behind
Thy godlike skill to quell the ills of human kind.

'Twas thine to grapple with the fiend of gain;
'Twas thine to toil and triumph in the field;
It can not be that *I* should faint in pain,
And like a craven, to the dastard yield.
On the starred mead, and in the o'erarching weald,
It hath been mine to *think* and to be blest;
And oft on mountain pinnacles I've kneeled
To pray I might be gathered to my rest
With glory on my brow and virtue in my breast.

Though anguish throbs through all my bosom now,
And wild tears gush whene'er I think of thee,
Yet like blue heaven upon Cordillera's brow,
Thy memory clothes me with divinity,
And lifts my soul beyond the things that be, —

The strife of traffic, falsehood's common fear,
Friendship betrayed, unguerdoned vassalry,
And every ill, that reigns and riots here,
In this dark world, so far from thine immortal sphere.

My earliest smiles were thine, my earliest thought,
Like rosy light in morn's translucent sky,
First from thine eye, my spirit's sun, were caught;
And as it gleams on days that vanish by,
It turns to thee, my fountain shrined on high!
My Sister! is she with thee? where *thou* art
Thy children fain would be! On starbeams fly
Spirits of Love! and in my raptured heart
Make Heaven's own music till my soul in transport part,

And teach me with an awed delight to tread
The darksome vale that all must tread alone,
And gift me with the wisdom of the dead,
Justly to do, yet all unjustly done,
Freely to pardon! Till the crown is won,
Be with me in the errings of my lot,
The many frailties of thine only son;
And when brief records say that he is not,
Hail his wronged spirit *home* where sorrow is forgot.

AN EVENING SONG OF PIEDMONT.

Ave Maria! 'tis life's holiest hour,
The starlight wedding of the earth and heaven,
When music breathes its perfume from the flower,
And high revealings to the heart are given;
Soft o'er the meadow steals the dewy air,
Like dreams of bliss the deep blue ether glows,
And the stream murmurs round its islets fair,
The tender night song of a charmed repose.

Ave Maria! 'tis the hour of love,
The kiss of rapture and the linked embrace,
The hallowed converse in the dim still grove,
The elysium of a heart-revealing face,
When all is beautiful, for we are blest;
When all is lovely, for we are beloved;
When all is silent, for our passions rest;
When all is faithful, for our hopes are proved.

Ave Maria! 'tis the hour of prayer,
Of hushed communion with ourselves and heaven,
When our waked hearts their inmost thoughts declare,
High, pure, far-searching, like the light of even;

When hope becomes fruition, and we feel
The holy earnest of eternal peace,
That bids our pride before the Omniscient kneel,
That bids our wild and warring passions cease.

Ave Maria! soft the vesper hymn
Floats through the cloisters of yon holy pile,
And 'mid the stillness of the nightwatch dim
Attendant spirits seem to hear and smile!
Hark! hath it ceased? The vestal seeks her cell,
And reads her heart — a melancholy tale!
A song of happier years, whose echoes swell
O'er her lost love 'mid pale bereavement's wail.

Ave Maria! let our prayers ascend
For them whose holy offices afford
No joy in heaven — on earth without a friend —
That true though faded image of the Lord!
For them in vain the face of nature glows,
For them in vain the sun in glory burns,
The harrowed heart consumes in fiery woes,
And meets despair and death where'er it turns.

Ave Maria! in the deep pine wood,
On the clear stream and o'er the azure sky
Bland twilight smiles, and starry solitude
Breathes hope in every breeze that wanders by.
Ave Maria! may our last hour come
As bright, as pure, as gentle, heaven, as this!
Let faith attend us smiling to the tomb,
And life and death are both the heirs of bliss!

THE

SISTERS OF SAINT CLARA.

A TALE OF PORTUGAL.

CANTO I.

I.

'Tis the bridal of nature, the season of spring,
When Pleasure flits round on her diamond wing,
And the spirit plays brightly and softly and free,
Like gem-dropping beams on a boundless blue sea,
And the young heart is lit by the beams of love's eye,
Like an altar of perfume by fires of the sky.
'Tis the heart-blooming season of innocent love,
When the green growing mead and the whispering
grove,
And the musical stream, as it purls o'er the dale,
And the flowers whose lips zephyr woos in the vale,
Are seen with the spirit of thrilling delight
As visions of beauty too passingly bright,
And heard like the songs that come o'er us in dreams
When the soul's magic light through infinity gleams.
The gay Earth is vestured with verdure and flowers,
And hope sings away the sweet sunny hours,
While bathing in sunbeams, or over the sky
Her star-pinions waving through glories on high.

The citron groves throw on the wings of the breeze
Their balm-breathing flowers, and the green orange
trees
Harp sweetly in airs from the hill and the sea,
Like lyres heard unseen singing joys yet to be.
O Eden of beauty! Lusitania! the sun
Loves to linger a while, when his journey is done,
On the lofty twin Pillars, whose brows in the sky
Gleam bright when the sun-god rides flashingly by,
Which stand in their might 'mid the waves of the sea—
Abyla and Calpe—unconquered and free.
And Cintra's dark forests look smilingly on
Apollo descending from his chariot throne,
While Estrella's lagoon, green Escura receives
Sheen tints of his rays from the wood's gilded leaves,
And Tajo's broad bay like a mirror reposes
'Tween a heaven of light and a garden of roses.

II.

The sun's last beam of purple light
Blazons proud Calpe's castle height,
And over Lusitania's sea
Looks with a smile of melody.
The volcan fires of Ætna glow,
Brighter as sinks Hyperion low,
And, 'mid the gathering twilight high
Stromboli flames against the sky,
O'er dark-blue ocean's billowy foam,
To light the wandering sailor home.
Child of the sun, the dusky Moor
Watches the horizon, bright obscure,
And, while the proud muezzin calls
Devotion's hour from Ceuta's walls,

Throws his keen eye's far-searching glance
O'er the dark billows as they dance
Along the Mauritanian shore,
And listens to their surging roar
Around Abyla's basement deep,
Lest in tired nature's twilight sleep
The foe upon his guard should steal,
And gain the pass ere trumpet peal.
Adverse, the gallant Briton's eye,
From Calpe's height gleams o'er the sky,
And marks with all a sailor's pride
The vast sail gleaming o'er the tide,
While every breeze that comes from far
Wafts music from red Trafalgar.
Evening's dim shadow o'er the close,
Fair Lusitania ! and the rose
Of morning blushes o'er thy plains
With the same rich and gorgeous light
As when his warlike, wild Alains,
O'er forest, flood, and vale, and height,
From Volga's banks Respedial led
To Tajo's darkly wooded shore,
Though where they warr'd or why they bled
None know or name forevermore.
And the sun rolls his last faint beam
O'er princely dome, rose-margined stream,
And almond grove and jasmine bower,
With the same smile as when the earth
Blushed in the beauty of her birth.

III.

The full-orbed moon is gleaming bright
On Cintra's dark and rocky height,

And on verandah, turret, tower,
Palace and fane at this still hour
Glows with a radiant smile of love,
And gilds the music-breathing grove
With those pure beams of light serene,
Which sanctify the peaceful scene.
From wave and dome and field and grove
Rise the soft notes of pleading love,
And many a strain is heard from far
Of wandering lover's sweet guitar,
And in the songs he fondly sings
His glowing heart finds rainbow wings,
Which bear his spirit's powers afar
Unto his being's guiding star.
Dian—the queen of sighs and tears,
Her richest robe of beauty wears,
And smiles to hear the vows that rise
Beyond her empire in the skies,
While still she weeps, in prescient pain,
That passioned love is worse than vain.

IV.

St. Clara's dark and massy pile,
Where sunbeams fall but never smile,
'Mid the dense cypress grove uprears
Its ivied turrets, gray with years,
And, where the shadowy moonlight falls,
Uplifts its blackened prison walls,
Within whose solitary cells
Tearless despair forever dwells,
And sin, beneath devotion's name,
Reposes in its sacred shame,
While deeds 'twould sear the tongue to tell
Are done in murder's fatal cell.

Within St. Clara's cloistered gloom,
A living grave, a vital tomb,
Two lovely vestals, young and fair,
In misery dwelt and dark despair.
Their loves and hopes and feelings chained,
Lone sorrow o'er their being reigned,
'Till hope arose upon their eye,
And love's ecstatic witchery
Woke the fond hearts that had been crushed,
And the soul's sunlight current gushed.
Like roses budding on one stem
Or blending hues of opal gem,
Lonely they sat within their cell,
Silent till expectation's swell
Burst o'er each thought and feeling high,
Like sunshowers from the azure sky.
Round them the full heart's stilness hung,
'Till Zulma's glowing feelings sprung
To words that flowed like morning's beam,
Or song from lips of seraphim.
" Sweet Inez ! fast the fearful hour
" When we shall spurn monastic power,
" Doth hasten, and our spirits' might
" Must dare the ordeal of to-night.
" The church's power, or father's ire,
" And Heaven perchance, will all conspire
" To cloud young love's ascending sun ;
" Then, Inez, 'til the deed is done,
" And we have passed their power's extent,
" Let not thy dove-like heart relent
" Nor fancy picture punishment."
" Oh, lovely Zulma ! hope is light
" Within my trembling heart to-night,

" And fain this bosom yet would prove
" The silent joys of blissful love.
" But, ah ! my path in life hath been
" So full of grief, and every scene
" Of joy so soon hath changed to woe,
" Life's common bliss I ne'er shall know
" Till my lone heart hath ceased to beat
" Within the snow-white winding-sheet."
On her pale cheek and blanching brow
Hope's feverish hectic ceased to glow
And o'er her bosom came the blight,
The darkness of perpetual night,
The gloom of days that long had vanished,
And thoughts, that never could be banished.

V.

Zulma's high spirit at the view
Of peril more undaunted grew,
And glowed 'mid sorrow's gathering gloom
Like angel faith above the tomb.
In danger's hour she stood alone,
'Mid fearful things the fearless one,
And, as her sunlight spirit burned
O'er the deep darkness of despair,
The trembling fears of all she turned
To hopes, and left them smiling there.
Her broad high brow the throne of thought,
And features into spirit wrought ;
Her star-beam eye and face of light,
And moulded form that chained the sight,
And swan-like neck, and raven hair,
And swelling bosom, richly fair,
Which rose and sunk, like moonlight seas,
In its deep passion's ecstacies,

As if her mighty heart were swelling
In sun-waves for its heavenly dwelling;
All spake a spirit proud and high,
A wandering seraph of the sky,
And such was Zulma; sorrow's night
Might its dark shadows o'er her cast,
But the deep gloom her spirit's light
Changed into rose-beams as it past;
She had one aim, and none beside
Could bend her lofty lightning pride,
And, ere she drooped, she would have died.
Vemeira knew his daughter well,
And chained her spirit in a cell
Ere she could know the desolate
And hopeless woe of such a fate,
And 'twas to bless an elder child
He crushed that soul, so proud and wild.

VI.

Timid and fearful as the fawn,
That searches ere it treads the glade,
Yet lovely as a spring-time dawn
In robes of rosy light arrayed;
Warm, feeling, soft and delicate
As the last blush of summer eve,
Yet trembling at the frown of Fate,
Lest, while her heart did sadly grieve,
Sin should assume the garb of woe,
And shroud in gloom devotion's glow:
Inez, though fair as forms that rove
Round Fancy's fondest dream of love,
Was tender, gentle, fragile, frail,
And shrinking as the violet pale
Which blooms in solitary vale,

By zephyr fanned and breathed alone,
Unseen, unsought, unprized, unknown.
Feelings suppressed and thoughts untold
Flowed silently, like molten gold,
O'er her fond heart, while virtue's sun
Threw glory o'er them as they run.
Her smiles and tears alike were born
In purity of virgin love,
And, like bright Eos, child of morn,
She drank at streams that gush above:
For sweetness such to her was given,
Her faintest prayer was heard in heaven.

VII.

When Zulma heard her sister's plaint,
And saw her gentle spirit sink,
Her soul arose in power—"To faint
" While standing on dark ruin's brink
" Were madness worse than mirth in death
" When love and bliss our flight await
" To quail, to droop despair beneath
" Were folly that deserved the fate."
" But if we fail"—" It cannot be!
" Love, like the mountain breeze, is free,
" And, amid peril, wrong and ill,
" Strong as the gale that sweeps the hill,
" Or severing ocean in its might,
" Brings long lost treasures into light."
" But will beholding heaven approve
" Our broken vows for earthly love?"
" St. Mary shrive thee! would'st thou be
" A vestal in hypocrisy?
" Oh, gentle Inez, guard thy love!
" Count Dion's daring quest would prove

"But folly's dream in evil hour,
"If thou dost spurn the boy-god's power."
Inez arose, her blue eye flowed
In gushing tears of pearly light—
"Zulma! my heart were ill-bestowed
"If Dion called me false to-night."
"Vemeira's daughter still!—O Heaven!
"Love's messenger his call hath given!
"Inez! that rose, by Dion thrown,
"Lay on thy heart—it is thine own—
"And haste thee, for we must be gone!"
The soft strain of a sweet guitar
Now mellowed came as if from far,
But, skillful in its measured fall,
It rose by dark St. Clara's wall,
And, mastered by Prince Julian's hand,
Its sweet notes flowed so richly bland,
They told unseen the minstrel lover,
And Zulma's soaring spirit over
Threw breathless rapture as she fled
From her lone cell with footstep light,
While Inez' heart, at every tread,
Spake like deep voices of the night.

VIII.

'Queen of the skies! why should the beams
Of thy soft eye so richly glow
O'er scenes that darkest gloom beseems,
As fitting their soul-harrowing woe?
Why should thy smile alike illume
Despair and Hope, and Love and Hate,
The bridal mansion and the tomb,
Hearts full of bliss and desolate?

Empress of Heaven! oh, thou wert made
For blooming hearts and tearless eyes,
To light the spirit's serenade,
And high-soul'd love's fond ecstacies;
And, when young Time in Eden's bowers
Wore radiant crowns of fragrant flowers,
While innocence with him would rove
In soothing shade of fair-leaved grove,
And love was bliss and truth its own
Blest guerdon in the morning's sight,
When angels looked from Glory's throne
And threw around her robes of light;
Ere woe was born of sin, and crime
Blotted from man's corrupted heart
The fairest name that youthful Time
Had written there with magic art;
Ere the sad hour man's father fell,
And o'er his fall rose shouts from hell,
Thou, sky-throned Isis! from above,
Saw'st nought but pure unconscious love
Beneath the azure sky—whose sun
Smiled on each deed by mortals done.
Alas! thou now art doomed to gaze
Upon a world so dark and fell,
That thy most pure and lovely rays
Reveal man's heart a living hell!

IX.

On the young vestals' desperate flight
Thou didst look down with smile as gay
As it had been their bridal night,
And they were led in fair array
O'er bright saloons and marbled halls;
And on St. Clara's prison walls

Thy gleaming radiance shone as fair
As if delight were smiling there ;
And on the lovely Inez' eye
As she and Zulma fled in fear,
Thy rays were thrown from yon blue sky,
Unconscious that they lit a tear.
Crossing the cypressed cemetry,
They hurried on with unheard tread
'Till they had gained the boundary
Of the lone empire of the Dead,
When, ere the signal could be given
To those who watched beyond the wall,
Inez stretched forth her hands to Heaven,
Weeping as if the hour when all
Her hopes should die had come and spread
Its pall o'er life—and thus she said ;—
" Now, ere we part, sweet Zulma, say
" Thou lov'st me as in childhood's day,
" When we together fondly strayed
" Through arboured groves and green-wood shade,
" Plucked roses on the mead to crown
" The hours we loved to call our own.
" And felt that heaven looked smiling down,
' When none beneath the laughing sky
" Were half so gay as thou and I.
" Tell me the bloom of life's young flowers
" Still lingers round thy changeless heart
"And that the joy of happier hours
" Will never from thy soul depart !"
" *Now ere we part !* a strange prelude,
" Fair sister ! to the heart's high bliss ;
" Thy very spirit is imbued
" With doubts and fears—away with this !

"Thou art MY sister! droop not now,
"Remember thine and Dion's vow!
"They hear our rustling in the shade—
"Here is the cord-wove escalade—
"Now, INEZ, fearless follow me,
"Doubt not, we must and shall be free."
Unfaltering ZULMA scaled the height,
Cheering the lovely nun to speed,
And then flew down with footstep light
To JULIAN's arms, most blest indeed,
The solitary vestal stood
A moment ere she dared to climb,
And in that moment's solitude
Her stolen flight appeared like crime;
She was so pure, so lovely, sin
Tinged not a thought her soul within.
But Dion hung upon the height,
And step by step she climbed above,
Her hand was stretched, in wild delight,
To grasp that of her only love,
When fancied guilt and dark despair
Came o'er her as she lingered there,
And her brain reeled in dizziness;
She heeded not the cries below,
She could not see nor hear nor know
The insupportable distress
Of those who saw her form on high,
Delirium in her swimming eye!
One last shrill shriek of wild affright,
The falling form that met his sight,
The hollow groan, that rose and fell
Upon his heart like ruin's knell,

X.

" Away—away ! Prince Julian, fly !
" The alarum bell is pealing high,
" And ruthless hordes of vestal fiends
" Are rushing hither !"—Who ascends
Again that dreadful wall, so late
Scaled with a look that smiled at Fate ?
'Tis Zulma—" Julian ! leave me now,
" For I must share the death I wrought,
" And consummate my vestal vow
" In pain and darkness as I ought."
She rose to give her purpose deed,
When Dion barred her path and cried—
" Prince Julian ! as thou would'st in need,
" And when despair hath humbled pride,
" Crave mercy of the Power on high,
" Seize Zulma quick, and fly, fly, fly !"
In passion wild and wildered fear
The Prince obeyed the wise behest,
And grasped the heroic maiden ere
Her deed had left him thrice unblest,
And, ere a moment more had flown,
The high-soul'd nun and Prince had gone.
Count Dion watched till they had fled,
Then sprung below among the dead,
Where headstones gleamed to mock the gloom,
The desolation of the tomb.
Gently he raised the unconscious nun,
And laid her bleeding on his breast,
Thus—even thus, a blessed one
To pillow such a form to rest ;
While, as he gazed in speechless woe
On her soft, lovely features graven

With death's dark lines, he saw below
Nor love nor joy, nor hope in heaven.
But scarce the space of lightning's glare
Was left to muse of his despair,
Or soothe the suffering Inez there,
The cloister horde by Clotilde led,
Exulting that their holy hate
Could now be poured on beauty's head
And virtue's bosom desolate,
Rushed like hyena troops upon
The gallant Dion—but, appalled
By his proud port, though all alone
He stood—they paused and shrilly called
The faggot priest, their alguazil,
To guard the holy cloister's weal.
Folding his bosom's dying bride
With one strong arm unto his breast,
And with the other waving wide
Iberia's sword that many a crest
Had cloven in the deadly fray,
He bade the throng yield ample way,
And sprung upon the ladder's height;
Then came the alguazil, the light
Of hell was in his scowling eye,
Dashing the trembling host aside
Like war-ship rushing in its pride.
The lover there that moment stood,
Not like a warrior trained in blood,
But like that Spirit who on high
His four-edged sword flashed o'er the sky,
And bade the sinning mortal die.
"Yield thee, blasphemer! Heaven commands."
"Chain, then, the bold blasphemer's hands,

"And bind his madden'd spirit down
"Low as thy master's and thine own."
"Darest thou the monarch's alguazil?"
"Bid ye the whelp-robbed lion kneel!"
"Dark ruffian! thou wilt rue this hour."
"Ruffian!—not while my sword hath power."
And with the word the unfailing blade
Low at his feet the opposer laid,
And Dion seized the escalade.
He springs with more than mortal might,
He rises—almost gains the height—
His hand is on the moss-grown wall—
This moment saves or ruins all!
A word, a thought, a look, a dream
May ratify the doom of years;
One glance, one quick electric gleam
May lead unto an age of fears!
Oh! Dion, nerve thy heart again,
One minute—spring—and thou art free,
O think—thy love—'tis vain—'tis vain,
Despair hath sealed thy destiny!
They tear away the cord-wove frame,
And thou art doomed to woe and shame!
Still Dion bears the double weight
With one torn, bleeding, numbing hand
Awhile—he falls—the scroll of Fate
Hath rolled its darkest record! "Stand,
"Exulting demons, stand ye there,
"And o'er all earth your triumph yell,
"And laugh o'er death and life's despair,
"For than ye worse reign not in hell!"

* * * * * * *

* * * * * * *

XI.

'Tis joy to gaze, from the tall ship s lee,
On the curling waves of the moonlight sea,
When the mellow airs of spring-time night
Come over the heart as it floats in light,
And the sleeping flowers exhale perfume,
Like a virgin's breath from lips of bloom,
And the dark-blue waters curl and gleam
In the diamond star-light's mirrored beam,
While the spirit burns o'er the glittering sea
'Till it longs a moonlight wave to be.
Oh, spirits that sail on the moonlight sea
Should have thoughts as vast as eternity,
And feelings as pure as the sleeping rose,
When its leaves in the dew of the sunset close.

XII.

O'er Lusitania's soft-blue moonlight bay
Swells the gay song of reckless gondolier,
While his bark dances, as the waters play,
On the shore waves that glitter bright and clear.

Dim in the distance, marked upon the sky,
Wave the blue pennon and the glimmering sail,
And oft is heard the master's anxious cry
While shoreward sea-boy answers to his hail.

Yet, save his song and their expectant cries,
The world is slumbering in a soft repose,
And spirits from their star-thrones in the skies
Breathe softly as a dew-lipped sleeping rose.

It is the hour when love's communion fills
Eye, lip and heart with rapture's magic light;
When waning Dian, throned on shadowy hills,
Smiles o'er young transports from her azure height.

Pomegranate, orange, lime and citron groves
Shadow gray turrets and time-honoured towers,
And heaven's pale queen amid their arbours roves,
And counts with tears the melancholy hours.

But hushed is song of happy gondolier,
And fast the shadowy sail ascends on high ;—
A step, a form, a voice—" Prince Julian's here !"
" Alfonso, haste ! this hour we 'scape or die !"

XIII.

Before the rising, shrill-voiced gale
Flies the yard-stretching, mighty sail,
Swelling o'er broad Atlantic billow,
Like swan upon her wavy pillow,
Dashing aside from her high prow
The wave, whose hissing foam-wreaths glow
Like jewels thrown in floating snow,
And hurrying on her watery way,
Between two oceans, heaven and earth's,
Like war-horse through the battle fray,
Whose mighty heart would burst his girths
In its high swelling, should his lord
Or check his speed or sheathe his sword.
With a long sigh, as if from dream
Of pain and anguish slowly waking,
From Julian's breast, with sudden scream
Wild as her bleeding heart were breaking,
Zulma rose and gazed around
On ocean's sons, on wave and sky,
And then fell back and deeply groaned,
While gleamed through tears her eagle eye.
" Inez ! sweet Inez !" Shudderings came
Over her like the sansar's breath,

As from her heart flowed that sweet name
Which now was linked with woe and death,
And, wrapt in silent suffering,
She saw nor wave nor sky nor lover,
Nor heard the light-winged breezes sing,
Like nymphs in sea-shells, ocean over;
All—all to her was pain and gloom,
Her thoughts of what she left behind
And o'er her angel sister's tomb
She heard the lonely wailing wind,
With spirit voice of wild distress,
Denouncing Inez' murderess!
Darkly with phantoms of her brain
Communing, o'er the billowy main
Zulma was hurried rapidly,
And the low murmuring of the sea
Seemed, when she heard the gulfing surge
Hymning the murdered vestal's dirge.

XIV.

The virgin huntress of the skies
Witn Ocean's daughters flies afar,
And Eos and her nymphs arise
Above the sun-god's throne, each star,
Orion's blazing sword of light,
And the twin-martyrs' glory bright,
And sea-born Beauty's radiance dimming,
While blue-zoned Tethys weaves a crown
Of pearls and corals brightly swimming
Through her vast empire fathoms down,
To deck Aurora's rosy brow
As her white steeds o'er ether fly,
And proud Hyperion, bright and slow,
Rolls unto heaven his glorious eye.

The bird of Jove his mighty wings
Waves o'er the crimson vault above,
And from his eye a radiance flings
Bright as the brightest glance of love.
The white-plumed sea-gull skims the sea,
The curlew sports around the bark,
And nature sings of liberty
And love as when from ancient ark
The beasts of earth and birds of heaven
To their bright fields and skies were given.

XV.

The rushing ship is sailing now
O'er the bright wave of Trafalgar,
And morn is blushing o'er the brow
Of Algarve's dusky mountains far,
With the same smile of living bloom
As when to ocean's billowy tomb,
Amid the sea-fray's carnage red,
Their requiem shouts of victory,
Shrouded in glory, England's Dead
Sunk with unclosed, war-lightened eye,
Whose last, bright glance from gory wave
Saw England's banner proudly streaming
Victorious o'er their ocean grave,
And England's sword triumphal gleaming;
And o'er his sons, with every surge,
Bright, billowy ocean sings their dirge.
And now the swelling sail is fanned
By zephyrs o'er that narrow sea,
O'er which on either margin stand
Those giant mountain twins which he,
Alcmena's son, with god-like power,
Severed and poured the sea between,

And which, since that rock-sundering hour,
The deadliest foes have ever been.
Thence onward holds the bark her way
Through the blue wave in fair array,
While to the northern view arise
The Appenines 'neath bending skies,
O'er whose snow-mantled summits erst
The Mauritanian hero led
His warlike host, by fate accursed,
To glory, as the warrior said,
And the proud spoils of mighty Rome;
In that soul-stirring hour of pride,
When his heart rolled in glory's tide,
Having dread Cannæ in his view
No more than he whom Waterloo
Doom'd to the Rock-Isle's living tomb,
Had of that desolating fray
On Lodi's or Marengo's day.

Before the view, where sun-beams smile,
Rises that rocky mountain isle,
Where he was born, the mighty one,
Whose gory course of fame is run;
And where, perchance, a guiltless boy,
His fellows' chief, his mother's joy,
He wandered oft, and played, and smiled
Amid the mountain's shrubbery wild,
An innocent and happy child;
Undreaming of his pomp and power,
His crimes, disgrace and exile fate.
Ah! few can tell in childhood's hour
What thoughts and deeds their manhood wait
Or who will bann or bless the name
That blazes on the scroll of Fame.

In him a mighty spirit burned,
But with a fierce volcano glare,
Oh, had that soaring spirit turned
To heaven and drank in glory there,
Earth would have bowed in rapture's mood
And held his name in sanctitude.
The Man, who guides a nation's way
To bloodless glory, o'er his name
Throws fairer wreaths of light than they
Who deck Earth's highest shrine of Fame.
But ah! he fell, and with him died
His empire, power, and pomp, and pride;
And nought remains of all he won—
Quenched is Napoleon's zenith sun.

Still onward fleet the ship careers,
Like rapid lapse of hurrying years,
While fades the bright foam of its wake,
Like all the joys we give or take,
And bears, with sail expanding high,
Its course, beneath a glorious sky,
Toward soft Campania's fairy land,
Where zephyrs sport with breathings bland
O'er ruins erst of pride and fame,
And gorgeous domes of deathless shame.
And, 'mid the night that robes the skies,
Julian directs sad Zulma's view
Where Ætna's fiery columns rise
In desolation's lurid hue,
Glaring between this world and heaven,
Like fiends to whom destruction's given.
The baleful light is flaring o'er
Trinacria's vine-clad, flowery shore,

Where Arethusa once gush'd forth
In lucid streams for bards to drink,
And Alpheus 'neath the sea and earth
Met his fair fountain bride—the brink
Bloomed like a garden of sweet flowers,
And, near, Ortygia's sacred grove
Delayed the rosy-footed hours
Of pure delight and raptured Love.
A weedy marsh now stagnates there,
And taints the thick and sluggish air,
As all man's hopes close in despair.
The lovers' course is almost done,
The lovers' goal is nearly won,
And how hath Zulma borne the flight?
Like one whose brighest day was night.
Like one whose heart hath caught a taint
Of crime, though fancied, dark and deep;
Whose dread remorse doth ever paint
Horrors, and ne'er is lulled to sleep
Since o'er a spirit proud and high
It reigns with three-fold energy.
Who backward looks and finds despair,
And forward, misery bars her there;
Who hath no hope on earth and none
Beneath high heaven's offended throne.
The more she thinks, the darker grows
The volume of her sins and woes;
No change comes o'er her agony;
Like Ætna's fire, it burns within,
And, dark'ning o'er the spirit's sky,
Burns ever with the gathering sin.
It was not madness; o'er her brain
Coherent thoughts ceased not to flow;

But 'twas that dread, oppressive pain,
That mountain weight of crushing woe,
Which follows, in a sinless mind,
A deed that spirits too refined
Brood into guilt—for priestcraft e'er
Riots in human woe and fear.
Reason was worse than vain, and speech
The dreadful mania could not reach,
That o'er her burning spirit shed
The baneful death-dew of despair,
The upas of a bosom dead
To all of beautiful and fair;
For Zulma sought no sympathy,
No comfort faithless as 'tis free,
But leaned upon the penal rod
And bowed her burning heart to GOD.

XVI.

The barque has passed the Tyrrhine sea
And anchored in the glorious bay
Of proud and base Parthenope,*
Where perfumed gales with sunlight play
O'er antique temple, giant tower,
And palace proud, whose mirrored dome,
Like a bright heaven, o'er many a tomb
Of many a mighty one laid low
Gleams with a rich, refulgent glow,
Like Freedom o'er lost Power.
The barque is moored—the lovers gone
Beyond the once fair Lucrine lake,
Where dark-browed Ruin reigns alone
O'er Baiæ lost in marshy brake,

* Neapolis, or Naples.

And all the fairy gardens, groves,
Meadows and dales erst loved so well
By him* (so reckless luxury proves
In one a nation's ruin fell)
Who shunning Glory's shrine when he
Had gained the fane, left mighty Rome
The victim of fierce anarchy,
Dreading yet hurrying on her doom.
Lucrine—the haunt of mirth is gone,
And there volcanoes glare alone!
Baiæ hath sunk to dust, and she,
Earth's mistress stands, like ancestry,
Scowling o'er sons whose highest boast
Had been their fathers' deepest shame,
To pride, to truth, to glory lost,
To honest hearts and patriot fame.

XVII.

Days, weeks and months have been and gone,
And lovely Zulma dwells alone
In solitary castle high
Between fair earth and fairer sky.
Julian had been, all lovers are,
Had knelt and sworn his deathless love,
And, like a sky-throned, radiant star,
Thrown light and beauty from above;
He had been all that being is,
Whom kindoms wait—I dare not dwell
On man's *intent* to offer bliss
To one who had for him farewell
Bidden all thoughts of earth and heaven,
And sole to him her full heart given.

* Lucullus

Prince Julian was Campania's heir,
And thus decreed his royal sire ;—
" Thou wed'st proud Austria's daughter fair,
" Or never com'st the sceptre nigher."
Julian was proud of pomp and fame—
The fair nun could nor trump his name
Nor plume his power—but she might be
The unseen queen of sovereignty,
The empress of his private hours—
The angel of his palace bowers.
So Julian thought, though he had tried
Her honest fame by speech oblique
And look lascivious, when his pride
And birth and state appeared most weak
Before wronged Zulma's Juno eye,
Whose glance spake pride and purity.
From day to day he talked of love,
While Zulma would not see his aim,
Save when the princely sophist strove
To prove all rites a needless name ;
Then flashed her eye and glowed her brow,
Like sunbeams o'er the mountain snow.
On love I will not moralize ;
It hath more wiles and snares than sighs ;
Sooth be the tale and fair I tell—
His deeds are man's true chronicle.

XVIII.

'Twas soft Campania's evening hour,
And earth and heaven were seas of light,
And Zulma in her rose-wove bower
Sate gazing on the horizon bright,
Where white clouds float and turn to gold
In many a bright and glorious fold,

And fancy pictures angel pinions
Far waving o'er those high dominions,
'Till, as she thought of pleasures gone,
And Inez, tortured, dying, dead,
And her own misery there alone,
Her hopes destroyed, her true loves fled,
Her bleeding heart left desolate,
And all the ills and woes of fate,
She seized her harp and mournfully
Sung of those joys no more to be.

THE BANKS OF ZEVERE.

The bright sun is sinking o'er Italy's sea,
And kissing Campania's fair gardens of flowers,
But, oh, his smile brings no pleasure to me,
For my heart ever grieveth o'er childhood's sweet
hours:
Sweetly gay rise the notes of the lover's guitar,
As he greets his heart's bride in the valley cot near,
But, ah, all my songs of delight are afar,
Like a spirit's voice heard on the banks of Zevere.

How oft have I sat with sweet Inez upon
Those rose-cushioned banks in our being's gay hours,
And fancied delights ever new to be won
In the great World of beauty and music and flowers!
How oft, O thou dear one! I slumbered with thee
In our moon-lighted bower in the spring of the year
And heard the birds singing on our apricot-tree
When we woke to delight on the banks of Zevere!

How often when nature in vain bloomed around
I turned in my heart-stricken sorrow to thee,
And in vigil and penance and weariness found
Thy sweet love a solace and treasure to me!

But, alas! thou art dead, and I am alone,
Far from all that on earth or in heaven were dear;
Fare thee well, lovely Inez! dark shadows are thrown
O'er our bower on the banks of the lonely Zevere.

Julian had stood beside the bower,
And heard, unseen, the mournful song,
While every blushing, dewy flower
Reproached him with fair Zulma's wrong;
But nature's voice, so soft, so still,
Fails to o'errule ambition's pride,
Or with atoning sorrow fill
A lordly heart unsanctified.
Julian drew near and greeted fair
The sad, forsaken, lovely maid,
And, eloquent in praise and prayer,
Rehearsing all he oft had said,
Implored compliance with his love,
Acceptance of his treasures—all—
And she should ever—ever prove
The queen of banquet, bower and hall,
And be his heart's eternal bride,
His life his sun, his hope, his heaven,
And, when he gained his throne of pride,
His royal name should soon be given.
But, while the Prince besought and prayed,
How sat and looked the insulted maid?
Like her of Enna's rosy vale
When wooed by him of Acheron;
Her marble brow, her cheek so pale,
Her tearful eye—all brightly shone
With pride and shame, disdain and scorn,
And thus—"Why was I ever born

" So to be scoffed at ?" quick began
The nun, while fierce her hot blood ran,
And her small form, dilating, grew
Like towering angel on the view.
" Prince Julian, cease ! I charge thee, cease !
" Are these thy notes of love and peace ?
" Art *thou* to be a nation's king ?
" Thou—false, deluding, faithless thing !
" The thoughts that lightened spirits high
" In the old days of chivalry,
" Throw not a wandering gleam o'er thee,
" Thou craven night of loselry !
" Vemeira is a noble name,
" And it can never be that fame
" Should Zulma's memory link with shame.
" Shall I thy leman be ? O no !
" Never while I can wield a blow,
" While poison drops or waters flow.
" Rede thou a woman's spirit well
" Ere mock her thus with words from hell,
" And know that virtue is her heaven,
" To things like thee, oh, never given !

* * * * * *

* * * * * *

" O Julian, Julian ! love like mine
" Is quenchless, deathless, for 'tis pure ;
" E'en now it doth around thee twine
" Fondly, and cannot but endure
" The same as when thine eye first shone
" O'er the same mirror as my own.
" Hadst thou been what I thought thee erst
" As knightly as thou wert at first,
" Though doomed to groan in poverty,
" 'Mid malice, misery, wrong and ill,

" The slave of fear—a lord to me—
" I would have loved—obeyed thee still,
" And, with unsorrowing brow and eye,
" Forsaken not and unforsaking,
' When sleeping, kissed thy misery
" Away, and sung to thee when waking.
" But these are dreams of passion yet
" Surviving when its hope hath set;
" Vain mockeries of my bosom's sun,
" Quenched ere his journey hath begun!
" I leave thee, Julian! and be thou
" Thy own just judge—no worse! and now—
" There are thy gifts!"—From neck of snow
Her carcanet—and then her zone
Of jewels and her chains and rings
She loosed and threw, disdainful, down;
" There, Julian, take the gilded things,
" For which thou thought'st that I would sell
" My honour—and now fare thee well!"

XIX.

Bewildered, lost in guilt and shame,
And torrent passions wildly warring;
Defied, despised in deed and name,
Each wild-fire thought another marring;
Prince Julian stood unmoving where,
In all the grandeur of despair,
Zulma, like empress throned in power
More than deserted nun, had left
Her lover in that sundering hour
When her proud heart of hope was reft.
Zulma had hurried from his view—
Her form of love, her voice, her smile,

No more enchantment o'er him threw—
No more his sorrows could beguile;
She had been his—and now was not—
He had been hers in grief and woe—
Now she had gone—to be forgot—
And he was left alone to—" No!
"By Heaven! it cannot, shall not be!
"Crown, sceptre, kingdom—what are ye
"To love and love's true paradise?
"The earth preferred unto the skies!
"Ambrose!" "My lord!"—"Caparison
"The fleetest steed in all my stalls,
"And bring the courser here anon—
"And guard thou well the castle walls!
"I will the maid regain or die,
"For Honour is man's majesty!"
He vaulted on his gallant steed,
And vanished in the forest dun,
Then rose the hill, and o'er the mead
Rushed 'neath the last beam of the sun.

THE

SISTERS OF SAINT CLARA.

CANTO II.

I.

O LAND of my birth! thou fair world of the West!
With freedom and glory and happiness blest!
Thou nation upspringing from forest and grove,
Like wisdom's armed queen from the brain of high
Jove!
Though thy winds are the coldest the North ever
blows,
And thy mountains the drearest when covered with
snows;
Tho' the warm fount of feeling is chilled while it
gushes,
And pleasure's stream frozen as brightly it rushes;
Tho' thy sons, like their clime, are oft chilling and rude
And rough as the oak in their own mountain wood;
Yet I love thee, my country! as fondly as Tell
Loved the Alpine Republic he rescued so well.
For thy yeomen can circle the winter-eve hearth,
Undreading oppression, and talk of the Earth,
Whose bosom yields nurture to father and son
Leaving hearts pure and gay when the glad work is
done:
While the pæans they shout over glories by-gone
Are echoed by virtues for ever their own.

O thou home of the rover o'er ocean's rude wave,
Asylum of sorrow and fort of the brave!
Advance in thy glory o'er forest and sea,
Unrivalled, unconquered, heroic and free!
Though the rose bloom and fade in its holiday hour,
And the sun-god is palled in his glory of power
Tho' winter's cold breath blanch the blossoming rose,
Unlike the bright clime where the sky ever glows,
Yet thy virtues bend not to each soothing breeze,
Whose syren song lures through the soft shading trees
Like the gay, grovelling sons of the tropical clime,
Whose skies are all glory—whose earth is all crime.
None love thee so well as thy sons far away,
None bless thee more oft than the bard of this lay.

II.

The sunniest rose that ever blowed
In velvet vale of soft Cashmere;
The loveliest light that ever glowed
O'er heaven in spring-time of the year,
Ne'er blushed and beamed more purely bright
Than gentle Inez' sinless heart
Upon that dread unholy night
When doomed with all it loved to part.
No spirit, gazing from above,
With eyes impearled in pity's tears,
Cherished more heavenly thoughts of love
In glory's highest, brightest spheres,
Than that pure child of love and light,
Dragged, 'neath the covert of the night,
To the dim arch'd refectory;
Where, telling fast their rosaries,
And lifting many a saint-like eye
To heaven with muttered groans and sighs,

The demon conclave met to doom
To living grave, to breathing tomb,
The apostate, suffering, dying nun.
The word hath passed—the deed is done!
Ere morn gleams through the pictured glass
Of prison cell, or o'er the wall
Of dark St. Clara light doth pass,
Dimly and thick and sickening, all
Of that dark bigot band, save one,
Are kneeling at the tapered shrine,
Before the Omniscient's holy throne,
Where every thought should be divine,
To chant their impious prayers to Him,
In whose creation-searching eye
Not even the heavenliest seraphim
Are pure in their great piety!
Alas! that Heaven's most blessed boon,
Religion, breathing peace and love,
In man's polluted heart so soon
The veriest creed of hell should prove!

III.

Unseen, unfelt, unknown, her fate
O'er the fair vestal's head had past,
And she was left all desolate—
The doom was sealed—the die was cast—
Ere, waking from her dreadful dream,
She faintly said—"I heard a scream
"Of death, methought, O Dion! say
"Is Zulma safe?" Then, as she lay
Leaning against the dungeon wall,
She turned—groaned—and fell back again;
"Oh, Dion! love! oh, tell me all,

"Where—where is Zulma?"—Awful pain
Came o'er her then and dimmed the eye
Of yesternight's dread memory,
And through her spirit's drear opaque
She could not look—she could not take
Perception of her agony;
She knew 'twas so—but how or why
It baffled her delirious brain
To tell;—and then she thought again,
And more distinct her memory grew
Of what had passed—and chill the dew
Of death hung on her writhen brow,
Where love still shed its parting glow,
As dim she caught the past and gone;
Yet she could not—the dying one,
Think why she thus was left alone.
She spake again, but faint and low—
"O Dion! thou hast often said
"Thy love could master every woe,
"And o'er all griefs its radiance shed;
"It cannot be that thou should'st now
"Forsake thy love, forget thy vow—
"Now, when I feel—O Dion, come
"And bear me hence—I must go home!"
She listened then for some faint sound,
And strove to rise and look around;
But all was midnight gloom, and she
Alone there in her agony.
Still memory gathered link by link—
And still life's current quickly bled—
With a death-thirst she longed to drink
What flowed around her dungeon bed;
She scooped the fluid in her hand,

And bore it to her lips—'t was blood!
And then her spirit lost command
'Mid horror, gloom, and solitude,
While thought, no words of man can tell,
O'er all the past began to swell,
And well she saw her hopeless doom,
There buried in eternal gloom,
Whence shrillest shriek and wildest cry
Could never reach the shuddering sky.
No missal there nor cross had she,
O'er which to breathe her parting breath;
To cheer her in her misery,
And change to bliss the pangs of death;
For they had banned the dying nun
And barred redeeming penitence!
Demons! their hate her glory won—
Her amulet was innocence!
So malice works its own reward,
And weakest proves when most on guard,
For never yet hath hatred wrought
The deadly ruin which it sought,
Untended by a deadlier blow
Than that which laid its victim low.

IV.

A sound disturbed her solitude—
High chanting from the chapelry;
Like wailings from a gloomy wood
When echoed by a stormy sky,
The distant swell of cloister strain
And matin hymn came o'er her brain,
And roused to life her slumbering pain;
It was her dirge—that morning song,
And slowly rolled the notes along

The cypress groves—the vaults—the cells—
Like murder's midnight groan which tells
The fearful deed most fearfully;
And there the lovely Inez lay
In suffering's last extremity,
While not a solitary ray
Of light relieved the heart-felt gloom
That palled her spirit in the tomb.
It was a mockery of her woe—
The mass of hell yelled out below—
That pæan, like a death-doom sent
Through farthest vault—through deepest cell,
To agonize the punishment
Of the fair one Heaven loved so well.
But oh, no fiend with things can cope
Whom God hath left to their own will—
Giv'n o'er beyond all reach of hope,
At hate's hell-cup to drink their fill;
The deadliest demon, banned the most,
May fill the archangel's holiest throne
Ere mortal once—forever lost,
Can for his damning deeds atone.
The light of heaven may beam o'er hell
Dimly and touch the apostate there;
But man, abandoned, bids farewell
To hope, and weds his own despair.

V.

Another sound the stillness broke,
And Inez' bleeding heart awoke.
It was the wailing of a dove,
The death-song of a simple bird
O'er her who died for heaven and love,
And gladly were the soft notes heard.

Perched on a cypress o'er her cell,
The bird hailed not the glorious sun,
But sadly sung the last farewell
Of the pure, sweet, expiring nun,
To earth and earthly sins and woes
And life so early in its close.
As Inez listened to the strain,
And longed to waft it back again,
The shade of death was in her eye,
The pulses of her being beat
Faintly, and death's last agony
Came o'er her like a shadowy bloom,
A soft voice stealing from the tomb,
A light to guide the parting spirit
Beyond the woes that all inherit.
Feebly she sunk—the crimson tide
Gushed forth no more—her heart was still;
Yet her lips trembled as she died—
"Dion—forgive—my wrongs!" and 'till
Her features sunk collapsed in death
That name was breathed with every breath.

VI.

A taper gleams amid the gloom—
A white-robed form approaches near—
It pauses by the dungeon tomb,
And listens tensely as in fear,
Or hope—and now it moves again
And lifts the iron-bolted grate,
And gazes o'er the cell of pain,
Doubting its lovely tenant's fate.
Demon! go in—thy victim's gone!
Unseen, unheard, like guilt alone,

Clotilde doth listen there awhile,
And then descends—and with a smile
Deadly and dark moves round the corse,
Whose features are an angel's still.
" Dead?—Ay, 'tis well—it had been worse
" Had justice half fulfilled my will
" Or hadst thou lived till now!"—She turned
The lovely vestal's body o'er,
And laughed aloud; and then she spurned
The corse upon its gory floor,
And smiled as if she gave it pain;
And then she raised the beauteous nun—
" Ay, 'tis a blessed fate, sweet one!
" That thou hast wrought thyself—again
" Thou would'st not do the deed!" She threw
The pale, cold corse in scorn away,
And yet more dark her features grew,
As death had robbed her of her prey;
And still she stood, with fiend-like eye,
Revelling in hatred's demon feast,
And with low curse and muttered cry
Banning e'en HIM who had released
The vestal from her deadly power
And raised the soul to Eden's bower,
When a loud crash rose high—and far
The echo as of bolt and bar
Shooting, went forth!—Where art thou now,
Proud abbess? Ah! thou soon wilt know!
The iron portal to the cell,
The lifted grate had fallen—how
It nought avails for me to tell;
Perchance, the wind had laid it low,
Or death-winged angel might have thrown
The dreadful bars in anger down,

Eternal justice to dispense
To suffering, murdered innocence.
Howe'er it was—proud Clotilde there
Was doomed to perish with the dead,
In silence, darkness and despair,
And meet the fate her sentence said.
There could be no relief—no, none—
She had gone forth, unseen, alone,
And from that subterranean cell
No cry arose to human ear;
It was a dark monastic hell,
Beyond hope's sun-illumined sphere.
She shook the bars—but they were fast—
She shrieked—but echo mocked her pain;
She gazed around—but shadows past
Like fiends, and she sunk down again.
And then remorse was leagued with fear,
And both like vipers gnawed her heart:
And horrid sounds were in her ear
That cried—"What dost thou here? depart!
"Seek thou the hell of thy dark creed,
"Thine be the doom thou hast assigned,
"The unpitying bigot's bitter meed,
"The quenchless ruins of the mind!
"Depart! depart!" how awful e'er
Is guilt when phrenzied by its fear!

VII.

Unshrived, she there must die in all
Her unforgiven guilt and woe;
On either side a dungeon wall,
And wrath above and death below
Unsoothed, unpitied and alone,
Without a single orison,

Without a tear to mourn her fate,
Or look of grief compassionate,
Or holy right or orris pall
Or requiem chanted forth by all
The holy vestal sisterhood,
Who round her erst admiring stood
As if St. Marie had been given
To them in other form from heaven.
But such be guilt's dark fate for e'er!
She there must perish dust to dust,
Unshriven in the dungeon drear,
Accursed below—among the just
All entrance barred eternally!
Now guilt forestalled redemption's hours,
And madness sprung from agony!
Darkly the storm of misery lowers,
And darker yet it soon shall be;
For Sin uprears her giant form
And mad Remorse, her spectre, stands,
Gashed by the fangs of guilt's dark worm,
Lifting on high his gory hands
To warn too late—to tell at last
The victim that her day hath past,
And yet more awful thoughts arise
More fearful shadows blast her view,
And wilder are her echoed cries,
And colder is the dungeon-dew.

VIII.

Time flies—strength fails—but madness grows
Stronger and darker in its mood,
And fevered Fear delirious throws,
O'er all the gloom a robe of blood;

And now she sinks beside the nun,
There like a song-lulled angel sleeping,
And smiling as her woes were done,
And she in heaven were vigils keeping.
She starts as if an adder stung!
A demon voice of mirth had rung
Through all the chambers of her brain;
She listens—now it comes again,
Blended with laughter wild and rude,
And echoes through the fatal cell,
And cries aloud—"Thy soul's imbued
"With blood of innocence;—'tis well
"That on thy victim's lifeless breast
"Thou should'st sink in eternal rest!"
Her maniac heart could bear no more,
The last extremity had come;
She grovelled on the cold earth floor
In speechless anguish at her doom;
Gazed with a madden'd eye, that told
What horrors o'er her bosom rolled,
Upon the nun who slept as still
As infant that has drank its fill;
Then with a shriek that might appal
The fiend, against the dungeon wall
Dashed headlong—groaned and died!—'Tis past,
The more than mortal suffering.
Alas! I would it were the last!
But earthly minstrel dare not sing
Of fates beyond the farthest ken
Of starry-eyed philosophy;
Among the abodes of mortal men
He finds enough of misery

To break the heart and rack the brain
That feels or thinks of human pain.
Her fate hath past—her soul hath fled—
And peace attend the voiceless Dead!

IX.

Life scarce had parted and her fate
Passed o'er the haughty abbess there,
Ere steps approached the iron grate,
And voices, as in last despair,
Echoed above the fatal cell.—
The portal's raised and they descend,
The sisterhood.—Now note ye well,
Fair vestals! ere ye ween to wend
In sin's broad path, sin's woful end!
The highest bliss of heaven may prove
The bitterest dreg in misery's cup,
And spirits born of heaven and love
By guilt be lost and given up
To state abhorring and abhorred—
And not adoring and adored!
Long was the anxious search and quest
Ere they could trace their abbess there,
And anguish searched full many a breast
As they stood gazing in despair
On murdered and on murderess.
I pause not now to paint the scene—
The natural ills of life suffice
To fill with tears the sternest eyes,
When thought retraces what hath been,
To gloom the heart and cloud the way
That shone so brightly yesterday.

Together from the dungeon cell
The corses were in silence borne,
While lingering tolled the funeral knell,
And sullen echoes moaned forlorn;
And shrouded in their vestments white,
They laid them side by side, and kept
Their vigils through the livelong night,
While breathlessly the dead ones slept,
As softly as two infants, born
Perchance, to be each other's scorn!
The wakeful sisters watched alone,
And many a holy rite was done
To foil the fiend and save the soul
Of her who once held high control
O'er penance stern and vow austere,
For many a long and sinful year.
The lovely innocent that there
Too holy was for grief or prayer,
Lay like a picture of the blest,—
'Twas her last hour and loveliest!
They watched—they prayed—night waned and morn,
Like holy hope in Eden born,
Blushed the stained glass and casement through,
And gave the gloomy scene to view.

X.

To die—to feel the spirit fainting
In the mansions of the breast,
While yet the vivid eye is painting
Life and vigor unpossessed;
To see the mortal frame decaying,
The temple's pillars breaking down,
And know the soul will soon be straying

Over climes and realms unknown ;
While warm affection hovers o'er
The couch of death, with wailing prayer
Imploring lengthened life once more
In all the anguish of despair ;
And we behold and feel and know
All that is felt for us and yet
Beside perceive the overthrow
Of hopes on which the heart is set,
And picture in our dying hour
Anguish unknown till we are dead,
And conscious, hopeless misery's power,
And tears from being's fountains shed—
Oh, 'tis a time, an hour of gloom
Worse than the midnight of the tomb !
But, ah, 'tis worse to think that we,
The proud, high, sentient lords of earth
Must moulder into dust and be
Or clay or nothing ! At our birth
It was decreed that we should die,
But not that we should rotting lie
With every foul and loathsome thing
Blending our ashes.—Fling, oh, fling
My corse in ocean's booming wave,
Or burn it on the funeral pyre,
But lay it not in reeking grave
To glimmer with corruption's fire !
St. Clara's funeral bell is knelling
With the solemn voice of death,
And far the mournful notes are swelling
While from postern far beneath
Issue the white-robed virgin train,
Chanting low the requiem strain,

Over the dark and dismal tomb
Of one in being's roseate bloom,
And one in sallow withered age,
Departed from life's tragic stage.
Where sorrow never wakes to weep,
And ill and wrong distract no more,
And homeless wanderers sweetly sleep,
And hate and pride and pain are o'er,
They lay the vestals finally.
Above them waves a cypress tree,
Intwined with briar and rosemary,
And round them sleep the mighty dead,
Who centuries since forever fled ;
A silent nation gone—alas !
Where living thought can never pass.
The ceremonial pomp is past—
The vestals vanish, one by one—
The holy father is the last,
And even he hath slowly gone.
And stillness reigns o'er all the scene,
That is so peaceful and serene ;
A stillness greatly eloquent
When pious spirits bow and feel
Delicious melancholy, sent
From heaven o'er all their being steal
With purifying breathings mild ;
And they become like little child
Gentle and docile, purely good,
In their communing solitude,
And look from earth to heaven with eye
Of sage reflecting piety,
Comparing man's allotment here
With glories of a brighter sphere.

XI.

O Love! the holiest name in heaven,
The purest, sweetest thing below!
Why are thy joys to torture given?
Thy rapture's unto wailing woe?
Why should thy fondest votaries prove
Faithful even unto death in vain?
Or why, despite thy vows, O Love!
Should all thy blisses close in pain?

No voice was heard—no form was seen
Within the churchyard's lonely bound,
And Dion, from his weedy screen,
Rose mournfully and gazed around.
Long had he watched each lone—lone hour
For some faint note of joy or grief,
'Till destiny's most dreaded power
To him had almost been relief.
But nought allayed his dread suspense
'Till Inez and her murderess
Were borne to that lone mansion whence
No tenant ever found egress.
Then flashed the whole revealment dire
O'er Dion's burning heart and brain,
And death became a wild desire,
A refuge from his penal pain.
With rolling eye, and brow of gloom,
And pallid cheek and trembling tread,
Dion approached the robbing tomb
Where Inez slept among the dead,
And bowed his throbbing head upon
The dark funereal tablet stone
Despairingly, while forth his tears
Unbidden gushed.—" In youthful years

"I little recked of fate like this;
"I thought the world was full of bliss
"And man most blessed in life—Alas!
"I am not now the thing I was;
"And nought remains for me to dare
"But misery, madness and despair;
"The darkness of a breast that bleeds
"O'er the wild thought of damning deeds,
"The doom that never will depart
"From the dim mansions of the heart."
He drew his poniard, looked on high
For the last time with gleaming eye,
Then laid him down the grave beside
And clove his heart! The purple tide
Gushed like a torrent and—he died!
The last glance of his spirit turning
To her for whom his heart was burning.

XII.

The autumnal sun's rich evening beams
Blush o'er Cantabria's billowy sea,
And Lusian fields and groves and streams,
Like angel smiles, celestially;
And clustering vines hang purpling o'er
The shrubbery-mantled palisade,
And golden orange, cypress hoar,
And cork-tree rough, and yew, whose shade
The dead alone doth canopy,
And sunken glen and dim defile,
Alike in nature's bounties free,
Return the soul-inspiring smile
Of Autumn—queen-muse of the heart!
And as soft evening's hues depart,

Like holy hopes that smile in death,
And twilight robes the fading sky
With beauty felt, not seen—beneath
The spreading palm, the lover's eye
Burns as he tunes his soft guitar,
And sees his own dear maid afar,
Approaching her rose-woven bower
To solemnize love's sacred hour.
And lordly prince and shepherd hind,
And lady proud and simple maid
Enjoy alike the season kind,
When flowers grow lovelier as they fade.
Eve shadows dim the varied scene,
And the calm sunlight wanes away,
While one lone cloud of lustre sheen
Still wears the rays of parting day,
And hangs upon the zenith sky,
Like hope the sad heart lingering by.

XIII.

Looming in shadowy twilight o'er
Tajo's broad bay afar is seen,
Scudding toward the Lusian shore,
A quick, unladen brigantine;
And now it grows upon the eye,
White sail, dark hulk, and swan-like prow;
And swells upon the evening sky
Like castle turreted with snow;
And full the rushing wake is heard,
Blent with command's shrill-uttered word,
And many a heart throbs fondly now
To meet its loves and find its home,
As the light vessel crinckles slow
The waters which no longer foam.

The brigantine is moored—the crew
Are busy, boisterous, glad and gay,
And jovial crowds are there ;—but who
Through the dense throng makes rapid way
With looks so proudly desolate ?
Tis ZULMA, who hath borne her fate
And yet will bear 'till being's close,
All she hath lost and still can lose,
With an unshrinking spirit none
Can tame or crush ;—she is alone
In desolation—but she bears
Her lofty brow unblanched, and throws
Around an eye undimned by tears,
And, as she hurries on, she grows
Stronger, as if her spirit stood
Prepared for woe of all degree,
And agony and solitude,
And horror, and deep misery.
With hurried step though tearless eye,
She came, where still the massy towers
Of her own convent rose before her
And cast time's deepened shadows o'er her.
From many a tongue too soon she heard
The fatal story of the past,
Told too with many a needless word,
That fell like Lybia's desert blast.
Zulma shrieked not, but fiercely rolled
O'er brain and heart the worst—the last
Wild storm of ruin ; hope fell dead,
And her high spirit 'neath its own
Intensity was crushed ; she said
Nothing responsive—sigh nor groan,
Nor scream nor cry was heard ; she threw

Her bleeding eye to heaven and bowed
A moment as in prayer—then grew
Like desperation calm.—A crowd,
As toward St. Clara's towers she went,
Followed in mute astonishment
That she should thus defy despair
And her own certain ruin dare.
Soon ceased their marvel—Zulma came
Beneath the window of her cell,
And upward gazed—and sighed the name,
The memory of the victim nun
The loved, the lost, the lonely one,
Who shed o'er life the only spell
The true heart loves and prizes well.
And as she gazed with mournful eye
On dusky wall and cypress grove,
The soul whose pride could never die,
The spirit of immortal love
That never sheds a human tear,
Was journeying to a holier sphere.

XIV.

"Jesu Maria! who art thou?
"Christ and the Virgin shield us now!"
A war-steed dashes through the throng—
A horseman leaps upon the ground,
And rushes like a maniac strong
Toward dying Zulma, while around
Gather the crowd to mark the scene—
For one so mournful ne'er had been.
Zulma looked up—a faint smile passed,
Like silvery moon-beam on the wave,
O'er lip and eye and then it cast

Behind the death hue of the grave.
Low bowed the horseman, Julian, there,
And fearful was his agony;
He kneeled, like statue of despair,
In hopeless, speechless misery;
But quivering lips and burning brow
Were worse than vain and idle now.
"Zulma"—he said at last, but wild
Came then the memory of his shame,
And Zulma's eye so proudly smiled
He trembled but to speak her name,
For she was calm as all must be
Who triumph o'er the demon—man,
And hold their pride and purity
Above corruption's blight and bann.
But life was ebbing fast away
From Zulma's broken heart and now,
While yet was left a conscious ray
Or never more his words must flow.
He spake at last—his words were few
But full of dark remorseful power,
The out-pourings of the soul's mildew,
That taints each lovely blooming flower,
Making all life a waste!—The fire
Of being, that had sunk and waned
In Zulma's bosom, burned again
Brightly a moment and there reigned
A majesty 'mid all her pain
That daunted Julian, as she strove
To rise upon a maiden's breast;—
"Prince Julian! that thou had'st my love,
'And that in thine I was most blest,
'Tis bootless now to own; my doom

"Is sealed forever and the tomb
"Must be the resting-place of one
"Who once—who yet loves thee alone;
"Thou hast my pardon while I live—
"*Forgive thyself as I forgive!*"
Backward she fell—faint grew her breath,
Life left her cheek, her brow, her eye;
Slow o'er her heart came chilling death—
Zulma is in eternity!

THE HOUR AT WILL

PART I.

'Tis only when the heat and dust and toil
Of day have passed, my better heart can smile;
'Tis only when in weariness and pain,
My task hath ceased to bind my dizzy brain,
That gentler thoughts and holier feelings come
Like angel visitants, and guide me home—
Home to the hallowed temple of the mind,
Where heaven's own music rolls upon the wind.
And, oh, while wandering 'mid the cold and low,
And mocking Mammon with a smile and bow,
While doomed to wear o'er deep contempt, applause,
And crush my nature 'neath the world's vain laws,
How, like a lost child, seeking home once more,
My bosom brightens, and my soul doth soar!
How, like the eagle of my native clime,
Genius aspires beyond the reach of Time!
Then for a moment, glad oblivion throws
Its deep veil o'er my trials and my woes,

And trickling touches of a kindlier mood,
Like summer evening o'er the ancient wood,
Soothe evil passions, lull the heart to rest,
And blend the spirit with the pure and blest:
And I forget that Fortune is my foe,
And Man the fiend that reigns in human woe;
That lineal hatred o'er my childhood spread
The gloom, though not the slumber of the dead,
And yet prevails to sadden every scene
Where hope and love and loveliness have been.
All these pass from me in the hour of pride,
Like smouldering wrecks down ocean's billowy tide.
With downcast eyes and tiar'd head declin'd,
His gold-wrought purple floating in the wind,
Gazing on valley, forest, stream and flood,
Against a rock the Persian monarch stood;
While, far below, his vassal millions lay
Like bristling tigers couchant for their prey,
Ardent as eagles, joyous as the lark
Whose music melts along the silvery dark,
Full of high hope of conquest, power and fame,—
That golden shroud for every mortal name!
And, as he gazed upon this pomp of power
One trump had summon'd to his palace bower,—
The haughty Despot wept that Time should cast
Their names, like ashes, on the fire-winged blast,
That, ere three-score of hurrying years went by,
His glorious millions,—each and all would die!
Each for himself, philosopher or bard,
Must toil uncheered and be his own reward
Through evils countless as the midnight dews—
The victim votary of the thriftless muse—
Till bursts the sun of Fame's rejoicing day,

And the hours blossom like the buds of May,
And Youth's dim hope out-blazes like a star
High throned in heaven and gleaming from afar,
And flatterers crawl around the honoured one
Mocked when obscure and trampled when unknown!
What recks the world—stern, haughty and austere—
From whose swoln eye slow drops the undried tear?
What recks the world if care and grief assail
The heart that suffers though it will not quail?
If doubt and darkness gather round *his* way,
Whose spirit revels in the light of day?
If, poor and friendless, Genius must submit
And panier'd dullness crush the choisest wit?
If earth becomes, by man's inhuman guile,
A hell, the deeper that the sun-beams smile?
And Mind, new lighted at the throne of God,
Darken and sink and mingle with the sod?
What recks the world, ere wakes the son of Fame,
Who blights and execrates an unknown name?
Or who bands forth a menial miscreant host
And triumphs o'er archangel spirits lost?
—Dark are the shades that cloud thy mortal hours
Poor lonely wanderer from elysian bowers,
And few the joys, earth's silken sons possess,
Light the wild horrors of thy wilderness!

As sable clouds along the evening sky
Glow with the glories of the sun's bright eye,
So the dull toils of daily life assume,
When Genius smiles, the beauty and the bloom
Of unseen realms, where holiest spirits sing
'Mid the fair gardens of an endless spring.
Few and uncertain 'mid the cares of life,

The sin, the sorrow, and the hate and strife,
Are the brief hours devoted to the shrine
Of Love, whose purest worship is divine,
But these quick moments gladden and uplift,
And bear us through the sublety and thrift,
The coldness, darkness, solitude and want,
The woes that wither though they cannot daunt,
Raise and refine the grovelling works of man,
And lead us back where Life in Love began.
Like summer showers, when wanes the burning day
These hours of pride, athwart our weary way,
Gleam with a mellow gladness and repose,
That strengthen bleeding hearts to bear their woes,
And through all wrong and evil guide us on,
Though poor yet proud, though friendless not alone.
Then fruit and blossom mingle on each tree,
The soul soars gladly and the heart is free ;
Soft airs float by with music on their wings,
And the lyre warbles from a thousand strings ;
The heart's best feelings—all the joys of youth,
Dreams in the green-wood—hope and love and truth,
Thoughts by lone fountains, in their freshest bloom,
And chastened sorrow o'er affection's tomb—
All—all come back and win the soul afar
From earth's dark galley toil and rankling war,
Gild the dense gloom of error, fraud and sin,
And crown the altar of the heart within.

Yet, like wild lightning lifting, fold on fold,
Such awful gloom as wrapt the world of old,
To show how green and beautiful beneath
The earth lies covered with the veil of death,
These high revealments mock the dazzled mind,

Leave, as they vanish, deeper gloom behind,
Melt the touch'd heart that should be proud and stern,
And, like frankincense gushing from an urn,
O'erpower the vision, that should settle on
The thin cold ashes of the dead alone.
With feelings purified and sense refined
And the veil'd glories of a mighty mind,
The bard goes forth, from solitude sublime,
To meet and grapple with a world of crime,
Like a bright seraph in some distant star,
To feel his spirit with his fate at war,
To know his greatness and to bear the scorn
Of the miscreant menials on the dung-hill born,
To walk abroad, with radiant Genius crowned,
While crowded solitude hangs coldly round,
And seek, once more, the muse's lonely room,
And sigh to sink to slumber in the tomb!
Such is, hath been, will be the doom of minds
That cast their glories in the world's vain winds!

PART II

Stars of the heart! immortal lights that glow
Along life's lone and weary way of wo,
That lengthens, lingers like a pilgrim vowed
To some far shrine he parts from in his shroud,
How soft and soothingly ye come and spread
A blooming veil around the changed and dead,
Like the faint mind, inspire each drooping though
And hymn the magic beauty ye have wrought!
There's not a desert on the Earth so drear,
But fountains sometimes gush and gurgle near;

There's not a wilderness so sad and lone
Without its dweller and a kindred one;
There's not an iceberg in the arctic sea,
But bears life, feeling, joy and liberty;
And every heart, however worn and lost
To all it loved and idolized the most,
However pierced and manacled, and cast
A wreck and ruin on life's dewless waste—
Against the storm of grief may still bear up,
Though it hath drained affliction's poison cup,
And smile oft-times and blend its wonted powers
With minds unknown in childhood's leafy bowers,
Such Nature's best; while life prevails, there's hope,
And strength still given with despair to cope—
DESPAIR! oft uttered in a reckless mood,
By earth's victims never understood,
The grim, gaunt tyrant of the fiends who fell,
Born of Remorse—the quenchless fires of hell!
From bosoms dark and rugged gushes forth
Full many a stream to fertilize the Earth,
As from the black rock of the desert poured
The clear cold waters while the host adored;
And they, who walk in wisdom and in truth,
May oft, 'mid strangers, drink the joys of youth,
And find their sojourn gladdened by some voice,
That bids the fainting and sick heart rejoice.
Good, through victorious evil, oft appears,
Justice *may* mark the guiltless suppliant's tears,
Hope may rejoice in happier days to come,
And truth leave not the world in utter gloom.
Man clings to man through every wo and wrong,
And woman wins the daring and the strong.
To all, on whom the heartless world hath laid

Its ban—to all confiding and betrayed
By serpent lures, repulsed and cast aside
By the red Moloch hand of menial pride—
How bright, how cheeringly—the world forgot,
And all the evils of the poor man's lot—
Loved faces smile around their home of Love,
Loved voices breathe the gladness of the Dove,
And sooth the anguish of proud spirits stirred,
By the soft magic of a gentle word!
Passions as dire as winds in wildest wrath
And desolating as the lava's path,
Sink into slumber, broken and subdued
By the low voice of Love's sweet solitude.
Deep hate and wild revenge have oft foregone
Their fixed resolves while some belovod one,
With few kind words and one ambrosial kiss,
Filled a dark bosom with a seraph's bliss.
Laws, manners, morals and traditions old,
And customs antique as the banner's fold,
Fortune and faith—dominion, pride, and power,
And all that magnifies man's scepter'd hour,
Rose up, like spectres, when in secret spoke
Woman—and forth the Persian edict broke!
When War's deep trump awoke the world to arms,
Search out the cause in woman's fatal charms!
When peace flies smiling o'er the bloomy realm,
Lo! angel love directs the monarch's helm!
When the fierce Bandit leaves the work of death,
His wrong'd heart melts beneath affection's breath;
When the blest Sabbath o'er the city throws
A cheerful sanctity and hushed repose,
Gaze on the mother when her children kneel—
Few worship God—but every heart can feel!
When drops the dagger from the madman's grasp,

Who folds his writhing form in love's own clasp,
And with prophetic vows and burning tears,
Leads mind to triumph in the coming years?
Who on the Statesman, in his household bowers,
Bestows the tenderness of youthful hours,
And pillows on her breast the mighty mind
Revered, admired, and dreaded by mankind?
Who shield the weakness, guide the scornful pride.
And sooths—deserted by the world beside—
The bitter sorrows of ambition thrown
On the dark desert of despair alone?
Who casts o'er ruined hope and glory passed
Verdure that breathes and blossoms o'er the waste?
Who, like the sunset of an autumn even,
Gives unto Earth the glorious light of heaven?
Woman, devoted, cheerful and serene,
Lives in all laws and blends with every scene,
Pours proud ambition through each burning vein,
And tends the soldier on the battle plain;
Gives to the poet all his might of mind,
And gilds the desert fancy leaves behind;
Uplifts the feeble, quells the daring, throws
The hues of heaven o'er all desponding woes,
Moves upon earth the pilgrim bound to love,
And mounts, a seraph, to her God above!

Oft, when forsaken, trampled and reviled
While on my solitude no eye hath smiled,
When left to breast and buffet, as I might,
The faithless billows of a stormy night,—
Oft have I found in one beside me now,
(Her of the starry eye and sunny brow)
A tender solace and a mild content
Earth could not give with all her blandishment.

And she hath cheered me with a spirit free
To range the realms of high philosophy,
A heart imbued with such ethereal power
As wraps the saint in his sublimest hour,
While her fair features, soft as twilight's gush,
Lightened and flashed, and, with a solemn rush,
Her words of truth and hope and love came o'er
My heart, like moonlight on a rock-barr'd shore
And I have born the coward's dark attack,
Hate's dungeon ordeal, envy's midnight rack,
The scorn of fools, the sayings of the vile,
The branded felon's hypocritic smile,
The altered eye of friends, the sapient saws
Of dotard pedants, and the moral laws
Of convicts guiltier than the dungeon cell
E'er held in chains, or deepest vault in hell—
With a calm eye, a conscious brow that threw
The reptile back to feed on demon dew.
For still the angel of my pathway said
" 'Twere just—but oh, strike not the serpent dead!
" He bears a death—a living scorpion death
" In every pulse and vein and thought and breath,
" Leave him the doom thy righteous hand would end—
" Leave him on earth without a single friend!"
Shall I not praise the wise and winning art
That drew the lightning from my burning heart?
Shall I not feel as time leaves all my foes
In the oblivion of unblest repose,
And on our mingled tides of being run
In little channels glancing to the sun,
That wisdom dwells with loveliness and gives
A hallowed pleasure to our troubled lives,
A conscious trust of happier days in store,
For hearts undoubting, that in grief adore?

Without a fear that truth will not prevail,
Without a glance at slander's thrice-forged tale,
Prizing heaven's gifts too high to boast or vaunt,
Feeling a heart that danger cannot daunt,
And, with contempt ineffable and strong,
Beholding rioters in human wrong,
With thee, my bride!—and thee, my bright-eyed boy!
I share my sorrow—ye partake my joy.
Earth holds a home and coming time a name,
That may not vanish from the roll of Fame!

THE DEATH SCENE.

Glimmering amid the shadowy shapes that float
In sickly Fancy's vision o'er the walls
Of Death's lone room, the trembling taper burns
Dimly, and guides my fearful eye to trace
The wandering track of parting life upon
The burning brow and sallow cheek of him
Whose smile was paradise to me and mine.
The autumnal wind breathes pantingly and comes
With hollow sighs through yon high window o'er
Thy feverish couch, my love! and seems to sob
Amid the waving curtains as't would tell
My heart how desolate it will become
When left in its lone widowhood to weep
And wail and agonize at Memory's tale.
The outward air is chill, but, oh, thy breast,
My dying love! is scorching with the fires
That centre in thy heart, and thy hot breath

Heaves sobbingly, like the sirocco gale
That heralds death ; and thou art speechless now
Save what thy glaring eyes can tell, for life
Is parting from thy bosom silently.
Thy pulse is wild and wandering, and thy limbs
Are writhing in convulsive agony,
And, while thy spirit hovers o'er the verge
Of Fate, thou canst not speak to me nor bid
Thy chosen one a long farewell! O Heaven!
Let thy sweet mercy wait upon his end
And life's last struggle close—'tis vain to hope
For life—then take his soul on gentle wing
Away, and let the sufferer rest with Thee!
Alas! hath He who rules the universe
Replied to my wild wish? oh, give me back
The spirit of my love for one brief hour—'tis o'er!
'Tis o'er! my love, my happiness, my hope.
I sit beside a corse! How deadly still
Is the lone chamber he hath left! The moan
Of dying nature, and the bursting sigh
Of a heart breaking, and the murmuring voice
Of a delirious spirit—all are hushed!
The eye that kindled love in my young heart
And told me I was blessed, is lustreless—
And those dear lips, that oft illumed my soul,
Are stiffening now ; those features exquisite,
On which I often gazed as on a mirror
Beaming with beauty, genius, feeling—all
That love adores and honor sanctifies,
Collapse in their dread slumbers and assume
The ashen deadliness of soulless dust.
And must it be, my love! that thou wilt sleep
Where I can never watch thy wants and glide
Around, thy gentle minister? No more

Read voiceless wishes in thy pleading eye
And soothingly discharge them? Art thou gone,
Or is it but a dream? O thou dost dwell
Within my heart unchangeably as wont
And ever wilt!—I sit beside the Dead
Alone, while round me the world is bent
On pleasure—on a shadow from the dust!
The bright blue wave of Hudson rolls below
My solitary view and sounds of joy
Fling music o'er its waters and the voice
Of gayety is rising on my ear,—
Like banquet mirth amid the pyramids.
O the full consciousness of utter loss!
The single wretchedness of cureless woe
While all around are gay! The chaos wild
Of billowy thought, on whose tumultuous tides
Hopes, powers and passions—all the elements
Of heart and soul in foamy whirlpools toss
'Till whelmed in ruin!—Lovely babe! thou hast
No father now, and where, my orphan child!
Will close our wanderings? I have no home
For thee, dove of the storm without an ark
To bear thee o'er the waters of the Waste!
Cold, voiceless mansion of my ruined love!
I'll close thine eyes and kiss thy pallid lips.
And watch beside thee for the livelong night—
The last, last night I shall behold thy form!
O agony, and they will bury thee!
Will snatch thee from the pillow of my heart,
And lay thee in the damp unbreathing tomb!
Sleep, my sweet child! thou knowest not the pain
Of the sad bosom that thou slumberest on.
It is some joy that thou feel'st not the loss
Of him who would have worshipped his firstborn.

The world is silent round me ; pale the moon
Gleams on the clay-shut eyes of him who loved
Her gentle light in life, and o'er his cold,
Collapsed, unchanging, melancholy face
Plays her transparent beam of love. My heart!
Thy bleeding tears would drown my soul, if yet
One being lived not in my life to tell
How dear he was to me. Farewell, my love!
Our slumbers now will be no more as wont!
Yet e'en in paradise thou wilt behold
Thine earthly love and bend from heaven to shed
Immortal hopes o'er nature's funeral urn.

* * * * * *

* * * * * *

Days, weeks and months passed o'er me and were seen
Vanishing away with that pale, meek content
Which doth exist, against the spirit's will,
So glad was I to feel that burden, Time,
Dropping from my pierced heart ; for I did live
Among, but yet not with the living—tears
Suppressed within the fountains of the soul,
Congealed like waters in deep cavern-halls.
My being passed 'mid shadows, and the things
Familiar once assumed or unknown form
Or appendage unknown, and to my eye
The faces erst beloved appeared like those
Imagination images in dreams;
And oft I feared to speak, lest I should be
Abandoned to my woe ; and, if I spake,
My voice re-echoed round me like the cries
Of shipwrecked mariners at night. My brain
Was fevered with my dreadful anguish, which
Grew by repression, like the *Rebel Flower*,*

* The Camomile

Until it mastered reason, or whate'er
Name that observant faculty doth bear
Whose power is o'er the visible universe.
There was a dread unmeasured, in my thought,
A vague idea of something horrible,
And I lived on like one in broken sleep,
Forever searching for some lost companion,
And wandering in mazes dark as doom,
Where the heart faints and fails, and hope expires.
Yet amid all the estranging of my love
I still clung to my child; a mother's heart
Retains its deep devotion to her dear
And pang-bought offspring, when the woman's mind
Is laid in ruins; and her bosom burns
With love instinctive for an innocent
And lovely creature whom her spirit knows
Only as something worthy to be loved.
Folding the orphan to my heart, I went
Abroad the mansion witlessly, and searched
Its chambers desolate, and then returned
In wildered disappointment that the thing
I looked for could no where be found.—I sat
In the lone winter nights before the dim
And melancholy embers, and did hush
My breath while listening for the tread of him
Who ever spent his evenings with his love
In social converse;—but he came not, so
I sighed and murmured to my prattling babe
That he would soon return; but then I thought
That he had gone to a far land and left
His duties to my care and faithful watch.
And so I oped his escritoir and saw
His papers, pens and pencils and all things
Reposed e'en as he left them, and I felt

That I could not arrange them otherwise
If they were wrong;—his closet then I searched
And there his vestments hung familiarly
And appositely arrayed.—I returned
From such short wanderings sad, and sometimes thought
My love had told me he should dwell no more
Upon the earth—and then my heart did feel
As if it floated in a lava sea.
Thus passed my strange existence from the day
He died until disease my infant laid
Upon his suffering couch, and I became
His sleepless watcher. Long I sat beside
The lovely one, attending all his wants
And sick caprices uncomplainingly,
Yet all unconscious that he was my son,
Till one said he was dying—then there flashed
Through my dark spirit thoughts long dead, and tears
Quenched the dull fire that burned upon my brain.
And left my heart's fair path a desert way,
Calm though 'twas dreary. Life hath direful ills
And woes and sufferings, but the fiercest lie
In madness, e'er in dread of heaven and earth.
It cannot weep—it doth not think, and yet
It hath both tears and thoughts, the one of blood,
Of pangs the other; all its feelings coil
Like serpents round the heart and sting the core
Unceasingly, and all the sweet ideas
Of love and friendship round the racked brain twine
Like knotted adders, venomous and blind.
Pierce, O thou Holy One! the heart, but spare
The spirit! Let thy judgments fall upon
The affections, but preserve the immortal soul!

My child was spared me ; and the tale I tell
Was gathered from the loved ones who beheld
But could not soothe my agony, and those
Impressions I retain of sights and sounds
That floated by me in bewilderment.

* * * * * *

It was the Sabbath's herald eve ; and pained
With melancholy musings, such as hearts
Bleeding with sorrow nourish, forth I went
To gaze on nature's pensive face and smile
Of virgin softness, and I felt the sense
Of her deep loveliness stealing o'er my woes
While watching her pure countenance, now veil'd
In moonlight and her changeful robes of green,
Azure and silver-blended, while she looked
Like one who was to me what angels are
To paradise—the living fount of joy.
A diamond star was floating 'mid the waves
Of pearl, that danced along the silver wake
Of Dian's bark, and it did seem like love
Adorning innocence ; while in the midst
Of ether hung the rosy isles of bliss,
Where spirits as they bear the hests of heaven
And warder Zion's towers, lift up the songs
That soaring souls forever sing above.
The thought of meeting my beloved again,
Filled all my soul with gladness ; for we part
But for a little season—a brief day,
From earth to heaven, and, like the evening star
Upon the azure verge of summer's sky,
The soul embraceth two eternities.

A sea of voices waked me from my dreams
Of holier spheres, and told me of the earth,

That held in its cold bosom all my loves,
Save one sweet babe, the image of its sire
Upon his lonely widow's heart! O Earth!
Cold is the couch thy sons must sleep upon,
And dark the chambers of their slumber deep.
I looked around me and the vestal moon
Was silvering the waters, o'er which scud,
Swan-like, full many a silent sail bound far,
Perchance, to fathomless eternity!
And dazzling lamps, that seemed in the pale moon
Like crime obtruding his unholy light
Before rose-beaming virtue, glared above
The blushing waters as they laughed in scorn.
And in a sea-dome, studded o'er with lights
That mocked the diamond, many a voice arose
In merriment well feigned, and many a form
Of outward splendour glided round to find
Something to tell how happy all must be
Who woo and win the pleasures of the world.
Like earth's gay hopes, full oft a column rose
Of fire far in the azure vault of night,
And then it burst and vanished! some did watch
The glittering fragments till they fell—then sighed—
And I sighed too—they told me of my joys!
It was no scene for me—the sights I saw
Were once shared with those eyes that wake no more;
The voices that I heard were all unknown;
The arm I held was not my wedded lord's!
'Tis bitter to compare our passing years!
The Dead! where are they now? The Living! what
Are they to those whose hearts are in the tomb?

* * * * * *

Slow I returned to my lone room, and kissed
My sleeping child, and looked to heaven—and wept.

www.ingramcontent.com/pod-product-compliance
Lightning Source LLC
LaVergne TN
LVHW020212110826
845151LV00003B/691

* 9 7 8 1 4 2 5 5 3 4 6 3 9 *